MEALS WITHOUT MEAT

ALISON & SIMON HOLST

MEALS WITHOUT MEAT
ALISON & SIMON HOLST

THE BEST-SELLING VEGETARIAN COOKBOOK

This edition published in 2016 by New Holland Publishers Pty Ltd
London • Sydney • Auckland

The Chandlery, Unit 704, 50 Westminster Bridge Road, London SE1 7QY, United Kingdom
1/66 Gibbes Street, Chatswood, NSW 2067, Australia
5/39 Woodside Avenue, Northcote, Auckland 0627, New Zealand

www.newhollandpublishers.com

First Published in 1990 by C.J.Publishing
Reprinted 1991 (twice), 1992, 1993, 1994 (twice), 1995, 1996, 1997
First published by New Holland Publishers in 1999

Copyright © New Holland Publishers Pty Ltd
Copyright © 1990 Alison and Simon Holst

All rights reserved. No part of this publication may be reproduced, stored in a retrieval system or transmitted, in any form or by any means, electronic, mechanical, photocopying, recording or otherwise, without the prior written permission of the publishers and copyright holders.

A catalogue record for this book is available from the National Library of New Zealand.

ISBN 9781742579061

Managing Director: David Cowie
Publisher: Christine Thomson
Design: Diana Russell
Production Director: James Mills-Hicks
Printer: Hang Tai Printing Company

10 9 8 7 6 5 4 3 2 1

Keep up with New Holland Publishers on Facebook
www.facebook.com/NewHollandPublishers

PREFACE

When we wrote *Meals without Meat* over 10 years ago, we did so with vegetarians (those who eat no chicken, fish or red meat) foremost in our minds, but hoped it would also have a wider appeal. Many subsequent reprints (with combined sales of over 250 000 copies) tell us that we were indeed successful!

The feedback we've received—from vegetarians, from cooks wanting to prepare some meatless meals each week, from those cooking for families including vegetarians and 'meat-eaters', and from those who panic at the thought of preparing meals for vegetarian guests—since *Meals without Meat* was first published has been incredibly positive. Simon has often been told that the availability of most of the ingredients plus their relative inexpensiveness makes the book easy to use and economical. People frequently tell Alison that the recipes are as popular with the meat-eaters in their family as with the vegetarians they cater for—often no easy feat.

Meals without Meat was written during the years that Simon was at university. He lived in a number of flats over that period and, as his interest in cooking grew, he prepared more and more vegetarian meals. Many of those meals had a particular emphasis on ingredients that were within students' budgets, and which could be produced from the store cupboard, fridge or freezer after classes were finished for the day.

Simon's ideas, recipes and cooked dishes were also welcomed in our family kitchen and dining room. Then, he asked me why I didn't write a book about meatless meals, since he and so many of his friends found it hard to get reliable recipes. When I replied that I was thinking about it, but hadn't quite got around to it, he suggested that we might work on it together. What mother could turn down such an offer!

Working at home together over two summer vacations, we talked, experimented, tasted, and wrote our recipes. During this time we cooked for very honest tasters from four different generations-these included vegetarians and semi-vegetarians, some who usually ate four or five meat meals a week, and others happy to eat meat at least twice a day, seven days a week. We got a lot of satisfaction when we produced food that everyone enjoyed.

Simon is now an author in his own right (*Simon Holst's Pasta Cookbook*, *Dish It Up* and *Fast & Fantastic*), but since our first collaboration on *Meals without Meat* we have worked on many other books together (including *Very Easy Vegetarian*, and *Meals Without Red Meat*). However, as *Meals without Meat* was our first book, it continues to have special associations for us. We hope that you will get pleasure from using our book, and eating the foods that you prepare with its help.

ALISON HOLST & SIMON HOLST

IMPORTANT INFORMATION

The following measures have been used in this book:

1 tsp	5 ml
1 Tbsp	15 ml
¼ cup	60 ml
½ cup	125 ml
1 cup	250 ml
4 cups	1 litre

All the cup and spoon measures are level, unless otherwise stated. (Rounded or heaped measures will upset the balance of ingredients.)

When measuring flour, spoon it into the measure lightly, and level it off without shaking or banging the cup, since this packs down the flour and means that too much is used. Small ¼ and ½ cup measures are useful for measuring these quantities of flour.

Most butter quantities are given by weight. These are marked on the paper around the butter. Small amounts of butter are measured by tablespoon. One tablespoon weighs 15 ml.

If you are measuring in inches using the following approximations:

5 mm	¼ in
1 cm	½ in
2.5 cm	1 in
10 cm	4 in
12 cm	5 in
15 cm	6 in
18 cm	7 in
20 cm	8 in
23 cm	9 in
25 cm	10 in
28 cm	11 in
30 cm	12 in
35 cm	14 in
40 cm	16 in
50 cm	20 in

If you are weighing in ounces and pounds, use the following approximations:

1 oz	30 g
2 oz	60 g
3 oz	90 g
3.5 oz	100 g
4 oz	120 g
5 oz	150 g
6 oz	180 g
7 oz	220 g
8 oz	250 g
1 lb	500 g
2 lb	1 kg

Abbreviations

cm	centimeter
C	Celcius
F	Fahrenheit
ml	millilitre
l	litre
g	gram
kg	kilogram
oz	ounce
lb	pound
in	inch
tsp	teaspoon
Tbsp	tablespoon

Temperatures and Approximate Equivalents

CELCIUS	FAHRENHEIT	GAS
100°C	225°F	¼
125°C	250°F	½
150°C	300°F	2
160°C	325°F	3
170°C	325°F	3
180°C	350°F	4
190°C	375°F	5
200°C	400°F	6
210°C	425°F	7
220°C	425°F	7
230°C	450°	8
250°C	500°F	9

MEALS WITHOUT MEAT

Always bring the oven to the required temperature before putting in the food which is to be cooked.

Most of the oven-baked recipes in this book were cooked in an oven with a fan. The fan circulates heat so that no parts of the oven are much hotter or colder than other parts.

If you use an oven which does not have a fan, you may find that you need to allow a slightly longer cooking time, or slightly higher temperature.

To help you judge when your food is cooked, I have given you other indications of readiness to look for, wherever possible, as well as indicating the probable time required.

MICROWAVE COOKING

Microwave cooking times vary, and cannot be given precisely. Microwave instructions have been given for a 650 Watt microwave oven with a turntable.

```
High ........................................100% power, about 650 Watts
Medium High ......................70% power, about 450 Watts
Medium.................................50% power, about 350 Watts
Defrost..................................30% power, about 220 Watts
```

IMPORTANT

Check the power levels and percentages on your own microwave oven, and alter cooking times accordingly, if your oven is different. The first time you microwave a new recipe, always watch it carefully during the second half of its cooking time, in case it is cooking more quickly. As soon as you can smell the food, you know that it is nearly cooked.

STANDING TIME

Food continues to cook after it is taken out of a microwave oven, e.g. a potato keeps baking for 1-2 minutes. The appearance and texture of the food change during this time:

- crumble toppings become crisper
- cabbage softens and brightens
- cake surfaces dry out

If you wait until food looks and feels cooked before you take it from the oven, you may well find that it is overcooked after standing. If in doubt, undercook. Take food out after the recommended time. You can always put it back in the oven if it is still undercooked after standing. It is much harder to render first aid to overcooked food!

CAN SIZES

You may find that you cannot buy cans of the exact size specified in this book. Do not worry if the cans are a little larger or smaller than those specified. Small differences are unlikely to make a difference to your recipe.

The following symbols have been used to give a quick indication of the characteristics of individual recipes.

- For special occasions; suitable for use when entertaining.
- Quick and easy; quicker than other recipes in the same section.
- Suitable for vegans, or, suitable for vegans when using the non-animal option.
- A food processor is necessary, or helpful.
- Recipe requires use of cook-top only.
- A microwave oven is used for all or part of the cooking, or a microwave oven is an option.
- A pressure cooker can be used with advantage, to speed up all or part of the cooking.
- This recipe is suitable for freezing.

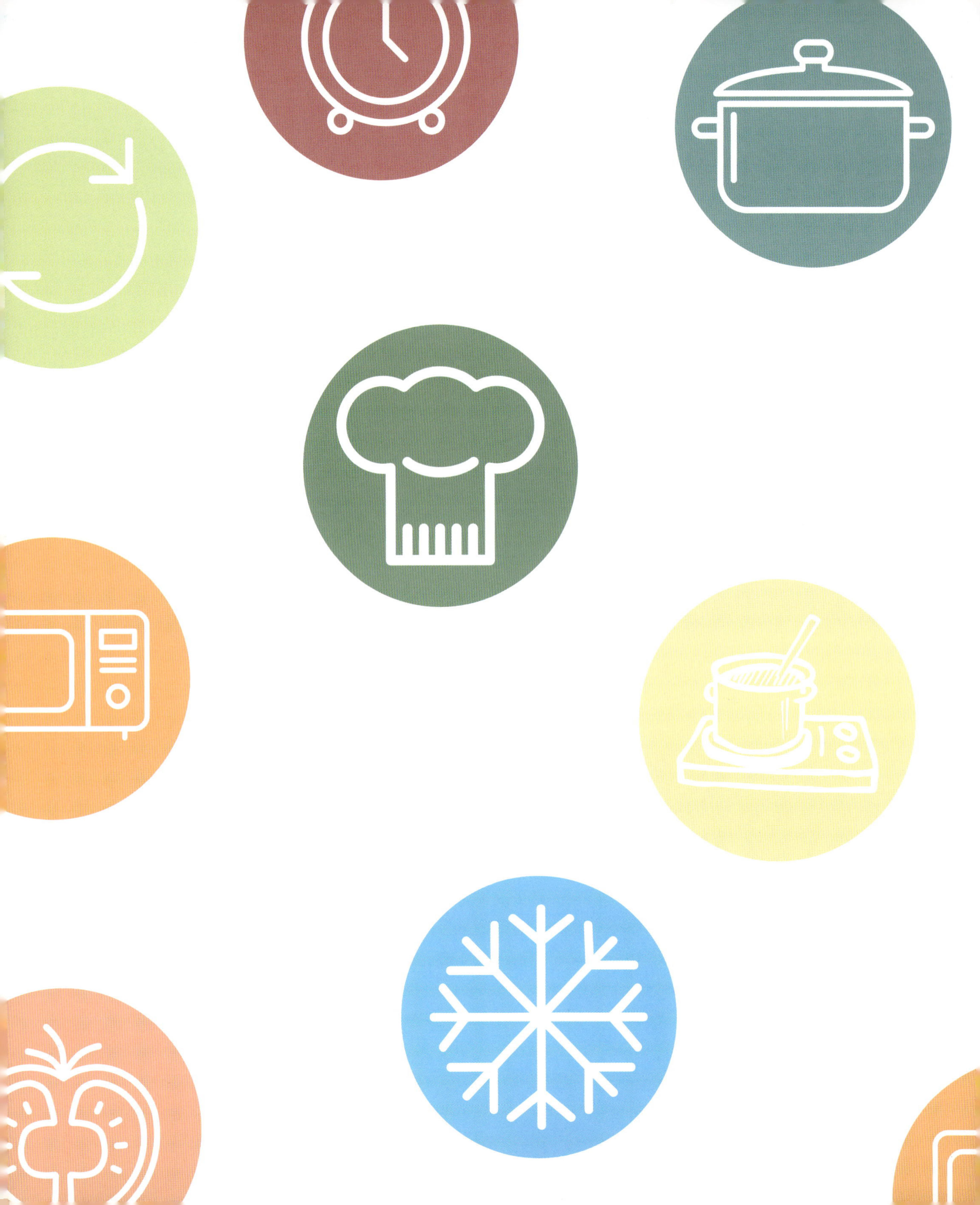

CONTENTS

SOUPS **11**

STARTERS & SNACKS **25**

BEANS & LENTILS **39**

POTATO MAIN COURSES **51**

PASTA BASED MEALS **59**

VEGETABLE MAIN COURSES **71**

BURGERS **83**

PIES & PASTRY **87**

EGGS & CHEESE **97**

TOFU DISHES **105**

RICE & GRAINS **109**

VEGETABLES & SALADS **119**

SAUCES & DRESSINGS **135**

BREAD & BAKING **141**

FAVOURITE DESSERTS **155**

BREAKFAST TREATS **159**

DRINKS **165**

TOMATOES **169**

BEAN BASICS **173**

EATING FOR HEALTH & HAPPINESS **177**

CONVENIENCE FOODS **178**

INDEX **180**

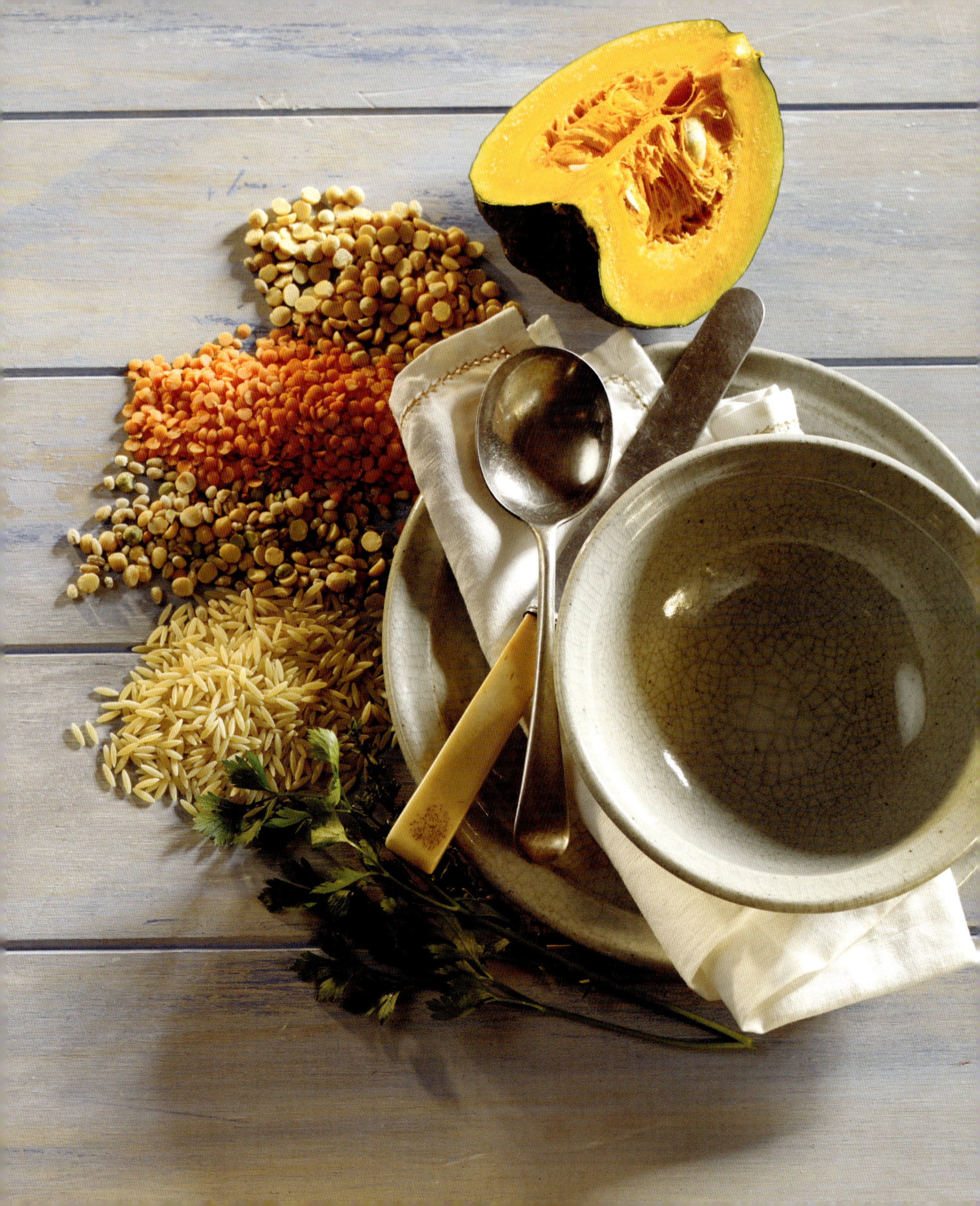

SOUPS & STOCKS

Soups are an important part of a vegetarian diet. They make good, easy one-pot meals where a variety of vegetables, pulses and grains may be served together. An interesting soup served with some sort of bread and raw vegetables and/or fruit in the form of a salad is as suitable for serving to friends as it is for an easy tray meal for one or two.

Here are some of our favourite soups. They seem to be popular with all adults and many children, vegetarians and meat-eaters alike. The soups vary in richness, protein content, thickness complexity and flavour. Remember that, when soup is the main part of the meal, it should be quite substantial.

SOUPS

Use your imagination when it comes to actually serving the soup. You can dress up the plainest of soups by serving it with a selection of extras.

Try small bowls of grated or parmesan cheese, croutons, little crackers, yoghurt, fresh herbs, diced peppers, sliced button mushrooms, cubed avocado, and chopped tomato.

Pass around extra hot chilli sauce, and black pepper or other spices for grinding.

It is not really worth making very small amounts of most soups. Even if you are cooking for one or two, try making the full quantity and freezing what you do not need immediately in small serving-sized amounts. Soup thaws fast, especially in microwave ovens. The thawed soup may need a few fresh additions, a little thickening and reseasoning, but it should not be very different from the original.

We hope that you will enjoy our recipes as they stand, then experiment with them later, making your own modifications.

SOUP STOCK

Many soups need the addition of flavoured stock to bring out the full flavour of other ingredients. There are a number of ways to prepare such stocks; choose the method that best suits your time and inclination.

INSTANT STOCK OR BOUILLON

There are a variety of vegetable stock cubes and powders on the shelves of supermarkets and 'health-food' shops. Some of these taste good and others can be disappointing. Always read the ingredient list on the container carefully as some manufacturers add animal fats to their vegetable-flavoured stocks.

When using instant stocks, work out what concentration suits you. In general 1 level teaspoon of powder (or 1 cube) to 1 cup of boiling water should give a strong enough flavour without being too salty.

'NEARLY INSTANT' STOCKS

As an alternative to using commercial stock preparations you can make stock almost instantly by dissolving any one of the following in 1 cup of boiling water:

1 tsp Vegemite or Marmite
1 tsp dark (Chinese) soya sauce
1 tsp light (Chinese) soya sauce
1 tsp Kikkoman soya sauce
1 tsp Kikkoman salt-reduced, soya sauce
1-2 tsp miso

1 tsp tomato paste, added to any of the above, improves its flavour.

It is worth experimenting with different combinations of these ingredients. Our favourite is a combination of 1 teaspoon each of the Chinese light soya sauce and tomato paste per cup of water. It is surprisingly good for something so easy and cheap, and is well worth a try.

These quantities should just be multiplied when larger quantities of stock are required.

VEGETABLE STOCK FROM SCRATCH

Making vegetable stock from scratch is often regarded as being an excessively time-consuming process. This is because of the long periods of time necessary to allow flavours to 'steep' from vegetables as they boil. Finely chopping the vegetables first (either by hand or, better still, in a blender or food processor) eliminates the need for prolonged boiling. This is the principle employed in this recipe, which makes a litre of fresh-tasting stock with an attractive colour in less than 20 minutes.

1 large onion
2-4 cloves garlic
1 large carrot
2 sticks celery
2 tomatoes or 2 tsp tomato paste

1 stalk parsley
¼ tsp freshly ground black pepper
4 cups (1 litre) cold water
½ tsp sugar
about 1 tsp salt

Quarter but do not peel the onion. Put in the food processor bowl with the unpeeled garlic cloves, the scrubbed but unpeeled carrot cut in chunks, the broken sticks of celery with their leaves removed, the tomatoes and parsley leaves and stalks. Process using the metal chopping blade until very finely chopped.

Transfer the chopped vegetables to a large saucepan, add the pepper then the cold water and bring to the boil. Simmer for 10-15 minutes, then press through a sieve, extracting as much liquid as possible. Add the sugar and salt to taste.

MACARONI SOUP

When you have made vegetable stock from scratch, you can use it to make lovely, easy soups. Here is one of the simplest we make.

for 4 servings
1 litre vegetable stock
2 tsp butter
½ cup macaroni or perciacelli
2 tomatoes, cubed finely
¼ cup chopped parsley

Bring the stock to the boil. Add the butter and macaroni and simmer until the pasta is tender, about 10 minutes. Cut the tomatoes into small cubes then add them and the chopped parsley to the soup. Bring it back to the boil then serve immediately.

Variations:
Add other quick-cooking vegetables such as sliced mushrooms, frozen peas, or finely chopped spinach. Add small cubes of tofu as well as quick-cooking vegetables. Replace the macaroni with fine ribbon noodles, or other small pasta.

CHEESE AND ONION SOUP

This is a rich, unusual and delicious soup, which may be made in a short time. Served with crusty bread and a salad it makes a satisfying and filling meal. Do not be too generous with serving size, since you may overwhelm those with small appetites.

for 6 starter or 4 main course servings:
3 medium-sized onions
2 cloves garlic
2 Tbsp oil or butter
1 tsp mustard powder
1 tsp salt
generous grind of black pepper
2 cups water
2 Tbsp butter
2 Tbsp flour
1½ cups milk
1 cup grated tasty cheese
1 Tbsp sherry
1 tsp dark soya sauce
½ tsp hot chilli sauce

Slice onions finely and chop the garlic. Melt the butter in a large pot, then sauté the onions with the garlic, mustard powder, salt and pepper until soft, without letting them brown. Add the water, bring to the boil, then cover and simmer over a low heat until the onions are tender.

In another pot melt the second measure of butter, then stir in the flour. Continue stirring while the mixture cooks for at least 1 minute. Add the milk and keep stirring until the sauce boils and thickens, allow to boil for a minute or so and then remove from the heat and stir in the grated cheese.

Add the cheese sauce to the onion mixture then stir in the sherry and soya and chilli sauces. Cook over a very low heat (avoiding boiling) for a further 10 minutes.

Serve immediately, or make ahead and reheat as required.

BROWN ONION SOUP

We all love this soup and have enjoyed variations of it over the years. When serving this soup as a starter, try adding a small handful of croutons to each bowl. If you are serving it as a main-course soup, it is delicious topped with thick slices of grilled French bread smothered with melting cheese.

FOR 8 SERVINGS:

500 g (4-6) onions
100 g butter (or ¼ cup oil)
2 tsp sugar
¼ cup flour
6 cups boiling water
2 Tbsp Chinese light soya sauce
2 Tbsp tomato paste
1 Tbsp dark soya sauce or Worcestershire sauce
black pepper
¼ cup sherry (optional)
hot pepper sauce

Cut the onions into 5 mm slices (a food processor does this perfectly). Heat the butter or oil in a large, heavy-bottomed saucepan. Add the onions and cook over a moderate heat for about 20 minutes, stirring frequently. Do not hurry this step as browning the onions is essential for the flavour of the completed soup.

Stir in the sugar. Cook for about 5 minutes longer until the mixture darkens even more, then stir in the flour. Dissolve the light soya sauce and the tomato paste in 3 cups of boiling water then add this to the onions. Allow the soup to boil, add the remaining water and return to the boil.

Reduce the heat and simmer for about 30 minutes before adding the dark soya or Worcestershire sauce, black pepper and the sherry. Taste and add a little hot pepper sauce and salt if desired.

CURRIED CASHEW AND CARROT SOUP

This delicious and unusual soup is made from a recipe given to us by a fellow cook. It is filling and substantial. Its flavour and texture will vary with the efficiency of your toasting and grinding of the cashew nuts. For best flavour have the nuts lightly and evenly toasted. The finer the nuts are ground the smoother and thicker the soup will be.

FOR 4 SERVINGS:

3 large carrots (500 g)
2 small onions
1 Tbsp butter
1-2 Tbsp curry powder
3 cups water
3 tsp vegetable bouillon powder
1 cup toasted cashew nuts

Slice the carrots and chop the onions finely.

Melt the butter in a medium-sized saucepan, add the curry powder and chopped onions, and sauté until the onions are soft but not brown.

Add the carrots, water and powdered stock and simmer until the carrots are tender.

In a blender or food processor, process the toasted cashew nuts to the consistency of ground almonds. (Cashew nuts can be toasted under a grill in a sponge roll tin with ½ tsp oil.)

Drain the cooked carrots and onion and put into the food processor with the ground nuts. Process adding the stock as required to get the desired consistency. Taste and adjust seasoning if necessary.

Reheat to serve. Top each serving with a spoonful of yoghurt sauce made with 1 cup unsweetened plain yoghurt mixed with 1 tablespoon finely chopped mint and 1 clove finely crushed garlic.

NOTE:
Home-made vegetable stock may be used to replace the bouillon powder and water. Check the seasonings before serving.

MINESTRONE

This is a colourful and popular soup consisting of a variety of vegetables and pasta in a thin vegetable broth. Although you can use quickly made 'instant' stock, it is nicer when made with the homemade stock on *page 7*.

FOR 8 SERVINGS:
2 Tbsp butter
1 large onion, chopped
2 cloves garlic, chopped
1 litre vegetable stock (see page 12)
1 potato, cubed
¼ cup perciacelli
½-1 cup chopped zucchini
½-1 cup chopped green beans
1 cup chopped cabbage
1 (425 g) can savoury tomatoes
1 (425 g) can kidney beans
sugar and salt to taste

Melt the butter in a large saucepan, add the onion and garlic, and cook gently without colouring for 5 minutes or until the onion is tender. Add the stock and bring to the boil.

Stir in the small cubes of unpeeled potato, and the perciacelli, and cook for 5 minutes, while you prepare the green vegetables. Add these, bring back to the boil and simmer for a few minutes longer before adding the liquid from the savoury tomatoes. Chop the contents of the can a little more finely, and add with the beans. It is not critical what size tin or colour of bean that you add, so use what you think will look and taste best. (We add the liquid from the beans, too, but you can please yourself about this.)

Cook gently for a few minutes after the last addition, then taste and adjust seasonings, adding any herbs that you like.

Top individual servings with grated parmesan cheese if you like.

CREAMY LENTIL AND VEGETABLE SOUP

This is an excellent main-meal soup that you can sit down to eat half an hour after you start to make it. You can change the ingredients, depending on the bits and pieces you have in the refrigerator, so it is never the same twice.

FOR 4-6 SERVINGS:
1 cup red lentils
1 litre hot water
25-50 g butter
1 or 2 onions
1 or 2 cloves garlic
1 or 2 carrots
1 or 2 stalks celery
1 tsp whole or ground cumin seeds
½ tsp grond coriander (optional)
½ tsp garam marsala
½ tsp paprika
2 Tbsp cream
2 Tbsp cornflour
1 cup frozen peas (or other frozen vegetables)
about 1 cup chopped tomato
about ¼ cup chopped fresh herbs (e.g., parsley, spring onions or chives, and small amounts of basil, thyme, oreganum)
1 Tbsp sugar (optional)
1-1½ tsp salt

As soon as you think about making this soup, measure the lentils and hot tap water into a bowl or jug so that the lentils start softening.

Melt the quantity of butter you want in a fairly large saucepan. Add the chopped onions, garlic, carrots and celery. If you intend to purée all or part of the soup, you can leave the vegetables in large pieces. If you want the soup unpuréed and fairly chunky, cut them into small, even pieces.

Add the cumin, coriander, garam marsala and paprika to the vegetables. (Leave out any of these which you do not have, or add 1-2 tsp curry powder, if you have none of them.)

Cook over moderate heat, stirring occasionally, for 2-3 minutes longer, without letting the vegetables brown.

Add the hot water and the lentils, cover, and simmer for about 20 minutes, or until the vegetables and lentils are tender.

Purée all, or part, or none of the mixture, and bring it back to the boil.

Mix the cream and cornflour to a paste with a little extra water, and pour into the soup.

Add the peas or other frozen vegetables and the tomato that has been chopped into pieces the same size as the peas. Add the sugar, then salt to taste. You will need at least a teaspoon, or the soup will be flavourless. Add small amounts, tasting carefully.

Add the fresh herbs, if you have leftover cooked vegetables, cut them into small cubes and add them too.

Serve with hot toast or croutons, French bread or bread rolls, and with a leafy green side salad or coleslaw, if you like.

WINTER SOUP

This thick, substantial soup may be served as the main part of a meal. It tastes as if it has simmered all day, but it can be served an hour after you start making it. If you like, spoon parmesan cheese over each serving.

for 4-6 large servings:
½ cup commercial cereal soup mix
5 cups hot water
1 large onion
2 cloves garlic
2 Tbsp butter or oil
1 carrot, chopped
100 g pumpkin or kumara or 1 potato, cubed
½ green pepper
½ red pepper
¼ tsp dried thyme
½ tsp dried basil
½ tsp dried oreganum
2 tsp yeast extract
2 Tbsp tomato paste
½ tsp salt
¼ cup chopped parsley

Put the soup mix and water on to simmer in a fairly large covered pot, while you prepare the rest of the soup in another pot or heavy frypan.

Chop the onion and garlic and cook over moderate heat in the butter or oil until the onion is evenly browned (but not blackened).

While this is cooking, chop the scrubbed carrot and the pumpkin or scrubbed kumara or potato into pieces the size of your little finger nail, then add them to the browned onion.

Cook for several minutes more, turning frequently, then stir in the chopped peppers and the herbs.

Tip the vegetables into the boiling soup mix, cover again, and simmer very gently for 45 minutes, until the dried peas etc. are tender.

Mix the yeast extract with enough hot water to dissolve it, then stir in the tomato paste. Add this to the soup, with enough salt to bring out the flavours, then add the chopped parsley.

Serve straight away, if necessary. If you have time, leave to stand for half an hour or more, to blend the flavours.

Note:
The cereal soup mix is made up of a mixture of barley, dried peas and beans, pasta, etc. It does not contain any stock.

CURRIED KUMARA SOUP

Kumara makes an unbelievably smooth purée. It has a mild, sweet but none-the-less distinctive flavour, and makes a very satisfying soup.

for 4-6 servings:
2 cloves garlic
½-1 tsp curry powder
75 g butter
500 g kumara

1 cup water
2 tsp vegetable bouillon or other flavouring (see page 12)
3 cups milk (approximately)
¼ cup cream (optional)

Add the crushed garlic and curry powder to the butter in a large saucepan.

Peel the kumara with a potato peeler and slice into pieces 1 cm thick. Cook in the butter for 1-2 minutes without browning. Add the water and bouillon, cover and cook for 10 minutes until tender. Purée, thinning with milk until it reaches the desired thickness.

Add the cream and reheat, but do not boil.

CARROT SOUP

Carrots are popular, cheap, and are available all year round. What's more, they can be made into a cheerfully bright, creamy soup which everybody seems to like. You can easily add your own gourmet touches to carrot soup, with herbs, cheese, or orange to modify its flavour.

FOR 6-8 SERVINGS:

2 cloves garlic
2 large onions
50 g butter
500 g carrots
2 tsp sugar
4 cups vegetable stock (see page 12)
¼-½ cup cream

Chop the onion and garlic very finely. Cook in the butter for 5-10 minutes without browning.

Add the finely grated carrot, sugar and stock, simmer for 10 minutes or until the carrot is tender, then purée.

Whisk in as much of the cream as you feel comfortable with, and seasonings. Reheat without boiling.

Variations:
Add finely chopped fresh thyme or ¼ tsp dried thyme as the carrots cook. Add the grated rind and the juice of one orange when you add the cream. Try replacing the cream with ½-l cup cheese sauce.

QUICK POTATO SOUP

This is a simple, quick and well-flavoured soup. Blending or processing gives the soup a wonderful smooth texture that is further enhanced by the addition of a little cream.

FOR 4 SERVINGS:

2 onions
3 cloves garlic
3 Tbsp butter or oil
3 medium-sized potatoes (about 500 g)
3 cups of vegetable stock (see page 12)
1 tsp sugar
a generous grind of pepper and nutmeg
1 sprig each of parsley and mint
1 pinch each of fresh or dried basil and thyme
¼ cup cream (optional)

Chop the onion and garlic. Cook in the butter or oil in a large saucepan over a medium heat for a few minutes, until the onion begins to brown. Scrub and dice the potatoes and add to the onion and garlic. Pour the stock over the vegetables, add the sugar, pepper, nutmeg and herbs, then stir together and cover. Simmer for 10-15 minutes or until the potato is tender.

Blend the soup until smooth. If you don't have a food processor or blender, force vegetables through a sieve. Add the cream and reheat (but do not boil) to serve.

If you find that the colour of this soup is not inspiring, try dressing it up by adding a swirl of cream and a sprinkling of chopped herbs to each bowl.

ALPHABET SOUP

This quickly made favourite family soup is easy enough for children to make for themselves, and takes less than 15 minutes. The 'alphabets' are fun for children who like to make their initials and names, but you can use any other pasta shapes. Vermicelli or narrow egg noodles are good for people who enjoy sucking up long, thin shapes, while big wavy noodles

SOUPS & STOCKS

give the soup a very substantial feel. The quantities given here may be varied to taste, but the order of additions is important and should be followed.

FOR 4 SERVINGS:
4 cups hot water
4 tsp vegetable bouillon or other flavouring (see page 12)
1 tsp sugar
2 tsp butter
3 Tbsp alphabet noodles (or up to ½ cup larger noodles)
1 small onion
1 stick celery
1 small carrot
1 small potato
1 tomato
1 Tbsp chopped parsley

Put the hot water in a medium-sized saucepan over high heat. Add the stock powder or selected flavourings and the sugar and butter. When this mixture comes to the boil add the noodles. Prepare and add the vegetables in the given order. Chop the onion and celery, grate the carrot and scrubbed potato and chop the tomato. The soup should be cooked about 10 minutes after the noodles are added. Stir in the chopped parsley and serve, or cool and reheat later.

FRESH TOMATO SOUP

When really ripe, red tomatoes are plentiful it is nice to know how to make soup from them. It is better to use canned tomatoes, however, when fresh tomatoes are not at their best. We like this soup when it is chunky, but you can purée it if you want to.

FOR 4 MAIN COURSE SERVINGS:
1 onion
2 Tbsp butter
2 cloves garlic
1 Tbsp flour
1 tsp sugar
1 tsp vegetable bouillon powder
½ tsp paprika
1 cup water
500 g ripe red tomatoes
basil, thyme, marjoram
cumin, black pepper hot chilli sauce
¼ cup chopped parsley

Chop the onion finely and cook in the butter without browning for 5 minutes or until it is tender. Do not hurry this step.

Stir in the chopped garlic and cook a minute longer, then add the next five ingredients. Simmer for another 5 minutes, while you halve the tomatoes and cut each half into 9 or 16 cubes, depending on their size.

Add the tomatoes and cook gently for 5 minutes more, adding fresh or dried herbs to taste, and the other flavourings, also as liked. Stir in the chopped parsley, adjust saltiness and sweetness if necessary, and serve.

For smooth soup, purée before adding the parsley.

Serve with big cheese-topped toasted slices of French bread, or with croutons or sour cream.

CHILLED TOMATO SOUP

Gazpacho (or chilled tomato soup) is really a cross between a soup and a salad. The base of this soup consists of well-flavoured tomato juice, or tomato juice with small chunky pieces of tomato in it.

FOR 4 SERVINGS:
1 (420 g) can diced tomatoes in juice
1 (425 g) can savoury tomatoes
1 tsp vegetable bouillon powder
½ cup boiling water
extra water
hot pepper sauce
4-8 iceblocks
1 avocado, cubed
1 green pepper, cubed
1 red pepper, cubed
¼-½ cucumber, cubed
about ½ cup chopped spring onion
    or mild red onion

1-2 cups small croutons
1 cup cubed tomatoes (optional)

Combine the contents of the two cans. Chop the pieces more finely using a food processor if available, or else mash with a potato masher, or strain off the solids and chop with a knife.

Measure the powdered stock into one of the cans, add boiling water to dissolve it, then rinse out the other can with this liquid. Make the total volume of tomato mixture up to 1 litre. Taste and adjust seasonings if necessary, adding a dash of hot pepper sauce, etc.

Refrigerate until needed, then serve in four fairly large bowls, each containing one or two iceblocks if the weather is hot.

Assemble the other listed ingredients in individual bowls, sprinkling lemon juice over the avocado to stop it browning. Pass these around so that diners can fill up their soup bowls with whatever combination and quantity of these that they want.

YOGHURT AND CUCUMBER SOUP

The mixture of cucumber and yoghurt is a useful and versatile one. Depending on its seasoning and concentration, it may be used as a soup, a sauce, a dip or a salad dressing. Although mint, garlic and dill are the herbs usually associated with this, you can please yourself. Try to allow standing time to allow the flavours to blend well.

FOR 4 SERVINGS:
2-3 long thin cucumbers
1 tsp salt
2-3 spring onions
2 sprigs mint
1-2 cloves garlic
1 sprig parsley
1 sprig dill (optional)
2 cups plain unsweetened yoghurt
2 Tbsp cream (optional)

Peel cucumbers only if skin is thick. Halve lengthwise. Scoop out and discard seeds. Grate remaining cucumber, sprinkle with salt and leave to stand for 5-10 minutes. Chop seasonings (in food processor with a little yoghurt). Squeeze cucumber to remove liquid and combine with seasonings and remaining yoghurt. Add cream for extra richness, and season. Process again if a smooth mixture is desired. Leave at least 30 minutes before serving.

PEA SOUP

Pea soup is comfortingly familiar to most people. It makes a good main-course meal when served with any crisp bread and a fruit or vegetable salad. Our version is particularly smooth, with a good flavour.

FOR ABOUT 8 SERVINGS:
1 cup yellow split peas
½ cup red lentils
10 cups water
2 large onions
2-3 sticks celery
2 carrots
2 cloves garlic
1 bay leaf if available
thyme, oreganum, and allspice
25 g butter
¼ cup flour
Milk, water or vegetable stock to thin.
salt and pepper

Bring the peas, lentils and water to the boil in a large pot. Add the onions, celery, carrots and garlic. There is no need to chop these finely since the cooking time will be about an hour and a half, and they are likely to disintegrate in this time. Add the herbs and spice listed, in quantities to suit your taste, or leave them out if you do not have them. Simmer this mixture until the split peas are mushy, then purée or push through a coarse sieve.

Rinse out the saucepan and melt the butter in it. Stir the flour into this, cook gently for 2-3 minutes, then add about a cup of the strained purée. Bring this to the boil, stirring constantly, then add another cupful and boil again.

Add the remaining mixture and bring to the boil, still stirring all the time. Simmer for 5 minutes.

This mixture will be very thick, and is suitable for refrigerating or freezing.

When the soup is required thin some of it with milk, water or vegetable; stock, to obtain the thickness of soup you want. Bring to the boil, taste, and season carefully. Serve very hot.

BLACK BEAN AND RICE SOUP

This is a simple but delicious soup made from only a few ingredients. We make it with small black tiger beans, but you could use bigger black beans if you like. The dark colour of the soup is unusual, to say the least! Sour cream or yoghurt swirled on top, a sprinkling of chopped spring onions, and a few drops of hot red chilli sauce make it look as good as it tastes.

Served with bread and a salad it makes a substantial main meal.

FOR 4 MAIN SERVINGS:
1 cup small black (tiger) beans
3 cups water
3 cups vegetable stock (made from vegetable bouillon powder if desired)
2 Tbsp olive or other oil
3 large onions
4 cloves garlic
2 tsp ground cumin
2 tsp dried oreganum
1-2 cups cooked brown rice
2 Tbsp wine vinegar

Simmer the beans in the water until they are very tender, and most of the water is absorbed. Add the stock, using enough powdered stock with hot water to get a good flavour (about a teaspoonful per cup) and simmer until the beans will break up easily. This should take about an hour altogether.

Measure the oil into a frypan with a lid. Chop the onions and garlic finely, with a food processor if available, and cook in the oil over moderate heat letting the onions colour lightly, but not browning them. Add the cumin and. oreganum after about 5 minutes. Remove from the heat and mix in the cooked rice and the vinegar.

When the beans are mushy, purée 1 ½ cups of them with enough of their cooking stock to make a thick liquid. Then combine the puréed and whole beans and stock, and the onion mixture.

Bring to the boil, and season to taste with hot chilli sauce, ground black pepper and salt. Add extra cumin and oreganum if the soup seems bland. (It should not need these if the cumin is fresh.)

Serve immediately or reheat when required, thinning with more stock if it thickens too much on standing.

Serve each bowl topped with sour cream, yoghurt, or a mixture of the two, chopped spring onion leaves, and a little more hot chilli sauce. Put more of these on the table if you like.

CREAM OF LENTIL SOUP

When cooked and puréed lentils and vegetables are combined with white sauce you get a delicious, creamy soup that is high in protein and appeals to most children.

FOR 4 SERVINGS:
2 Tbsp butter
2 onions
2 carrots
2 stalks of celery (optional)
½ cup red lentils
2 cups vegetable stock (see page 12)
1 Tbsp butter
1 Tbsp flour
2 cups milk

Melt the butter in a medium-sized saucepan. Chop the onions, carrots and celery, add to the saucepan and cook for about 5 minutes, stirring occasionally to prevent browning. Add the lentils and stock, then cover and simmer for 15-20 minutes until the lentils are tender.

While the lentils cook, make a thin white sauce by melting the remaining measure of butter, stirring in the flour and adding half a cup of the milk. Bring this mixture to the boil then add another ½ cup of milk, boil again then add the remaining cup of milk and allow to return to the boil.

Purée the lentil and vegetable mixture in a food processor or blender or by pushing it through a sieve. Add the puréed mixture to the white sauce, taste and season carefully if required. The flavour of this soup will improve with standing. Serve topped with croutons, or sour cream and chopped parsley or chives.

MUSHROOM SOUP

Although this soup tastes good when made with any mushrooms, for best flavour use mature mushrooms with brown gills. Of course it will taste best of all if you have been foraging and picked the mushrooms yourself.

FOR 4 SERVINGS:
3 Tbsp butter or oil
2 medium-sized onions
2 cloves garlic
2 carrots
250 g mushrooms
3 Tbsp wholemeal flour
4 cups of hot water
3 tsp instant vegetable bouillon or other flavouring (see page 12)
¼ tsp fresh thyme or a pinch of dried thyme
salt and pepper to taste

Heat the butter or oil in a large frypan with a close-fitting lid. Add the finely sliced onions, chopped garlic and grated carrots. Cook over a moderate heat until they are browned but not charred. Add the chopped mushrooms and flour and cook for 1 minute before adding the hot water, stock powder or other flavouring and thyme. Cover and simmer for 30-45 minutes. Strain off the liquid, purée or sieve the vegetables, then combine the two. Season to taste, and reheat just before serving.

NOTE:
For cream of mushroom soup, omit the grated carrot and replace half the water with milk. Do not brown the onion-and-garlic mixture, and add the mushrooms a little earlier, giving them time to soften before adding the flour.

ASPARAGUS SOUP

A few years ago, in England, I tasted some frozen asparagus soup. It was one of the nicest soups I have ever had, so I experimented making, freezing and thawing a rich asparagus soup.
This is almost as good as the original. You might like to try it. Eat it as soon as the soup is made, or, if you are lucky enough to have access to a lot of cheap fresh asparagus, make extra for your freezer.

FOR 6-8 SERVINGS:
50 g butter
2 cloves garlic, chopped
¼ cup flour
500 g tender asparagus
2 cups water
2 (150 ml) tubs Dairy Cream (or 1¼ cups fresh cream)
½ tsp salt
freshly ground black pepper

Melt the butter in a saucepan, over moderate heat, add the chopped garlic, and cook for 2 minutes without browning. Stir in the flour, then remove from the heat.

Grate the raw asparagus, using the appropriate blade of a food processor, or a hand grater. (Hold the bunch of asparagus at right angles to the grater.) Bring the asparagus and water to the boil, and boil for 2 minutes. When cooked, the asparagus should be bright green and barely tender.

Drain the asparagus cooking liquid into the butter and flour mixture, and bring to the boil, stirring all the time. Stir in the cream. Bring to the boil, add the cooked asparagus, and return to the boil again.

If serving immediately, thin to desired consistency with milk, vegetable stock, or water. If freezing, do not thin, but cool the thick soup as soon as possible,

SOUPS & STOCKS

so that the asparagus stays bright green. The fastest way to cool it is to stand the saucepan in a large container of cold or iced water, changing the water as it gets warm.

Freeze in covered containers, leaving head space. Use within 6 months. Bring thawed soup to the boil, thin as required, then adjust seasoning.

Serve with croutons or with grated cheese or with toasted cheese sandwiches.

CORN DAHL SOUP

This main-course soup combines an interesting selection of everyday vegetables and takes only half an hour to make. Its colour, flavour and texture make it popular with adults and children alike.

FOR 6 MAIN-COURSE SERVINGS:

½ cup moong dahl
1 litre water
1 Tbsp butter
1 large onion
2 cloves garlic
1 carrot
2 stalks celery
1 cup instant or home-made vegetable-stock
1 (440 g) can cream-style corn
2 silverbeet or 4 spinach leaves
2 Tbsp tomato ketchup
1 Tbsp cornflour
1 tomato
salt and pepper

Boil the moong dahl and water in a large pot for about 20 minutes, until the dahl is tender.

Meantime, melt the butter in a heavy-bottomed pan, finely chop the onion and garlic (in a food processor if available), add to the butter and cook gently for several minutes, without browning. Grate or finely chop the carrot and celery and add to the partly cooked dahl. Make up instant stock, using about a teaspoon with a cup of water, and add to the cooked dahl, with the corn and the green leaves which have been cut by hand into small squares.

Stir in the tomato ketchup and the cornflour mixed to a smooth paste with a little water, until the soup thickens.

Cut the tomato into small cubes and stir into the soup. Taste, and season as necessary.

Serve immediately, or reheat when required. Sprinkle grated cheddar cheese or parmesan on the soup if desired. Toast or warm crusty bread goes well with this soup.

PUMPKIN SOUP

The wonderful colour and smooth texture of Pumpkin Soup will brighten the bleakest winter day.

Pumpkins come in a huge range of shapes, sizes and colours, and all are good for soup. When they ripen, in autumn, you may find some real pumpkin bargains. As long as they are mature and their skins are unblemished, they will keep for months in a cool, well-ventilated place.

Once you cut a pumpkin it should be refrigerated and used in a few days.

Make more than you need and freeze the undiluted purée if you can.

FOR 6-8 SERVINGS:

1 kg pumpkin
2 onions, chopped
2 cups water
2 cloves garlic, chopped
2 tsp vegetable bouillon powder
2 tsp sugar
½ tsp grated nutmeg
2-3 cups milk
salt, pepper and sugar

Cut the unpeeled pumpkin into chunks and scrape away and discard the seeds and stringy part with a spoon.

Put all the other ingredients except the milk and final seasonings into a saucepan, lay the pieces of pumpkin on top, cover and simmer until the onion and pumpkin are tender. Try not to overcook the pumpkin or it will darken and lose some of its appeal.

Lift the pieces of pumpkin onto a large plate or board. As soon as they are cool enough to work with, scoop the cooked flesh back into the onion mixture and discard the skin.

Purée the pumpkin etc., getting it as smooth as possible. Prior to serving, thin purée to desired consistency with milk, adding a little cream if you want extra richness.

Season carefully. Reheat and serve.

Mushroom Soup

SOUPS & STOCKS

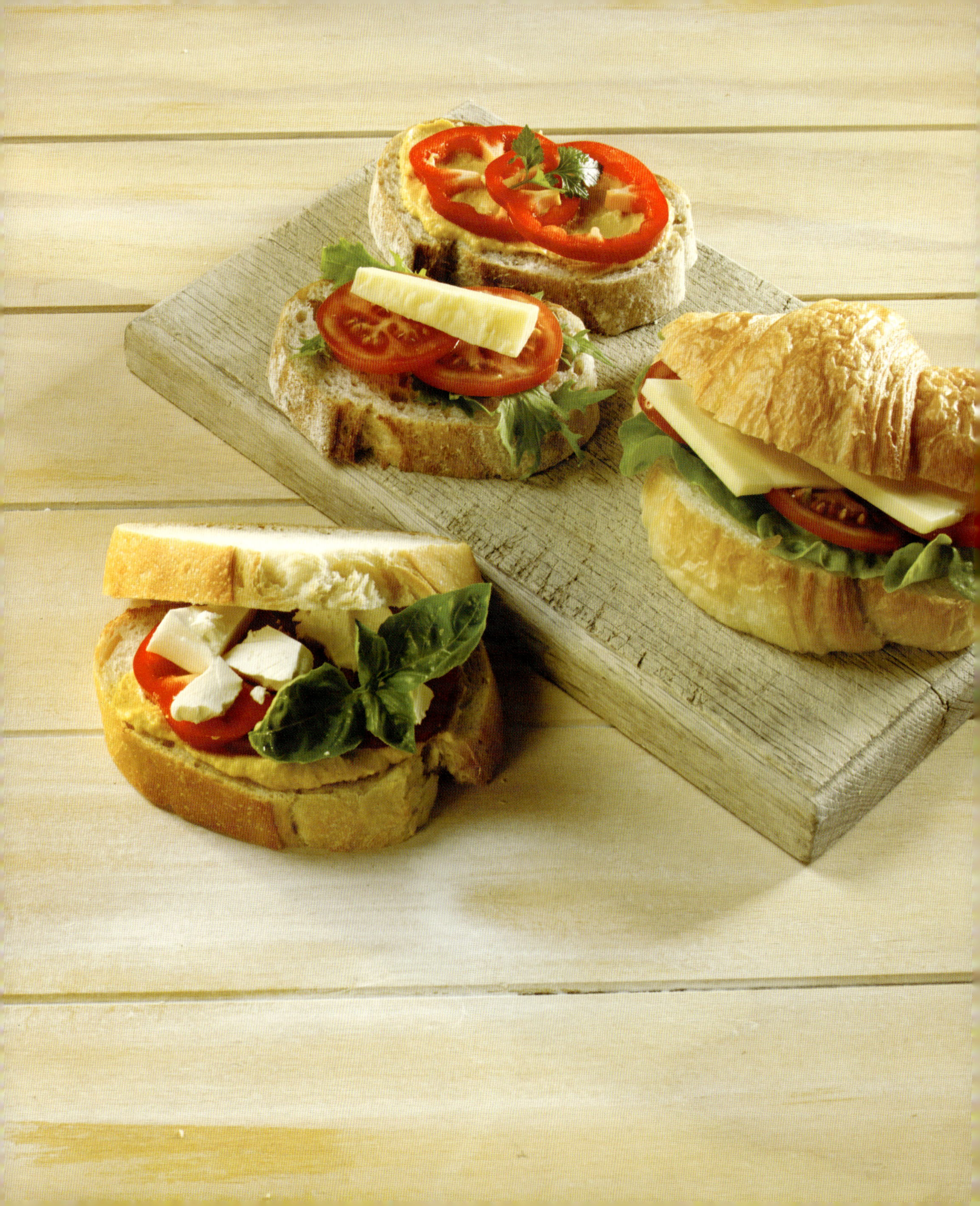

STARTERS & SNACKS

There are times when you want light, interesting foods to start a dinner, and there are other times when you come home tired, and do not feel like cooking or eating a substantial meal but would prefer to nibble a few snacks. On the next few pages are recipes for situations like these. Use one, or make several, depending on your situation.

AVOCADO DIP

This dip makes an avocado go a long way. It is a beautiful colour, and, rather surprisingly, does not darken on standing, so it can be made hours before it is needed. It looks very pretty piled in the centre of a flat platter, with corn chips and colourful vegetables arranged around it. Try it, too, on open sandwiches, with sliced tomatoes and hard-boiled eggs on top.

1 large avocado
½ cup sour cream
¼ cup oil
3 Tbsp lemon juice
½ tsp sugar
¼ tsp garlic salt
dash of tabasco sauce
salt to taste

In a food processor or blender, measure and purée the first seven ingredients, then add salt carefully, tasting all the time, until you get a good flavour. The amount of salt depends on the size and ripeness of the avocado. Chill until the flavours blend well and the dip thickens.

Note:

It isn't worth making this if the avocado isn't ripe enough to have a buttery texture. If there are any black, over-ripe bits, remove them or they will spoil the colour of the dip.

GREEN BEAN DIP

If you are a guacamole addict but are frightened by the price of off-season avocados, try this recipe. The replacement of avocado with fresh or frozen green beans may seem a little odd but the finished product is surprisingly good!

500 g green beans
3 hard-boiled eggs
½ cup cream cheese
1 small green pepper
1 tsp onion powder
1 tsp garlic powder
1 tsp (or to taste) hot chilli sauce
1 tsp mustard powder
½ tsp ground cumin
1 tsp sugar
1 tsp salt
juice of 1 lemon
black pepper
2 spring onions

Cook the beans until tender, then drain as much water from them as possible.

Put the beans and hard-boiled eggs into a food processor or blender, and process until smooth.

Add the cream cheese, diced green pepper, seasonings, and sliced spring onions and process again until well mixed. Pour into a bowl and refrigerate until you are ready to serve.

TOMATO SALSA

This easily made sauce is extremely versatile; it makes a good dip for corn chips or an equally good topping for a cottage-cheese-stuffed baked potato. Try it, too, spooned over a poached egg on toast, noodles or rice.

1 medium-sized onion
2 cloves garlic, minced
1 (425 g) can whole peeled tomatoes
1 tsp cumin
½ tsp marjoram
1 tsp chilli powder
black pepper
1 tsp (or to taste) hot chilli sauce

Put onions and garlic into a blender or food processor, and process until well chopped.

Add the drained tomatoes, and process again until the mixture is evenly combined, but still a little chunky.

Now add the seasonings (hot chilli sauce last, as you may wish to vary the quantity according to taste) and heat the mixture to boiling (either in a microwave or on the stove), then simmer for 5 minutes, reducing power level or temperature accordingly.

This mixture may be served hot or cold as a dip or sauce.

TOMATO AND CHEESE DIP

This tasty dip is substantial enough to be served with corn or potato chips and strips of raw vegetables as a light meal.

Tomato Salsa (as above)
2 tsp cornflour
1½ cups of grated mild cheese, preferably mozzarella

Mix the cornflour to a paste in a tablespoon of cold water. Add this to the salsa and heat until the mixture boils and thickens.

Stir in the grated cheese and leave to stand until the cheese begins to melt. Reheat before serving if necessary.

HERBED CREAM CHEESE PÂTÉ

This pâté does not harden on refrigeration. It is good alone, or as a spread under tomatoes or other vegetables. Try it just as it is, the first time you make it, then experiment with different fresh herbs, chopped capers, etc.

100 g soft butter
2 garlic cloves, chopped
  tsp salt
¼ tsp sugar
freshly ground pepper
¼ cup chopped chives
¼ cup chopped parsley
2 tsp thyme leaves
1 (250 g) carton cream cheese
2 Tbsp lemon juice
2 Tbsp milk

Cream soft (but not melted) butter. Add ingredients one at a time, in the given order, beating after each addition. Use food processor if available. Fill small pots with mixture, or, to unmould later, fill moulds previously lined with plastic film. Refrigerate until required.

HOT CREAM CHEESE DIP

This cheese mixture makes a delicious hot dip with corn chips, crisp raw vegetables, or slices of French bread.
Leftover dip can be stored in a covered dish in the refrigerator. It is especially nice spread on rolls, crumpets, English muffins, etc. and reheated under a grill.

1 (250 g) carton cream cheese
1 spring onion, chopped
1 clove garlic
1 Tbsp tomato sauce
5 drops or more tabasco sauce
¼ cup grated cheese
1 tomato (optional)
¼ green pepper (optional)

Soften the cream cheese by beating it with a wooden spoon until it is easily workable, or warm it briefly in a microwave oven.

Add the finely sliced spring onion and garlic, then the tomato sauce, tabasco sauce, and grated cheese. Stir in the finely chopped tomato and pepper, if desired.

Microwave 2-3 minutes on High (100%) power, stirring after each minute, until the cheese melts, and the mixture is hot and bubbling round the edges. Alternatively, put the mixture in a flameproof container and heat under a grill, stirring once or twice as the mixture warms, then leaving it to brown in parts on the surface.

Serve hot with corn chips, raw vegetables or sliced French bread.

AUBERGINE DIP

This popular Middle Eastern dip is traditionally served with dried, crisp pita bread. It is also good on hot toast, however. If you microwave the aubergine rather than grilling or baking it, you get a light green dip instead of a brownish one,.

1 small aubergine (about 300 g)
1 large clove garlic, chopped
¼ cup chopped parsley
2 Tbsp lemon juice
2 Tbsp tahini (sesame paste)
salt and pepper

Microwave the aubergine, after puncturing its skin in several places. Allow about 6 minutes per 500 g, and turn after half the estimated cooking time.

Or, roast in an oven heated to 180°C for 45-60 minutes, or turn over a barbecue until soft. However it is cooked, the aubergine should feel evenly soft when ready.

Peel or cut off the skin, and mash or purée the flesh with the remaining ingredients until well blended but not completely smooth. Stand for an hour to blend flavours before using as a spread or dip.

BLUE CHEESE DIP OR BALL

This tasty mixture has the flavour of blue cheese and the texture of cream cheese. With more liquid added, it makes a good dip. Made with a smaller amount of liquid it is firm enough to shape into a ball or cylinder, to coat with sesame seeds, nuts, or chopped parsley. It is a good way to make any of our delicious blue cheeses go further, or to introduce people gently to the flavour of blue cheese.

1 wrapped wedge NZ blue vein cheese or 100 g other blue cheese
1 (250 g) carton cream cheese
1 small onion
1 Tbp Worcestershire sauce
about ¼ cup (dryish) sherry
flaked almonds, chopped walnuts, sesame or sunflower seeds (for the ball only)

For the dip:

If you have a food processor, put everything in it. Break or cut the blue vein cheese into small cubes. Put the cream cheese in on top in dessertspoon-sized blobs. Cut the onion into eighths before adding it, then add the Worcestershire sauce and sherry. Process until smooth, using the metal chopping blade and wiping down the sides of the bowl with a rubber spatula when necessary. Thin the mixture with more sherry, cream or milk, if necessary. The mixture always thickens on standing.

Alternatively, mash the blue vein cheese into a large bowl with a fork. Add the cream cheese and beat with a wooden spoon or rubber scraper until smooth. Grate the onion or cut in half and scrape the cut surface with a teaspoon to get onion pulp and onion juice. Add to the cheese with the Worcestershire sauce and sherry. Thin as desired with extra sherry or cream.

For the ball:

Mix as above but use only 2 Tbsp sherry and no extra liquid.

Tip it out of the food processor (or other) bowl on to a piece of plastic on which you have spread toasted sesame seeds, toasted flaked almonds, finely chopped walnuts, or toasted sunflower seeds. Lifting up the edges of the plastic, roll the cheese mixture in its coating until it is the shape you want.

Although a ball looks lovely the first time it is served, it is hard to serve attractively a second time. A sausage or log shape is more practical, especially if you can persuade your guests to attack it from one end!

MUSHROOM AND WALNUT PÂTÉ

This pâté really looks the part! It makes an elegant (not to mention delicious) pre-dinner savoury, but it is equally good piled on toast or crackers for a quick snack.

FOR ABOUT 2 CUPS PÂTÉ

1½ cups green beans
2 eggs
1 Tbsp oil
1 medium-sized onion, diced
¼ cup walnuts, chopped
100 g mushrooms, sliced
1 tsp salt
½ tsp ground black pepper
2 Tbsp dry sherry

Cook the beans until tender, then drain well squeezing out any excess water.

Hard boil, then roughly chop the eggs.

Heat the oil and sauté the onion until it begins to soften. Add the walnuts and mushrooms and cook until the walnuts have darkened and the mushrooms are soft.

Put the beans, eggs and mushroom mixture into a blender or food processor (if using a blender, purée in small amounts). Process until smooth with the metal blade.

Add the seasonings and sherry, mixing in well. Transfer the pâté into a bowl and refrigerate prior to serving.

HUMMUS

We hope that you will not look at the ingredients for this dip, decide that they are uninteresting, and pass on to the next recipe! This mixture is quite addictive, once you acquire the taste for it, and may, in fact, be served as a complete meal, with dried pita or other bread, and vegetable dipping sticks. Try it made with any white beans. The flavour will change slightly, but the cooking time will be shorter. Black-eyed beans, for example, cook in 20-30 minutes, with no preliminary soaking.

1 cup dried chickpeas or other white beans
boiling water
juice of 2-3 lemons
3 cloves garlic
1 tsp salt
2-3 Tbsp tahini (sesame paste)
1 cup oil

Pour boiling water over chickpeas or other beans. Leave to stand for at least an hour, then boil until tender. If using black-eyed beans, boil without soaking for 20-30 minutes, or until tender. Drain cooked peas/beans and keep cooking liquid.

Put the cooked peas/beans in a blender with the lemon juice, garlic cloves, salt and tahini. Add half a cup of the cooking liquid and half the oil, then whiz the mixture until it is smooth, stopping the blender and pushing down the mixture several times.

Add the remaining oil slowly, then add extra seasoning if necessary. Refrigerate until needed (up to a week). Serve piled in a dish. For special occasions, sprinkle the surface with chopped parsley, toasted sesame seeds or a few whole cooked chickpeas, and pour a little extra oil over the surface, so it shines.

Variations:

Mash and sieve ingredients and mix by hand if a blender is not available. Use more tahini and more cooking liquid and little or no oil if desired.

SUSHI

If you are prepared to take the time to find the ingredients and prepare this, you will be rewarded by a dramatic and inexpensive dish which can be served as a snack or starter at any time of the day. You can make sushi without using thin sheets of seaweed if you make a large crêpe and use it to role the rice in.

Don't forget the dips of Japanese horseradish (wasabi) powder, mixed to a paste with water (or sometimes available in tubes), and of Kikkoman soya sauce. These really bring sushi to life!

FOR ABOUT 20 SMALL ROLLS:

1 cup short-grain rice
1¾ cups water
2 Tbsp dry sherry
2 Tbsp wine vinegar
2 Tbsp sugar
1 tsp salt

Cook the rice and water in a microwave oven on High (100%) power for about 10 minutes, or, if cooking conventionally, in a metal bowl standing in a pot of hot water, until it is tender.

Add the remaining ingredients and stir together with a fork. Taste, and add more of anything you think it needs.

Assemble the strips of vegetable that you will roll up in the rice. Select colour-contrasting vegetables, choosing from carrot, celery, red or green pepper, blanched spinach leaves and pickled vegetables. (Pickled oriental turnip is chewy and delicious.)

If using seaweed sheets, hold them over a hot element until they smell toasted, then lie one on a sheet of plastic.

If using a crêpe as a wrapper, make it in a large, preferably square pan, or trim its sides so they are parallel. Place it on plastic, too, for easy rolling.

Place a thin, fairly even covering of warm sushi rice all over the wrapper, then arrange on the end which will be rolled first, lines of your chosen vegetables. Lie blanched spinach leaves flat so that you will see a spiral of dark green when the roll is cut, later on.

Using the sheet of plastic to help you, roll up firmly to form a compact cylinder, with the vegetables in the centre. Wrap in plastic film, refrigerate until required (up to 2 days) then cut into short lengths with a sharp or serrated knife.

NACHOS

Nachos can be made and served in a number of different ways depending on the occasion. They can be made from bought corn chips, or if you have the time you can make your own from uncooked tortillas (uncooked corn tortillas may be obtained from some delicatessens or Mexican restaurants.)

If you are making your own corn chips, brush both sides of the whole tortillas with oil then cut them into pieces of the desired size

Traditionally tortillas are fried, but we have found that laying them out on a baking tray and then grilling them in the oven, turning once after a few minutes, works just as well.

Another possibility is to microwave tortillas treated in the same fashion — allow about 2 minutes on High (100%) power per tortilla cut into corn chips, turning at least once during cooking. This method is limited by the fact that you should cook no more than 2 tortillas at once, and thus it is best used when you only want to cook a few.

The range of toppings used on nachos can be varied considerably depending on what you feel like and what you have on hand to use. Spread the corn chips so they are several layers thick over an oven tray (if you don't mind 'communal' eating) or arrange them in a number of individual plates or bowls. Top with your choice of:

- refried beans (*see page 41*)
- sliced mushrooms
- chopped olives
- diced tomatoes
- diced peppers (or chillis)
- tomato salsa (*see page 19*)
- sliced avocado
- chilli sauce
- chopped spring onions
- grated cheese

If you are using refried beans, an alternative arrangement is to place a pile of the heated bean mixture in the centre of a plate or tray and pile the corn chips around this, then arrange additional topping over the top of this. The grated cheese is the only really essential component and should be sprinkled over last.

Place the tray or plates under a grill (or microwave them) until the cheese is well melted, add a dollop of sour cream and/or guacamole (*see page 31*) if desired, then serve immediately.

The list given above may sound complicated, but once you have tried a few times it's really very simple. Experiment with the range of toppings you use until you establish your own favourites. Using refried beans and sour cream can actually turn this snack into a fairly substantial light meal.

CRUDITÉS

Crudités are nothing more than fresh, crisp raw vegetables, cut into strips or pieces if large, for easy eating.
Arrange several of the following on a plate or platter, depending on the number of people to be fed. Serve little dishes of coarse salt and freshly ground pepper, and a generous supply of some variety of mayonnaise, e.g., garlic, herb, or chilli mayonnaise. If you are serving radishes, include a small dish of butter, since this is good spread on small cold radishes.

carrots	young beans
celery	tender asparagus
radishes	peppers
cucumber	mushrooms
snow peas	spring onions
cauliflower	witloof (endive)

GUACAMOLE

This simple sauce may be used as a dip, or spooned over refried beans for tacos and tostadas.

It is best made to taste rather than by definite quantities of added flavourings, since avocados vary so much in flavour and size.

Halve, stone, and remove the flesh from a ripe avocado. Mash or process the flesh briefly in a food processor, adding the juice from ½-1 lemon.

Add 1 or 2 finely chopped spring onions, a finely chopped tomato for colour, if desired, then season with salt or garlic salt, freshly ground black pepper, and hot pepper sauce. You might like to make other additions, too, such as a little sugar and ground cumin.

Spoon the guacamole into the empty avocado shells, or into a small bowl to serve. Cover until serving.

CHEESE SPREAD

This is a 'one stroke' sandwich filling which can be made quickly, keeps well for a week or two, and can be varied if necessary. By 'one stroke' I mean that it can be spread easily onto bread which does not need to be buttered first.
Creative sandwich-makers can have a good time adding an extra layer of filling for lunch-eaters who like variety.

100 g butter
2 tsp flour
1 tsp mixed mustard
½ cup milk
1½-2 cups grated medium or tasty cheddar cheese
1½ tsp wine or cider vinegar
1 lightly beaten egg

Have all your ingredients ready before you start cooking this mixture, since it can overcook or curdle if left too long at any stage.

Put some cold water in the sink so that it is ready when you need to cool the pan down quickly.

Melt the butter with the flour and mustard in a frying pan, stirring all the time. Add the milk and stir until the mixture bubbles and is smooth.

Without delay, lift it off the heat and add the grated cheese and vinegar, then stir over the heat until the cheese melts.

Take it off the heat again, and stir or whisk in the egg, which has been beaten just enough to combine the white and yolk, but not to become frothy.

Put it back on the heat for 5-10 seconds, until it becomes noticeably thicker. It is important that it is removed from the heat before the fat in it starts to separate, or the egg to scramble. Stand the pan in a sink of cold water and stir for about a minute, until it cools. This should stop any tendency to separate.

Spoon the spread into a jar, cover, and refrigerate, or keep in a cool place until you use it.

STARTERS & SNACKS

Note:
You may find that you want to alter the amount of flour or milk in this spread, to make it a little thicker or thinner. It may vary a little, depending on the cheese you use. If you use the filling at room temperature, instead of at refrigerator temperature, it will be softer; make sure it is soft enough to spread easily. Try it on toast, too.

FILLO TRIANGLES

Fillo pastry gives the feeling of lightness and crunchiness to savouries (*see page 88*).
The traditional filling of spinach and feta cheese is hard to beat. Use cream corn instead of spinach if this suits you better.

Fillo filling:
½ cup well-squeezed cooked spinach
½ cup crumbled feta cheese
1 egg
¼ cup toasted pine nuts (optional)

Chop the drained spinach finely. Mix with the cheese, egg and nuts, using a fork to combine them.
To make small triangular savouries, sandwich two sheets of fillo pastry together with a small amount of melted butter.

Cut the double sheet into six strips, each about 6-7 cm wide. Put a teaspoonful of filling on the end of one strip, about a centimetre from one edge and the bottom. Fold the corner with the filling over, so the bottom edge is against the side, and the filling is enclosed. Keep folding the pastry over and over, until the filling is enclosed by all the pastry in the strip. Fold any ends under, or cut them off. Brush the top surface with melted butter, and place on a lightly buttered baking sheet or sponge roll pan.

Make as many filled triangles as you want, then bake them, uncovered, at 180°C for 10-20 minutes, or until the pastry is crisp and golden brown. Serve immediately, or reheat when required.

POTATO SAVOURIES

These may be served with soup for lunch or tea, or served as small hot savouries. They freeze well, and may be thawed in a microwave oven, but are best reheated in a conventional oven, to retain their crispness.

for 12 savouries:
3 large slices thin-cut bread
butter for spreading
1 cup mashed potato
1 cup grated tasty cheese
1 egg
2 spring onions, finely chopped or 1-2 Tbsp onion pulp
paprika

Butter the sliced bread thinly but evenly, then cut away the crusts and cut each slice into four small squares. Press into patty tins, buttered side down.

Mix together potato, cheese and egg. Add chopped white and green leaves of spring onions. If these are not available, scrape the cut surface of an onion with a teaspoon to get onion pulp and juice. Add this to the potato mixture.

Put rounded, rough spoonfuls of mixture in each unbaked bread case and bake at 190°C for 20-30 minutes, until bread cases are evenly and lightly browned.

Note:
You will find filling may be used for more or fewer bread cases, depending on the amount of filling you want in each.

Take care when eating hot Potato Savouries. The filling gets very hot, and can burn your mouth!

CRUMBED CAMEMBERT

The idea of hot fried cheese is unusual, and has considerable novelty value. Serve it warm, with a tart jelly or sweet-sour pickle.

Chill a small whole camembert or brie cheese. Cut it into wedges the size that you want, then dip each in flour, then beaten egg, then in fine dry wine biscuit crumbs. Repeat the egg and crumb layers to get a thicker coating, if you, like.

Refrigerate again until required. About 15 minutes before it is required, lower carefully into very hot (200°C) oil, at least 3 cm deep.

Remove as soon as the coating is golden brown, and drain on a paper towel. Leave to cool a little before serving, since the inside will be very runny while it is hot. Serve on small plates with attractive garnishes.

BARBECUE BREAD

Don't save this savoury bread mixture just for barbecues. Warm it up in the oven or under a hot grill whenever you want something tasty, hot, and popular. You can mix the filling ahead of time and keep it in a covered dish in the refrigerator to use whenever you want to turn French bread or any bread roll into something exciting.

4 cloves garlic
100 g tasty cheese
100 g soft butter
3 Tbsp tomato sauce
1 Tbsp tomato paste (optional)

Chop the garlic finely in a food processor. Add the cheese, in cubes, and chop into small pieces. Add the butter, which has been warmed to easily mixed consistency, then add the tomato sauce, and if you like a definite tomato flavour, the tomato paste. Process until well mixed.

Or chop the garlic very finely. Mix with 4 cups of grated tasty cheese, the soft butter, and the tomato flavourings, and mix well with a rubber spatula, knife, etc.

Spread thickly on any long, thin loaf or roll which has been cut in slices without cutting through the bottom crust, so the bread still holds together in its original shape.

Wrap in foil, sealing joins, and heat through over a barbecue, under a grill, or in a hot oven, turning when necessary. Do not overheat. Fold back the foil so the top part of the loaf can brown and crisp up before serving. Serve hot.

Variations:
Add fresh or dried herbs to the mixture or replace the Tasty cheese with any other type that you have and like.

POTTED CHEESE

Small quantities of this strongly flavoured cheese mixture team well with pears, nuts, grapes, apples, crackers and celery. Matured cheddars 'pot' well. So do milder cheddars when mixed with blue cheese, although they have a greenish-grey colour.

50 g blue and/or matured cheddar cheese
25 g unsalted butter
pepper, mace or nutmeg
1-3 Tbsp sherry, brandy or port

Mash, grate or food process the cheese with half its weight of room-temperature, unsalted butter. Add a little pepper, mace or nutmeg. Then add whatever liquid you want to use, about a teaspoon at a time, until you have a soft spreading texture. Store and serve in small, covered pots. Spread on crackers or slices of apples, pears, etc.

TOASTED CHEESE SANDWICHES

Although you can make these in any frying pan or under a grill, it is simplest, especially for children, to use a thermostatically controlled electric frypan.

Preheat pan (to 180°C if electric).

Butter two slices of toast-thickness bread. Spread unbuttered side of one slice with cheese and pickle or chutney, for flavour and texture contrast. Top with remaining bread, butter side up.

Place sandwich on preheated frypan. Cook, uncovered, until golden brown, then turn and cook on the second side.

Cut into manageable shapes, and serve while hot.

FALAFEL

Falafel are little balls or patties which are made from dried beans. They should be crisp on the outside, and well herbed and spiced when you bite into them. They are a popular street snack in places where Middle Eastern food is eaten.

They make a good eat-in-your-hand meal if you pile them into split pita breads with lettuce, tomatoes, and a sauce made from toasted sesame seeds.

Although falafel are often made from chickpeas, the sky will not fall on your head if you make them from other white beans. Black-eyed beans give a good result, after half an hour's soaking. In Egypt, dried broad beans are used to make falafel.

FOR 50 WALNUT-SIZED BALLS:
1 cup dried white beans (above)
boiling water
1 large onion
4-6 cloves garlic
1 cup parsley sprigs
2 spring onions
¼ cup packed mint or coriander leaves
2 tsp ground cumin
1-1½ tsp salt
black pepper
hot pepper sauce
½ tsp baking soda

The beans for this recipe should be soaked so they are soft right through, Different beans take different soaking time. Pour a litre of boiling water over them and leave them to stand. The longest will take overnight, and the shortest, black-eyed beans, will be ready after 30 minutes, if they were fairly fresh. Chew a bean to see if it is ready, crunchy but soft, right through.

Chop the onion finely in a food processor. Squeeze it and remove any liquid, putting this aside, just in case the mixture is dry later. Chop the garlic, parsley, spring onion and mint or coriander leaves in the food processor with the squeezed onion. Remove from food processor.

Drain the soaked beans in a sieve. Process them alone until they are as fine as ground almonds. Coarsely ground beans will not stick together during cooking. Add the remaining ingredients, then the chopped herb mixture, and mix well.

Heat about 2 cups of oil in a suitable frying container (an electric wok is good) to about 200°C. The oil should be about 2 cm deep.

Take teaspoon-sized balls of mixture with two spoons. Roll each smooth in your hands or leave them rough if you prefer this. Drop about six balls carefully into the hot oil. Cook 4-5 minutes, turning once, when the lower part is brown. Drain on kitchen paper. Taste one of these and add more of any seasoning that it needs.

Serve with sesame cream sauce, as pre-meal snacks, or put in split pita breads with chopped tomato and lettuce, for a complete meal.

Sesame Cream Sauce
1 Tbsp tahini (sesame paste)
2 Tbsp lemon juice
2-4 Tbsp water
salt
few drops hot pepper sauce

If possible, make this sauce about half an hour before you want it, since its texture improves on standing. Measure the tahini into a bowl that holds about a cup. Add the lemon juice and enough water to mix it to a thin, smooth cream. Add salt to taste, and hot sauce until it is as hot as you like it.

POPCORN

Don't underestimate popcorn. Apart from the fact that few people can resist it when freshly made, popcorn is cheap, relatively low calorie, and a few dried kernels from your storecupboard make a potful in a short time.

2 Tbsp oil
2 Tbsp popping corn
1-2 Tbsp butter
salt, plain or flavoured

MEALS WITHOUT MEAT

Put oil in a frying pan or large saucepan with a lid. Add popping corn, put on the lid, and turn the heat to medium.

Wait patiently until you hear explosions in the pan. Shake frequently. When all the popping has stopped, tip the popped corn on to a tray.

Heat the butter and pour this over the warm popcorn. Sprinkle it with plain salt or with flavoured salt, like celery or onion salt.

Variation:

Candied popcorn; put 2 tablespoons sugar into the pan after the popcorn has cooked. When it turns to caramel, tip popcorn into pan and stir around.

ROASTING NUTS AND SEEDS

Roasting or toasting nuts and seeds really improves their flavour and often their texture also. Uncooked sesame seeds, for example, are virtually tasteless when compared to their toasted counterparts, which also have a more attractive colour and aroma. Sunflower seeds also benefit greatly from roasting, which transforms them into a crisp and delicious snack or topping.

To dry-roast seeds and nuts, cook them over a low heat in a heavy-bottomed pan, or spread them evenly over a baking tray and cook them in an oven heated to 180°C, or about 15 cm away from a preheated grill, until they are golden brown. Don't try to cook too many at once, since a single layer will always cook most evenly. It is also important to shake or stir them frequently as overcooking or burning really spoils the flavour.

If you are going to cook seeds or nuts in a microwave oven, add a little oil or butter, don't use too much or they will be oily and unpleasant. A teaspoon of oil is enough for 1 cup of nuts, which should take about 6 minutes on High (100%) power to cook. You may need more oil for smaller seeds—sesame seeds need about 1 teapoon per ¼ cup and will take 4-6 minutes on High (100%) power to cook. Again it is important to stir frequently in order to avoid burning. It also pays to remember that cooking will continue for a few minutes after the seeds/nuts have been removed from the oven.

Allow nuts or seeds to cool then salt lightly (try a variety of flavoured salts) if desired. If kept in an airtight container, toasted nuts or seeds should remain fresh for weeks. Try toasting the whole container of sesame or sunflower seeds as soon as you buy them so that they will always be ready on hand when you want them.

Note:

If microwaving, make sure that the container you select is heat resistant. Nuts and seeds get very hot and will melt some plastics.

OPEN SANDWICHES

One of the most useful quick snacks you can make is an open sandwich. Start with a bread base, remembering that you have many choices as far as texture, colour and flavour go.

For example:

Heavy-textured whole grain bread
Lighter, softer crumbed brown bread
Fruit bread
Interesting white bread
English muffins
Crumpets
Pita or pocket bread
Round split rolls or hamburger buns
Long (hot dog) rolls
Lengths of French bread, halved
Crispbread
All of the above, toasted

Choose several toppings, depending on your appetite, the time of day, how long it is since you had your last meal, and the time when you will have your next. Some of these open sandwiches are very substantial! Here are some open sandwiches which we think are worth trying:

STARTERS & SNACKS 35

- Thickly sliced ripe red tomato, on hot toasted rye or mixed grain bread. Spread with butter or cottage cheese or quark. Top with freshly ground black pepper, basil leaves, or alfalfa sprouts.
- Sliced tomato on a split length of French bread, topped with sliced mozzarella or gouda, browned under a grill, or heated in a microwave oven until the cheese melts. Add lettuce or watercress if you like.
- Sliced avocado on fresh French bread, with plenty of black pepper or several shakes of a not-so-hot chilli sauce. Sprinkle with alfalfa sprouts if available.
- Mashed avocado on hot toast or a toasted English muffin.
- Drained canned beans mixed with home-made pickle, chopped hard-boiled egg, and chilli mayonnaise, on a fresh crusty roll.
- Chopped, drained and canned beans mixed with chopped spring onion, sprinkled with Mexican Seasoning or cumin, topped with a slice of any cheese and a few thin slices of red pepper, heated under the grill until the cheese melts.
- Fresh crunchy peanut butter (or a mixture of tahini and peanut butter) and honey on crispbread.
- Peanut butter sprinkled with toasted sunflower seeds, on fruit bread, topped with sliced banana, drizzled with honey or a sprinkling of light brown sugar, and a little cinnamon, then grilled.
- Pita bread pockets formed by halving pita bread and spreading the sides, filled with a generous spoonful of hummus, finely chopped lettuce, bean sprouts, cucumber, and tomato, with whatever dressing is handy.
- Hot refried beans on toast, topped with grated cheese, shredded lettuce, and a slice of tomato.
- Hot refried beans, sliced avocado, and a little sour cream, sprinkled with hot pepper sauce, on a flour tortilla. Add alfalfa sprouts if available.
- Warm split rolls with one of the dips, spreads, or pâtés listed earlier in this section. Add suitable raw vegetables for extra colour and texture.

TWO-SLICE SANDWICHES

The days of small, triangular, wafer-thin sandwiches have passed. Sandwiches tend to be made of large slices of thicker (but fresh) bread, with generous amounts of filling.

Fillings made up of two or three different foods seem more satisfying and interesting than those made with only one. Try to include something which will stick the slices of bread together.

Try some of our favourite fillings listed below or use your imagination to try and create your own — remember variety is the spice of life!

- Modifications of the toppings suggested for open sandwiches above.
- Cream cheese, chopped nuts, with lettuce or alfalfa.
- Cream cheese, chopped sultanas and nuts.
- Chopped dates, walnuts and orange juice, heated together.
- Cheese, marmite, and lettuce or sprouts.
- Cheese spread (*see page 31*) with lettuce, tomato and sprouts.
- Peanut butter (or other nut butters) and tahini in equal quantities, mixed with honey or tofu, or chopped sunflower seeds.
- Coleslaw, raisin and cheese.
- Peanut butter, cheese and alfalfa sprouts.
- Tomato and cottage cheese.
- Tofu spread (see below), lettuce and sprouts.
- Egg and tomato, by itself or with lettuce and sprouts.
- Gherkin and cheese.
- Chocolate spreads or chips with sultanas or raisins.
- Grated carrot, raisin and lemon juice.
- Leftover salad and cheese or marinated tempeh or tofu.

TOFU SANDWICH SPREAD

FOR 4-6 SANDWICHES:
250-300 g firm tofu
3 Tbsp mayonnaise
1 tsp mild prepared mustard
¼ tsp turmeric
¼ tsp salt
2 Tbsp chopped parsley and chives
juice of ½ lemon (optional)
black pepper to taste

Drain the tofu then crumble it into a bowl. Add the remaining ingredients and stir gently until everything is well mixed and all the tofu is well coated. Season to taste then use in the same manner that you would usually use mashed hard-boiled eggs.

SQUIGGLES

The name may not give much away, but these are delicious deep-fried pea-flour snacks. Vary the seasonings according to your own taste.

1 cup pea flour
1 Tbsp poppy seed
1 Tbsp toasted sesame seed
4 tsp ground cumin
2 tsp ground coriander
2 tsp garam masala
1 tsp paprika
1 tsp turmeric
½-1 tsp chilli powder
½-1 tsp salt
½ cup water

Measure the dry ingredients into a medium-sized bowl, mix together lightly. Add the water and stir to form a dough the consistency of thick paste. If the dough seems too dry, add a little more water.

Preheat 1-2 cm of oil to 200°C. Transfer the dough into a forcer bag fitted with a fine ribbon or fine (2-4 mm) circular nozzle. When the oil is up to heat, begin to squeeze in the dough.

If you like regular shapes, hold the nozzle close to the surface of the oil, this should give you quite good control of the extruded dough. For more random shapes, hold the bag further above the surface (10-15 cm). This will allow the dough to form its own shapes. Be very careful when working around the hot oil as splashes may cause painful burns.

Cook for 3-5 minutes until crisp and brown, turning occasionally to ensure even cooking. Remove from the oil, and stand on paper towels to drain prior to serving.

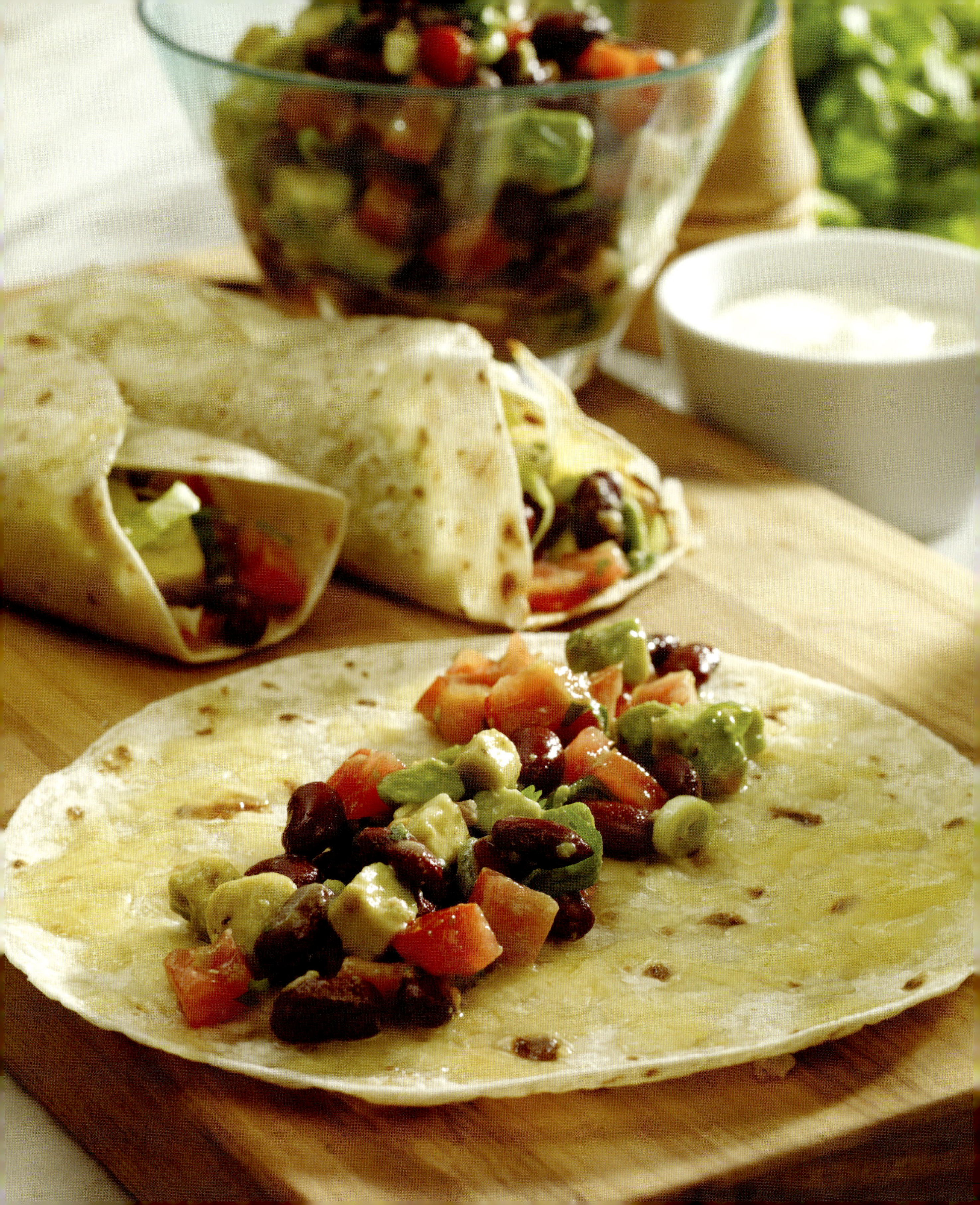

BEANS & LENTILS

Dried beans, etc., play an important part in vegetarian diets. You can use drained canned beans, or beans which you have precooked yourself, in the following recipes. For details, read page 116. It is very important to cook beans until they are completely tender before using them in these recipes.

BLACK BEAN CHILLI

Black beans come in a variety of shapes and sizes. The small black beans used for this South American recipe have an interesting smoky flavour.

FOR 4-5 MAIN COURSE SERVINGS

1-1½ cups small black (turtle or tiger) beans
1 medium-sized onion, diced
1 medium-sized green pepper, diced
2 sticks celery, finely chopped
3 cloves garlic, crushed
1 Tbsp oil
1 tsp ground cumin
1 tsp coriander
½ tsp chilli powder
1 tsp basil
1 tsp oreganum
½-1 cup tomato purée
1 cup cooking liquid from beans

Cook the beans until very tender, (*see page 175*) then strain, reserving the liquid.

Sauté the chopped onion, green pepper, celery and garlic in the oil for about 5 minutes, without browning. Add the seasonings, tomato purée and reserved bean liquid.

Pour over the drained beans. Simmer for half an hour, stirring occasionally, adding more liquid if necessary.

Serve over rice. Garnish with sour cream and chopped spring onions or chives for extra colour. A dish of cooked or raw peppers, and a green salad are good accompaniments.

NOTE:
Use the larger quantity of beans and tomato purée for a more substantial mixture.

BAKED BEANS

These beans, baked in herbed tomato sauce, bear little resemblance to the more mildly flavoured commercially canned beans. They make a popular main course.

FOR 4 MAIN SERVINGS:

1½ cups haricot beans
2 onions, chopped
2-3 cloves garlic
2 Tbsp oil
1 (425 g) can whole tomatoes, chopped
1 Tbsp tomato paste
2 Tbsp sugar
1 Tbsp dark soya sauce
1 tsp basil
½ tsp marjoram
¼ tsp thyme
black pepper
3 cups hot water

Cook the beans as described on page 116. Drain.

Chop onions into fairly large chunks and roughly crush and chop the garlic. Combine these in a medium-sized roasting pan or shallow casserol dish, and coat with the oil. Bake, uncovered, at 160°C for 30-40 minutes, or until the onion browns, stirring occasionally.

In a blender or food processor, or with a potato masher, combine the whole tomatoes, tomato paste, and all the flavourings.

Stir the cooked beans, tomato mixture, seasonings and hot water into the onions and garlic, and bake, uncovered, at 160°C for a further 90 minutes, stirring occasionally. If at any stage the mixture seems too thick, add more water.

Serve with crusty bread and a green salad or cooked vegetables, or as part of a buffet meal.

AFRICAN BEANS

This recipe is particularly quick because black-eyed beans cook faster than most other beans.
The sauce based on tomato and coconut cream is unusual and colourful.

FOR 4-6 MAIN COURSE SERVINGS:

1½ cups dry black-eyed beans
2 medium-sized onions, chopped
2 Tbsp oil
1 small (135 g) can tomato paste
1 (410 g) can coconut cream
2 tsp paprika
½ tsp chilli powder (to taste)
½ tsp cumin
2 tsp sugar
1 tsp salt
black pepper to taste

Cook the beans following the instructions on page 116. In another pan sauté the onions in the oil until they are soft and clear.

Add the tomato paste, coconut cream and seasonings, stirring until they form a smooth and creamy sauce. When the beans are cooked, drain and combine with the sauce. Serve immediately, or, for even better flavour and texture, leave to stand and reheat when needed.

Serve on brown or white rice, accompanied by a mixed green salad.

CORN AND PEA PATTIES

Although split green and yellow peas are often added to soups, they may be cooked and used as you would use red and brown lentils or dried beans. They have their own distinctive flavour and a rather mealy texture, and you need to cook them gently so that they do not break up, but they are worth experimenting with. In this recipe they add extra protein to an old favourite, corn fritters.

FOR 4 MAIN-COURSE SERVINGS:

½ cup split green or yellow peas
1½ cups water
1 clove garlic, crushed
1 tsp ground cumin
1 tsp oreganum
1 Tbsp oil
1 (450 g) can whole kernel corn
2 tsp vegetable bouillon powder 2 eggs
1 tsp paprika
1 tsp curry powder
1 cup self-raising flour

Put the split peas, water, garlic, cumin, oreganum and oil in a medium-sized saucepan. With saucepan lid ajar, cook peas gently for an hour, or until tender.

After about 45 minutes, or a little earlier if the peas look dry, add the liquid drained from the corn.

When the peas are tender and most of the liquid is gone, cool to room temperature, add the bouillon powder, the unbeaten eggs, the corn, paprika and curry powder. Mix with a fork, then fold in the flour, mixing only until combined.

Place several spoonfuls of mixture in a pan containing hot oil about 5 mm deep. Adjust heat so the bottom of each patty is golden brown after about 2 minutes. Turn carefully, and cook the second side similarly.

Keep cooked patties hot on a paper towel in a warm oven until all are done.

Serve immediately, with several cooked vegetables and/or salads, with sauce or chutney if desired.

RAPID REFRIED BEANS

Although you can make refried beans from dried kidney beans and freeze them ready for those occasions when you want something really quick and easy, you may not always manage to be as organised as this. Don't despair! The following recipe takes less than 10 minutes from start to finish, as long as you have a can of beans in the cupboard. You can use this mixture to make delicious nachos (one of our staple light meals) or serve the refried beans on rice, with a

BEANS & LENTILS

shredded lettuce or tomato salad to compete the meal.

for 4 servings as nachos or for 2 main course servings:

1 large onion
2 cloves garlic
1 Tbsp oil
1 small green pepper (in season)
½ tsp chilli powder
1 tsp ground cumin
½ tsp oreganum
½ tsp salt
½ tsp sugar
1 (310 g) can kidney beans
1 Tbsp tomato paste

Dice the onion, chop the garlic finely, and sauté in the oil. When soft, add the chopped green pepper and seasonings. Cook, stirring occasionally to prevent sticking, until the pepper softens, then reduce the heat.

Drain the can of beans, keeping the liquid, and add the beans and the tomato paste to the rest of the ingredients in the pan. Heat through over moderate heat. Mash the mixture with a potato masher or fork, or, for a smoother mixture, process in a blender or food processor. Thin down with a little of the bean liquid if desired. Taste, and adjust seasonings to suit.

For nachos, pile in the middle of a flat plate, top with grated cheese if desired, and surround with corn chips.

Notes:

If you want to use a 425 g can of beans for this recipe, use 1½ times all the other ingredients.

Make sure that the oreganum and cumin you use are fresh and full of flavour.

To streamline refried bean production even further, replace the seasonings from chilli powder to sugar in this recipe with 2-3 teaspoons of the following seasoning mixture which can be mixed up in bulk and kept especially for this purpose and/or used to give any dish a Mexican flavour.

Mexican Seasoning Mix

1 Tbsp chilli powder
1 Tbsp onion powder
1 Tbsp garlic powder
4 tsp ground cumin
2-3 tsp dried oreganum
2 tsp sugar
1 tsp salt

Put all ingredients in a screw-topped jar or other airtight container and shake until well combined.

Note:

Dried oreganum can be bought in both powdered and crumbled leaf forms. The powdered version is better for use in this recipe. If you use the fine leaf variety, use 3 rather than 2 teaspoons and try to grind it a little finer in a food processor, blender, or better still with a pestle and mortar.

MEXICAN BEANS

This recipe is based on the Mexican staple—refried beans. It is very popular and is delicious with corn chips and fried tortillas, plain or folded, large or small. The mixture should have the consistency of thick spaghetti sauce.

for 6 cups:

500 g red kidney beans
6 cups hot water
2 large onions, chopped
3-4 cloves garlic, chopped
2-3 medium-sized carrots, chopped
2 tsp whole cumin seeds
¼ cup tomato sauce
2 Tbsp tomato paste
1 Tbsp cider or wine vinegar (or 2 Tbsp lemon juice)
2 tsp salt
2 pickled Jalapeno peppers or enough tabasco sauce to make the mixture taste hot

Cook the beans in the water until they are tender (*see page 175*). Do not drain.

Add the onions, garlic, carrots and cumin seeds and cook for 30 minutes more, or until all vegetables are tender.

Add the tomato sauce, tomato paste, vinegar or lemon juice, salt and the finely chopped pickled peppers or tabasco sauce.

Simmer for 10-15 minutes longer, then mash or purée roughly in a food processor. Taste, and add extra ground cumin, salt, tabasco, etc., if the flavour is not as strong as you like it.

Refrigerate until required, or freeze for long storage.

RED LENTIL LOAF

This loaf has proved to be popular with vegetarians and meat-eaters alike over the years we have made it. It is good served as a meat loaf would be served, with mashed potatoes, green beans or broccoli, and a fresh tomato sauce to go with the loaf.
Sorry about the long list of ingredients, but all the additions are important! With luck, you can serve the leftovers cold or reheated for a second meal, and sit with your feet up, tomorrow.

for 6-8 servings:

1½ cups red lentils
3 cups water
1 bay leaf
2 cloves garlic, chopped
2 onions, sliced
25 g butter
2 eggs
2 cups grated cheese
1 cup chopped tomatoes
3 slices wholemeal bread, crumbled
2 tsp salt
½ tsp curry powder
½ cup chopped parsley

Simmer the lentils gently with the water, bay leaf and garlic until they are tender and the water is absorbed. Meanwhile, sauté the onions in the butter until transparent. Remove from the heat and add the eggs, cheese, chopped fresh or canned tomatoes, breadcrumbs, seasonings, and parsley.

Remove the bay leaf from the cooked lentils and drain off any remaining water.

Stir the lentils into the rest of the loaf mixture, then spoon into a well-greased or baking-paper-lined loaf tin (alternatively, pour into a casserole dish and serve from this, without unmoulding).

Bake, uncovered at 180°C for about 45 minutes, or until firm in the middle.

MEXICAN TORTILLAS ETC.

Mexican food, long popular in California, where we first enjoyed it twenty years ago, is now making a global impact. It is well worth hunting down sources of Mexican ingredients, because they fit so well into a vegetarian diet.

Tortillas are a type of Mexican flat bread. The commercial variety is usually made from a special type of corn meal, but there are wheat flour tortillas too (*see page 144*).

Tortilla terminology can be confusing! Uncooked corn tortillas, cut into small wedges and fried, are corn chips or tostaditos. Taco shells are made by folding and frying corn tortillas until crisp. Tostadas are tortillas fried flat until they are crisp. Enchiladas are tortillas which are briefly fried, removed from the pan before they go crisp, spread with sauce, then rolled, folded, or stacked. The term Burrito refers to any filling rolled in a flour tortilla.

If you want to make tostadas, taco shells, corn chips or enchiladas yourself, start with unfried, flexible tortillas, which you buy fresh or frozen from delis or some Mexican restaurants.

Our favourite way to serve tacos, tostadas and burritos involves setting out dishes containing the following toppings:

- Mexican or rapid refried beans, hot or warm
- Grated cheese
- Shredded lettuce
- Chopped spring onions (or onion rings)

BEANS & LENTILS   43

- Sour cream
- Extra chilli sauce (optional)
- Chopped olives (optional)
- Sliced avocado or guacamole (optional)

This allows our family and friends to help themselves to whatever they want. The only suggestion we make is that they start with a layer of the beans. If you have guests or family members who may not have eaten this way before, go first yourself, showing the others what to do.

Note:
Don't forget to provide many large paper serviettes as there is no tidy way to eat this type of food.

VEGETARIAN SHEPHERD'S PIE

There are many times when it is really useful to know a recipe which is suitable not only for vegetarians, but which meat-eaters will feel happy to eat, too.

This recipe was immensely popular when we first made it. Everyone around the table kept helping themselves to more, until the dish was clean. It had not been described as a vegetarian specialty—it was served with several vegetable side dishes as any meat dish would be.

A recipe like this one cannot be assembled on the spur of the moment, because the beans and the potatoes need to be precooked. However, if you use canned beans and microwaved or instant potatoes for the topping, the pie will take a much shorter time to put together.

The beans must be cooked to the stage where they are tender enough to mash with your tongue against the top of your mouth, before you combine them with the other filling ingredients.

4-6 main course servings:
Topping:
1 kg potatoes
2 Tbsp butter
1 cup grated cheese
milk

Filling:
1 cup kidney beans
2 large onions
2 Tbsp butter
1 red or green pepper
3 Tbsp wholemeal flour
1 tsp vegetable bouillon
1 tsp dried basil
1 tsp dried oreganum
1 tsp paprika
2 Tbsp chopped parsley
1 tsp dark soya sauce
1½ cups bean cooking stock
2 Tbsp tomato paste

Cook the beans as described on *page 175* until very tender. Leave them to stand in their cooking liquid until required, then drain, reserving 1 ½ cups of cooking liquid.

Peel the potatoes, and cook in lightly salted water. Drain, and mash with the butter, half the grated cheese, and enough milk to get a good consistency. After mashing, beat with a fork until light and fluffy.

In a large pot or pan, cook the chopped onions in the butter until tender and medium-brown. Do not hurry this step. Stir in the chopped pepper, then the flour. Stir over moderate heat until the flour has browned slightly, then add the next six seasoning ingredients. Stir in the bean cooking liquid and the tomato paste, and bring to the boil, stirring constantly. Add the drained beans, taste, and adjust the seasoning if necessary.

Spread the mixture on the bottom of a lightly sprayed or buttered pan about 20 x 25 cm. Cover with the mashed potato. Sprinkle the remaining grated cheese over the surface.

Reheat at 180°C for 20-30 minutes, or in a microwave oven until the bottom centre feels hot to your hand. In either case, brown the top attractively under a grill.

If preferred, brown the top under a grill straight after preparing it, before refrigerating or reheating.

For easier serving, leave to stand for a few minutes before cutting.

A green vegetable such as brussel sprouts, beans or broccoli is good with this. You don't need anything else, except perhaps a glass of wine or beer.

BEAN STROGANOFF

Using soybeans in this recipe gives it an especially high protein content, but you may find their rather crunchy texture disconcerting. If so, replace the soybeans with any other beans, or add more lightly cooked button mushrooms or other vegetables to the delicious sauce.

for 4-6 servings:
1 cup soybeans
2 onions
3 Tbsp butter or oil
150 g mushrooms
¼ cup flour
1 Tbsp paprika
½ tsp salt
black pepper to taste
1 cup milk
2 Tbsp sherry
1 Tbsp dark soya sauce
½ cup sour cream
1 Tbsp fresh (or 1 tsp dried) parsley

Cook the soybeans (or substituted variety) until tender enough to eat without any more cooking (*see page 175*), then drain and leave to stand while preparing the sauce mixture.

Dice the onions. Heat the butter or oil in a large pan or heavy-bottomed pot, sauté the onions until soft and golden brown. Add the mushrooms and cook until soft.

Stir in the flour gradually, to prevent lumps forming. Add the paprika, salt and pepper and cook a little longer, stirring continuously. Gradually stir in the milk to make a thick sauce, then stir in the sherry and soya sauce.

Reduce the heat and add the sour cream, chopped parsley and cooked beans. Allow to heat through and then serve on noodles or rice.

BEAN AND CHEESE CASSEROLE

This is an interesting and tasty casserole which is extra-rich in protein. It makes an inviting winter dinner.

for 8 main course servings:
2 cups pinto or kidney beans
3 onions
2 large or 3 medium-sized cooking apples
2 Tbsp oil
1 tsp chilli powder (or to taste)
1 tsp mustard powder
1 tsp cumin
1 tsp oreganum
1 tsp salt
black pepper
4 tomatoes, chopped
¼ cup white wine
2 cups grated cheddar or mozzarella cheese

Cook the beans as described on *page 175*, until they are as soft as you like them, then drain. Although they get baked again later on, they will not become any softer, so do not hurry this step.

Chop up then sauté the onion and apple in the oil, until the onion is transparent and the apple is tender. Add the chilli, mustard powder and other seasonings.

Combine the beans, onion mixture, chopped tomatoes and wine in a large casserole dish.

Cover and bake for 30 minutes, at 180°C. Stir in the grated cheese and then return to the oven for another 10 minutes.

Serve with several plainly cooked vegetables such as carrots, beans, broccoli or kumara, and with crusty bread if desired.

SHORT-ORDER CURRIED BEANS

Don't forget that plain canned baked beans are good, ready-to-eat, protein-rich food. Make sure that you keep a few cans in your store cupboard so that you don't get caught out when you have to produce a fast meal.

FOR 2-3 SERVINGS:
2 onions
1-2 apples
2 Tbsp oil
1 tsp curry powder
2 tsp vegetable bouillon powder
½ cup water
1 (450 g) can baked beans
1-2 tsp cornflour
chopped parsley, etc.

Peel and chop the onions and apples into small cubes. Mix with the oil in a small frypan and sauté until golden brown. Stir in the curry powder.

While they cook, prepare microwave baked potatoes or toast split rolls, or toast, etc. Add bouillon powder and water to the browned onion mixture and simmer for 2-3 minutes. Add beans, and bring to the boil. Either simmer until mixture thickens, or thicken with a little cornflour and water paste. Add parsley or fresh or dried herbs, if available. Taste and adjust seasoning if necessary.

Serve on buttered toast, over split microwaved potatoes, on toasted split rolls, or on reheated rice or pasta.

NOTE:
Add any leftover cooked vegetables you might have, either before or just after adding the water.

RED BEANS AND RICE

Don't be put off by the name of this recipe, thinking that it sounds boring. It appears on hundreds of New Orleans menus, and is eaten by visitors and locals at all hours.

FOR 4-6 SERVINGS:
2 cups red kidney beans
6 cups water
50 g butter
3 onions, chopped
4-6 cloves garlic, chopped
1 green pepper, chopped
½ cup chopped parsley
2-3 bay leaves
1 tsp dried thyme
12 drops tabasco sauce, or chilli powder to taste
1 tsp salt
2 cups brown rice

Put everything except the salt and rice into a large saucepan. Boil vigorously for 15 minutes, then turn down and simmer for 3-4 hours, until the beans are meltingly soft and quite mushy, forming a thick sauce.

Remove the bay leaves, add the salt, and adjust the seasonings, adding more herbs and chilli sauce if you like.

Cook the rice so that it will be ready when the beans are cooked (rice seasonings are not given here, see page 80).

Serve the beans on the rice, with or without a knob of butter on each serving.

If you think it needs more colour and texture, depart from tradition and serve cubes of brightly coloured peppers to sprinkle over the top, or stir them into the beans a few minutes before serving.

BEAN FEAST

This is a very useful and tasty bean mixture. It tastes good served hot, warm, or at room temperature. It can be served as soon as it is cooked, but its flavour and texture improve with standing. You can serve the mixture as the main part of a meal, or include it in a buffet. Use whatever beans you like. I like haricot beans because they cook relatively fast, are reasonably priced and have a good flavour and texture.

FOR 8-12 SERVINGS:
2 cups haricot or other beans
8 cups water
¼ cup oil
2 large onions
2 scrubbed potatoes
2 cubed carrots

MEALS WITHOUT MEAT

2-3 stalks celery
2 tsp salt
1 tsp paprika
2 tsp sugar
¼ cup tomato paste
1 tsp dried basil
1 tsp dried oregano
2 cups cauliflower pieces
1 green pepper, sliced (optional)
about ½ cup chopped parsley

Soak the beans overnight, then boil the water until tender enough to squash with your tongue on the top of your mouth (*see page 175*).

Cool the beans in their cooking liquid until you are ready to make the rest of the recipe. Put the oil, onions, potatoes, carrots and celery in a large saucepan. Stir over moderate heat until vegetables are very hot, then add the next six ingredients, the drained beans and 1½ cups of their cooking liquid, and simmer, stirring frequently, for 15 minutes. Add the pieces of cauliflower and sliced green pepper and cook for 5 minutes longer. Remove from the heat and add the chopped parsley.

Serve reheated, warm or at room temperature, sprinkled with more parsley. Always taste before serving, and adjust the seasoning if necessary.

LENTIL AND VEGETABLE CURRY

Brown or red lentils, teamed with small amounts of several vegetables, and a well-flavoured sauce make a good meal the day before you go shopping to replenish your supplies. Use the last, rather tired vegetables that are hiding in paper or plastic bags, and add any leftover cooked vegetables from little dishes in the refrigerator. Or, if you have a garden, go out and pick a little bit of this or that.

For this recipe to have an interesting colour and texture, you must take care not to over or undercook any of the vegetables you use.

FOR 4 MAIN COURSE SERVINGS:
1½ cups red or brown lentils, or moong dahl
2-3 cups water
2 bay leaves
2 Tbsp oil or 25 g butter
2 onions
2 cloves garlic
1 tsp turmeric
1 tsp ground cumin
1 tsp ground ginger
2-3 cups chopped vegetables
1 tsp salt
1 cup hot water
about ½ cup coconut cream (optional)

Cook the lentils or dahl in the water with the bay leaves until tender, adding more water if necessary. Red lentils and dahl should take 20-30 minutes, and brown lentils 40 minutes.

While they cook, prepare the second mixture, preferably in a large non-stick pan with a lid.

Heat the oil or butter, add the chopped onion and garlic, and the spices. Cook without browning for 5 minutes.

Prepare and cut up the vegetables into evenly sized cubes or pieces, starting with those that take longest to cook. Add each vegetable as it is prepared, tossing it with the onion, and covering the pan between additions. Add the salt and water after the last addition and cook until all vegetables are barely tender. Add the cooked lentils and (optional) coconut cream. Taste, and adjust seasonings, thickness, etc., boiling down or thickening with a little cornflour paste if necessary.

Serve in a bowl or on rice. A salad of tomatoes and peppers with a yoghurt or French dressing makes a good accompaniment if you want to dress this up.

BEANS & LENTILS

PEA FLOUR PATTIES

Pea flour is made from finely ground dried peas. It is high in protein and forms a good fritter batter when mixed with water. It does not need the addition of eggs or milk.

In this easy recipe the raw vegetables are surrounded by batter flavoured with Indian spices. We like to make the patties small, because they cook quickly and have a high proportion of crisp coating. They make excellent finger food, and go very well with beer before a meal, but they are also excellent served with vegetables or salads as the main part of a meal.

Experiment, making them with different vegetables, but don't leave out the onion. To shorten their cooking time you can partly cook dense vegetables before coating them with batter, if you like.

FOR 4 MAIN COURSE SERVINGS OR SNACKS FOR 8:

1 cup pea flour
about ½ cup water
1 tsp turmeric
2 tsp ground cumin
2 tsp ground coriander
2 tsp garam masala
2 medium-sized potatoes
1 onion
1 cup frozen peas, or cauliflower florets etc.
oil for frying

Mix the pea flour with water and the flavourings to make a fairly stiff paste, Leave to stand for 5 minutes or longer if you can.

Scrub the potatoes, and cut them and the onion into pea-sized cubes. Cut other vegetables into cubes the same size.

Mix all the vegetables into the batter just before you intend to start cooking. They will thin down the mixture. Add extra pea flour or water to make a batter thick enough to hold spoonfuls of the vegetables together.

Heat oil 2 cm deep in a frypan. Drop teaspoonfuls of mixture carefully into it. Adjust heat so patties brown nicely in about 4 minutes, then turn them and cook the other side for the same time. Faster cooking will leave vegetables raw. Drain, and serve as soon as possible, with a sauce made by combining the following in amounts to suit your taste:

- lemon juice
- plain, unsweetened yoghurt
- chopped mint
- salt

This dip or sauce improves on standing.

DAHL

This is a mixture of spaghetti-sauce consistency which is nice served with rice and curry side dishes. You can have a wonderful time surrounding the big bowls of dahl and rice with little plates of sweet and savoury, raw and cooked, crunchy and soft foods which will provide interesting accents for your meal. Be limited only by your imagination and your purse!

FOR 4 MAIN COURSE SERVINGS OR 6-8 SIDE DISH SERVINGS:

1 cup red or brown lentils or moong dahl
4 cups water
2 Tbsp oil
2 onions, chopped
2 cloves garlic
2 tsp cumin seeds
1 tsp ground turmeric
2 tsp grated root ginger
1 tsp garam masala
1 tsp salt

Boil the lentils or dahl in the water until tender and mushy — about 20 minutes for moong dahl, 30 minutes for red lentils, and 40 minutes for brown lentils.

In another pan heat the oil and cook the next five ingredients over moderate heat until the onion is tender. Stir in the garam masala and the salt and

48 MEALS WITHOUT MEAT

remove from the heat.

Add the onion mixture to the pulses when they are soft, and simmer together for 5 minutes, boiling fast if mixture needs thickening, or adding more water if it is too thick.

Serve immediately, or reheat, adjusting seasonings just before serving.

BULGAR AND BEAN 'CHILLI CON CARNE'

The bulgar in this sauce thickens it and gives it body in the same way that minced beef gives substance to spaghetti sauce, while the beans add extra interest. The final combination of chopped wheat, beans and rice is not only interesting to eat, but nutritionally well balanced too! Try it if you want a quick-cooking dinner — although you may find, as we do, that leftovers taste even better.

for 4-6 main course servings:

¾ cup bulgar
1½ cups boiling water
2 large onions
2 cloves of garlic
2 Tbsp oil or butter
2 tsp ground cumin
1 tsp oreganum
½-1 tsp chilli powder (to taste)
1 Tbsp soya sauce
3 Tbsp tomato paste
2 tsp sugar
½ cup hot water
juice of 1 lemon
black pepper
1 (425 g) can kidney beans

Pour the boiling water over the bulgar and then leave to stand, stirring occasionally while preparing the rest of the recipe.

Dice the onions and finely chop the garlic, heat the oil or butter in a large pot or frypan and sauté these until the onion is soft and beginning to turn clear. Stir in the cumin, oreganum and chilli powder and continue to cook for a few minutes.

In a small bowl or cup mix together the soya sauce, tomato paste, sugar and hot water. Pour the resulting purée over the onion mixture, then stir in the lemon juice, black pepper (to taste) and the drained, rinsed beans.

Add the bulgar and combine everything well. The mixture should be about the consistency of a thick spaghetti sauce. If you think that it is still too thick, add a little more water (some batches of bulgar seem to absorb much more water than others). Allow to simmer over a low heat for 5-10 minutes, stirring occasionally to prevent sticking on the bottom.

Serve over brown or white rice, topped with sour cream and spring onions or chives, accompanied by your favourite salad or cooked vegetables.

Note:
Bulgar is sometimes called Burghul.

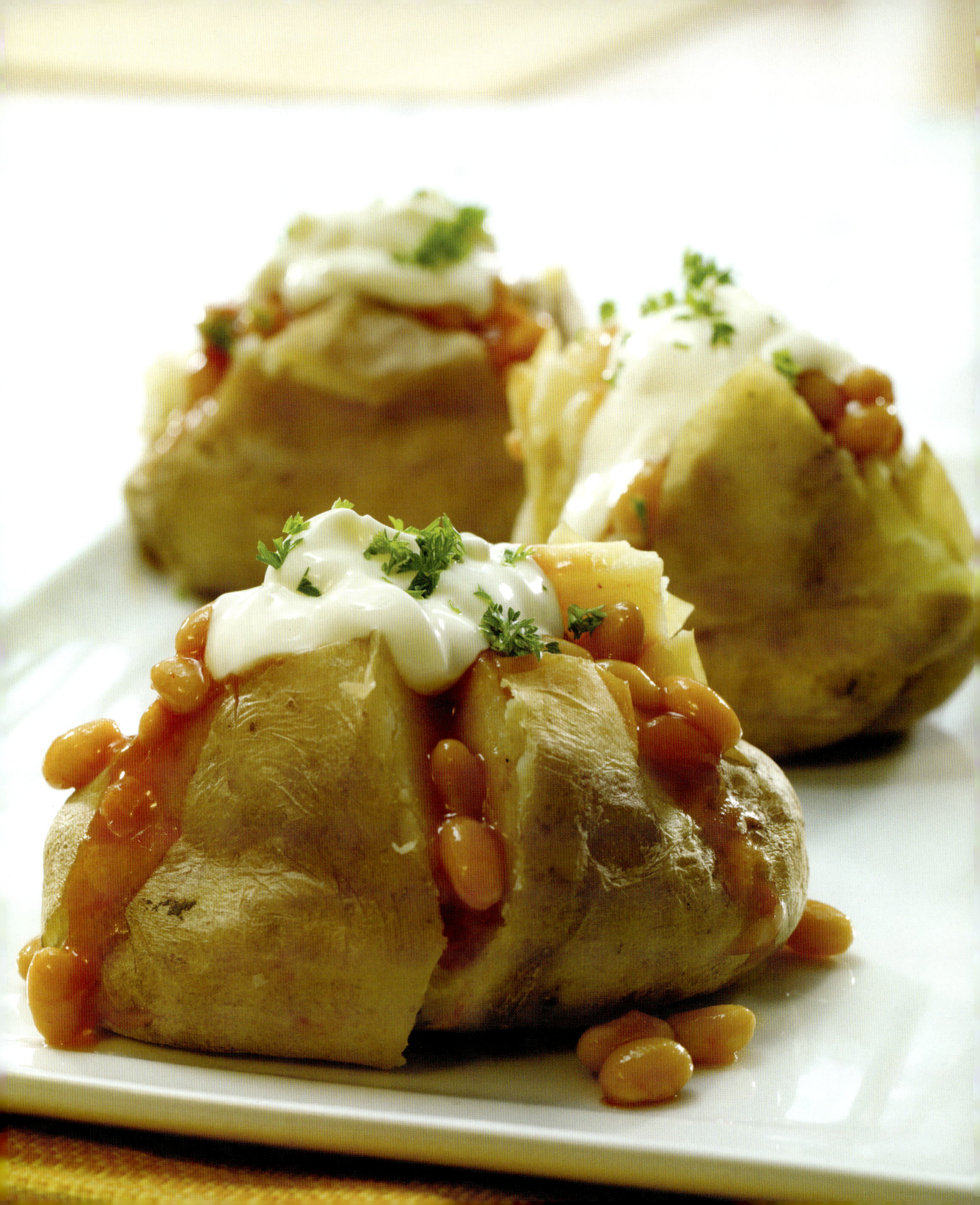

POTATO MAIN COURSES

Potato recipes are always popular and make good main courses, for family meals, or as part of a buffet

STUFFED BAKED POTATOES

Everybody likes potatoes which have been baked, emptied of their cooked insides, filled again with mashed potato and exciting additions, and reheated.

Scrub large potatoes, bake at 200°C for about an hour, or microwave on High (100%) power, for 4-6 minutes per potato. Potatoes are cooked when they 'give' when pressed.
Remove a slice from the top, or halve the cooked potatoes.
   Scoop out the flesh with a small spoon, and mash it with one or more of the following:

- butter/ quark
- grated cheese
- cubed cheese
- tofu
- mayonnaise
- milk
- sour cream
- cream cheese
- yoghurt
- cottage cheese

Season with:
- chopped spring onion or chives
- chopped parsley
- finely chopped thyme, basil, marjoram, dill, mint, etc.
- pepper
- chutney, pickle, or relish
- garlic or garlic spreads
- mustard
- chilli sauce
- chopped gherkins
- chopped red or green peppers

Stir in:
- sautéed mushrooms
- sautéed onions
- chopped avocado
- chopped nuts
- corn
- asparagus
- baked beans
- Mexican beans

Taste and season if necessary. Pile the filling back into the potato shells. Reheat at 200°C until heated through and browned, for about 15 minutes, or microwave until heated through, for about 2-3 minutes per potato. Brown under a grill if desired.

POTATO PANCAKES

Potato pancakes seem especially popular with children—they enjoy their texture and mild flavour. Because the potato browns on prolonged standing, do not mix the batter before you plan to cook it. If you like, you can mix the first six ingredients in a bowl and add the potato and flour just before cooking. In this recipe the potato is grated straight into the bowl, and is not squeezed first. If the mixture seems a little wet, add 2-3 tablespoons of extra flour. This will depend on the potatoes.

for 6 servings:
2 eggs, unbeaten
2 Tbsp milk
1 onion, very finely chopped
1 tsp curry powder
1 tsp salt
½ tsp celery salt
500 g raw potatoes
¼ cup flour
oil

In a basin mix the eggs, milk, onion and seasonings. Stir with a fork until mixed. Just before cooking, grate the scrubbed (or thinly peeled) potatoes into the mixture and add the flour. If wholemeal flour is used, increase the quantity slightly. Fry spoonfuls of the mixture in hot corn or soya oil, about 5 mm deep, for 3 minutes per side, until golden brown. If the cooking time is too short, the potato will not be cooked in the centre.
   Serve alone, or with tomatoes or mushrooms.

MEALS WITHOUT MEAT

POTATO AND EGG CASSEROLE

This is probably our most popular potato recipe—'comfort food' at its best! It does take some time and effort to prepare, but it can be organised ahead, leaving plenty of time to clean up before the meal.

for 4-6 servings:

4 (800 g) cooked potatoes
4 hard-boiled eggs
50 g butter
2 large onions
¼ cup flour
1 tsp dry mustard
½ tsp salt
black pepper to taste
2½ cups milk
1 cup grated cheese

Topping:

1 Tbsp butter
1 cup fresh breadcrumbs

Slice the cooked potatoes into a large buttered casserole dish, then add the quartered, sliced or chopped hard-boiled eggs.

Melt the butter in a saucepan and cook the chopped onions until they are tender, but have not browned. Stir in the flour, mustard, salt and pepper. Add 1 cup of milk and bring to the boil, stirring constantly. Stir in the remaining milk and bring back to the boil again. Remove from the heat and add the grated cheese, stirring until smooth.

Pour the cheese sauce over the potato and egg mixture, and stir to combine. Cover with the topping made by tossing the melted butter and bread crumbs together.

If making ahead of time, refrigerate at this stage until needed. Bake, uncovered, at 180°C for 30-45 minutes, until the crumbs are golden brown and the filling has heated through completely.

EGMONT POTATOES

We have eaten casseroles like this for years. Everybody loves them. Whenever one is served as part of a buffet meal, people seem to bypass exotic and expensive foods to take second helpings!

for 4 servings:

800 g potatoes
¼ cup water
2 Tbsp butter
4 onions
1 (250 g) carton sour cream
herbs, chopped
about 2 cups grated tasty cheese

To cook the potatoes for this recipe very quickly in a microwave oven, scrub or thinly peel the potatoes and slice them 5 mm thick. Put them in an oven bag or small-lidded microwave casserole with the water and half the butter. Close the bag with a rubberband, leaving a finger-sized hole, or cover the casserole, and microwave on High (100%) power for 10 minutes, or until tender, shaking the container once after about 4 minutes. Alternatively, if cooking conventionally boil the potatoes until they are cooked, then slice them thinly.

While the potatoes cook, slice the onions, and cook them in the butter, in a covered frying pan, with the heat high enough to brown them lightly. Stir them several times as they cook.

Thin down the sour cream with enough milk to make it pourable, then pour this over the cooked potato, and mix well. Add chopped herbs to this then spoon half the creamy potatoes into a buttered dish, about 20x20 cm.

Sprinkle with half the cheese and half the onions, then arrange the remaining potato on top. Cover with the rest of the onions and cheese.

Grill for about 5 minutes, until the top is brown. For most even browning, have dish 18-20 cm from the heat.

If potatoes on the bottom have not heated through completely, microwave on High power until bubbling. This is nicest if left to stand for 5 minutes before serving.

SPICED POTATOES AND PEAS

When you use several spices to flavour a coconut cream-flavoured sauce, you can turn potatoes and peas into a whole meal—and a interesting one at that. The mixture will not be 'hot' unless you add the chilli powder.

FOR 4 LARGE SERVINGS:

1 large onion, chopped
2 cloves garlic, chopped
2 Tbsp oil or butter
½ tsp ground cumin
½ tsp ground cardamom
½ tsp ground coriander
¼ tsp ground celery seed
¼ tsp ground cloves
1/8 tsp chilli powder (optional)
¾-1 tsp turmeric
1 (410 g) can coconut cream
    600-700 g small potatoes, preferably new
3 cups frozen peas
1 Tbsp sugar
½ tsp salt

Put the chopped onion and garlic into a large frying pan with the oil or butter. Cook gently for 4-5 minutes, until transparent. Add the next seven spices. Stir over low heat for 2-3 minutes longer. Add the coconut cream and bring to the boil.

Scrub, scrape or peel the potatoes, and halve or quarter if large. Add to pan, cover and simmer, turning potatoes occasionally, until they are just tender, usually 15-20 minutes. Add the peas, sugar and salt and cook for a few minutes longer until peas are tender.

Adjust thickness of sauce by boiling briskly for a few minutes if too thin, or adding a little water if it is too thick. Taste, adjust seasonings if necessary, and serve.

CHEESY POTATO BAKE

This layered potato and cheese 'cake' is much more interesting than it sounds from its contents. It can be made from any cream soup that you like, remembering only to select a flavour that goes well with potatoes and cheese. If you find a suitable packet cream soup, this will do just as well as the can when made up with 2 cups of liquid.

This 'cake' firms up on standing after cooking, and is just as nice reheated a day or two later when it can be cut in wedges and served like a pie.

FOR 4-6 SERVINGS:

5-6 large potatoes (1 kg)
1 (440 g) can cream of vegetable soup
¼–½ cup milk, cream or sherry (or any
    combination of these)
2 cups (200 g) grated tasty (or Raclette) cheese
paprika

Cook the potatoes, then cut them into slices no more than 1 cm thick. Open the can of soup and measure the contents into a small bowl, add enough milk, cream, sherry or a mixture of these to make the soup up to 2 cups.

Grease a large, shallow ovenware dish, then cover its bottom with half of the potato slices. Sprinkle over half of the cheese, then pour over half of the soup. Repeat this process using the other half of the potato, cheese and soup mixture. Sprinkle the top with paprika and bake, uncovered, at 200°C for 45 minutes.

Leave to stand for half an hour or so prior to serving. This will allow the flavours to blend and the potatoes to absorb all the remaining liquid. Serve with a green or tomato salad and crusty bread rolls.

RACLETTE

This is an updated version of a Swiss tradition, where an easily melted type of cheese is heated and served on boiled potatoes, with pickled cucumbers and beer or white wine, as a complete meal.

Use New Zealand-made Raclette cheese which has the texture and aroma, when heated, of its Swiss counterpart. For a milder flavour use 'standard' mild cheddar or try Pyrenees, St Paulin or Poitevin cheese.

Boil the potatoes conventionally or microwave them before melting the cheese. To microwave new or maincrop potatoes, cut 500 g of scrubbed potatoes into even-sized pieces (smaller pieces cook more quickly). Microwave on High (100% power) in a covered dish or oven bag with ½ cup water for new potatoes, or ¼ cup for maincrop potatoes, for 6-8 minutes. Allow 2-3 minutes standing time. (If the potatoes shrivel they are overcooked.)

Heat slices of cheese in shallow dishes until soft and bubbly around the edges. Use the microwave oven, or the grill of your conventional oven.

Note:
Cook more potatoes and more cheese than you think you will need, since you may be surprised by the amount eaten.

Although not traditional, mixed salad and bread rolls make fine accompaniments for this meal too.

Raclette

POTATO CAKES

Enormously popular, these potato cakes don't need to be made to any precise formula—vary the seasoning each time, using what is available. Use potatoes which have been boiled or microwaved (preferably the day before) or leftover mashed potato. Do not mix the flour and potatoes until you are ready to cook them as the mixture sometimes turns sticky with prolonged standing.

FOR 4 SERVINGS:

2 cups of grated cooked potato or
    2 cups mashed potato
1 cup self-raising flour
1 tsp celery salt
1 tsp garlic salt or onion salt
½ tsp curry powder
4 spring onions, chopped
¼ cup chopped parsley
up to 1 cup cooked cold carrots, peas
    or mixed vegetables (optional)

Mix the cold grated (or mashed) potato with the remaining ingredients, adding other fresh or dried herbs and spices if desired.

If the dough is too dry to mould into a 10-cm-wide cyclinder, add a little milk. If it is too moist, add a little extra flour.

Cut into 1-cm-thick slices with a sharp serrated knife. Turn in a little extra flour and cook in a preheated (preferably non-stick) pan in a small amount of oil or butter. Allow about 3 minutes per side.

Serve with a salad or cooked vegetables.

POTATO FRITTATA

Make a variation of this recipe; at weekends when you want something quick and easy, and at times when you haven't bought any special ingredients, but want to use up leftovers.

You will also find this a useful recipe if you want to take something substantial for a picnic and don't have time to make a pie.

FOR 4-6 SERVINGS:

50 g butter
3 onions, sliced
3-4 medium-sized potatoes (500-600 g)
2 zucchini, sliced (or other vegetables)
4 eggs
2 Tbsp water
½ cup grated parmesan cheese

Melt the butter in a large heavy pan.

Cook the sliced onions in the butter, over moderate heat, until they are evenly browned.

Add the sliced, unpeeled potatoes, stir well, cover pan and cook for 15-20 minutes, stirring occasionally.

After 10-15 minutes add the zucchini or other vegetables, so they will be cooked when the potatoes are.

Beat the eggs with the water and half the cheese.

Pour over the pressed-down vegetable mixture, and cook over gentle heat for 10 minutes or until the sides and bottom are cooked.

Sprinkle remaining parmesan cheese over the top, then brown under a grill, until the top puffs up and browns lightly.

Serve hot, warm or at room temperature, with a salad if desired.

Variations:

Add chopped garlic with the potatoes, and fresh or dried herbs with the egg mixture.

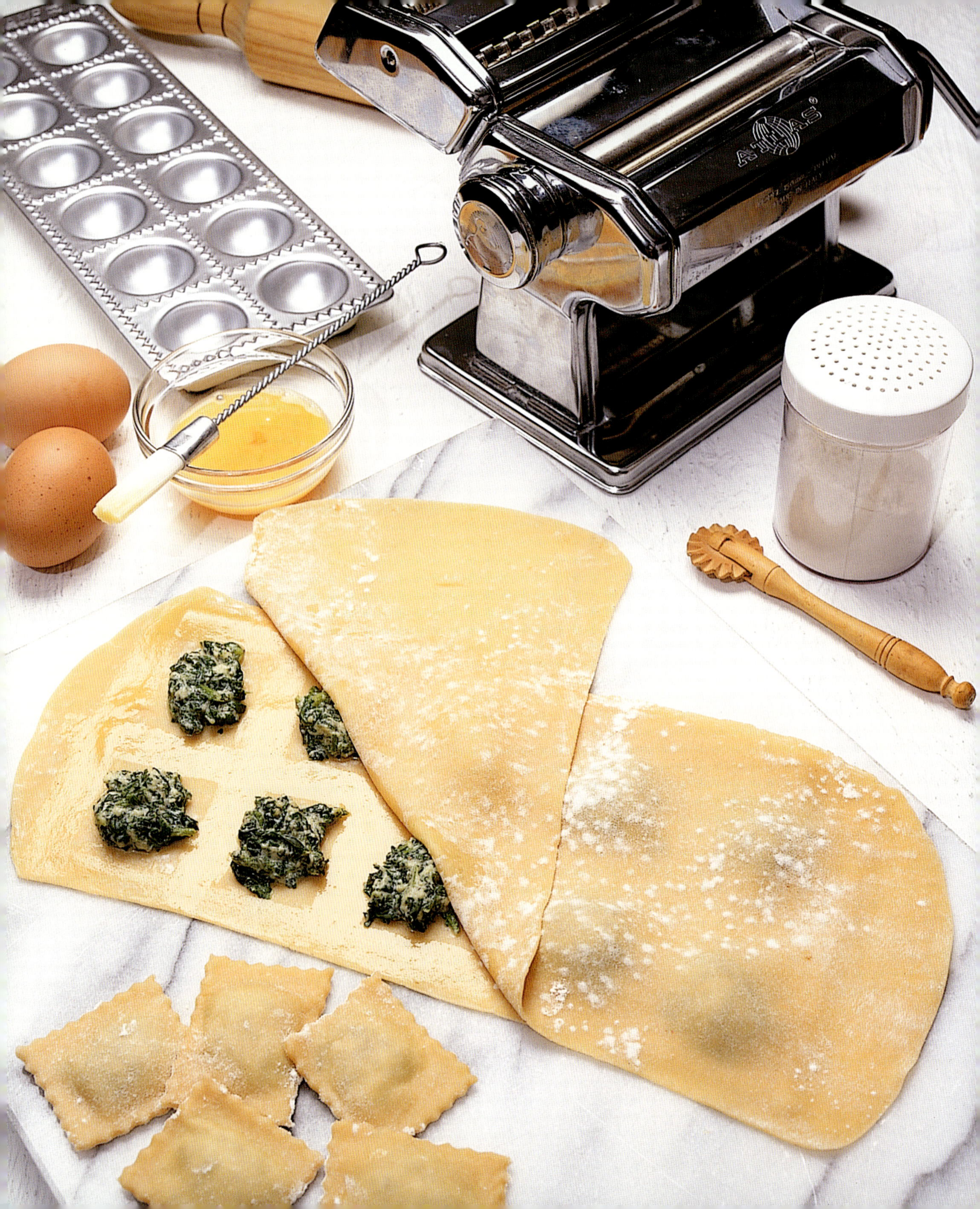

PASTA BASED MEALS

Pasta comes in a remarkable range of sizes and shapes. It cooks quickly and can be served with many interesting sauces. Don't limit yourself to only a few pasta recipes. Keep trying different ones and experiment with different pasta shapes, too.

TO COOK DRY PASTA

To fully enjoy a pasta meal, you should cook the pasta carefully. Make sure that it has no uncooked centre core, but do not overcook it so that it is soft and floppy. Try to judge the exact stage, when it is tender, but has some 'bite'; when it keeps its shape well, and has some bounce as it sits on the plate. Pasta served at this stage absorbs sauces and coatings well, and seems particularly satisfying to eat.

FOR 4-6 MAIN COURSE SERVINGS:
500 g spaghetti or other pasta
2 litres (8 cups) water
1 tsp salt
1 Tbsp oil
extra butter or oil

Select your pasta variety. Read the information on the pack to see if it has any special requirements.

Unless otherwise instructed, bring the water and salt to the boil in a large saucepan. Add the tablespoon of oil.

Add the dry pasta gradually, stirring occasionally, and trying to keep the water boiling. When it has all been added make sure that it is moving freely round the pan. Boil, uncovered, until tender. It should still feel rather firm when bitten. This stage is described as 'al dente'. (Pasta usually cooks in 8-12 minutes.)

Drain, and toss lightly with a little butter or oil, to stop the pieces sticking together.

Use as required. In general, use as soon as possible after cooking.

NOTE:
If pasta slightly overcooks, or if it must stand some time before use, drain, then rinse with cold water to cool it down quickly. Add more oil or butter than you would if you were serving immediately. If you have olive oil, use it in preference to other oils.

Cooking times of different pastas vary with size and shape. Judge by sight and feel, not by rote.

PAINLESS PASTA

When you are in a hurry, tired, or at a low creative ebb, remember that you can serve pasta without elaborate sauces and toppings. Simply stir several of the following into a pot of hot pasta (cooked according to the instructions given above), then enjoy!

- butter
- olive oil
- chopped fresh herbs
- garlic sautéed in olive oil
- diced tomato
- diced green or red pepper
- chopped spring onion
- pre-grated cheese
- pesto (see page 139)
- sour cream
- cream cheese
- lemon rind
- sautéed pine nuts
- toasted sunflower seeds
- nutmeg
- peanut butter thinned with soya sauce
- cottage cheese
- crumbled blue cheese
- chilli sauce
- grated parmesan cheese
- black pepper
- quark or frontage frais
- yoghurt
- sesame oil

FRESH PASTA IN SAVOURY TOMATO SAUCE

Look in delicatessens and supermarket specialty food cabinets to see whether they stock fresh ravioli, tortellini and other fresh pasta, stuffed or unstuffed. To cook these, follow the instructions on the packets. Serve with a well-flavoured sauce, preferably one with a contrasting colour.

MEALS WITHOUT MEAT

FOR 3-4 SERVINGS:

1 large red pepper
2 Tbsp butter
2 cloves garlic
1 ½ cups peeled canned tomatoes or 750g fresh tomatoes, peeled
1 tsp sugar
2 tsp cornflour
¼ cup water or wine
fresh basil (if available)

Cut pepper into small cubes. Cook gently in butter, with garlic, without browning, for 10-15 minutes, in a covered pan.

Add chopped tomatoes and liquid from can, and simmer, uncovered, for 10 minutes. Stir in mixed sugar, cornflour and water or wine.

If necessary, add more water or wine so sauce is lightly thickened.

Add fresh basil, taste, and adjust seasoning carefully. Serve over ravioli etc. as a first or main course.

CHUNKY VEGETABLE AND TOMATO SAUCE ON PASTA

This sauce has a good rich flavour and seems more substantial than it actually is. It is a good choice when you want a spaghetti sauce that will please both vegetarians and meat-eaters.

FOR 4-6 SERVINGS:

2 large onions, chopped
2 cloves garlic, chopped
2 tsp oil
1-2 cups sliced dark-gilled mushrooms
1-2 red peppers
1-2 green peppers
basil, oreganum, thyme
freshly ground pepper
¼-½ cup water
1 (400 g) can whole peeled tomatoes
2-3 Tbsp tomato paste
about 500 g fettucine or spaghetti (plain, spinach or wholemeal)

In a large non-stick frypan with a lid, cook the chopped onion and garlic in the oil until browned. Add a little water to soften the vegetables during the first few minutes of cooking, if desired, then turn up the heat until it evaporates. Add the chopped mushrooms after the onions have started browning, and cook until the mushrooms have browned.

Stir in the chopped peppers, add herbs according to your taste (about 1 tsp each of basil and oreganum, and ¼ tsp dried thyme) then add the water, cover, and cook over high heat until the water evaporates.

Stir over lower heat for 2-3 minutes, then add the chopped canned tomatoes and their liquid, and enough tomato paste to give a good colour and flavour. Simmer for about 10 minutes, adjusting the thickness by boiling it down, adding a little cornflour paste, or thinning it with extra water. Taste, and adjust seasonings if necessary.

Cook the pasta as described above, adding chopped herbs and parmesan cheese as well as the butter or oil if desired. Arrange in nests on the required number of plates, and pour the sauce over it.

MICROWAVED MACARONI CHEESE

This macaroni cheese uses only one microwave-proof dish. If you use pregrated cheese, you don't even get a dirty grater! If you like a crisp topping, make it before you cook the macaroni cheese. Microwave a mixture of 2 cups fresh breadcrumbs, 1 tablespoon melted butter and 1 tablespoon chopped parsley until crumbs turn golden, 2-4 minutes.

FOR 3-4 SERVINGS

75 g butter
1 tsp garlic salt
2 cups (200 g) macaroni, spirals, etc.
2 cups boiling water
2 cup milk
2 cups grated cheese
2 Tbsp flour

Cut butter into 9 cubes. Melt in fairly large, flat-bottomed microwave dish, for about 1 minute on High

PASTA BASED MEALS

(100%) power. Stir in garlic salt and macaroni, or any other shape of pasta that holds a lot of sauce, e.g. spirals. Pour boiling water over pasta.

Cover. Cook on Medium (50%) power for 10-15 minutes, until pasta is tender, stirring every 5 minutes. Stir in milk immediately. Mix grated cheese with flour. Stir into hot pasta mixture. Stir gently for 30-60 seconds until cheese melts.

Microwave for 2 minutes or until mixture bubbles all round edge. Stir again. Leave to stand for 3 minutes. Sprinkle with prepared crumbs, if desired.

MACARONI CHEESE

Don't forget about macaroni cheese. It is an old-fashioned 'comfort food', enjoyed by all age groups. If you come across somebody who is in a panic and doesn't know what to cook for vegetarians, you can solve the problem by suggesting this!

for 2-4 servings
1 cup (125 g) macaroni
2 Tbsp butter
2 Tbsp flour
1½ cups milk
2 cups grated cheese
salt and pepper

Boil macaroni until tender in plenty of boiling salted water, then drain. Melt butter, add flour, and heat until bubbly. Add milk in thirds, stirring and boiling between additions. Stir in the grated cheese. Season to taste. Heat only until cheese melts. Stir macaroni into cheese sauce.

Reheat, browning top in oven for best results, otherwise sprinkle with paprika and serve immediately.

Variations:
Add ½ cup drained crushed pineapple.
Replace ½ cup milk with pineapple juice.
Add cooked celery, broccoli, etc.

FRESH TOMATO SAUCE

If you have ripe red, flavourful tomatoes on hand, by all means use them to make sauces for pasta. You will be wasting your time, however, if the tomatoes are pale, or watery, or out of season. If this is the case, open a can instead, and save yourself disappointment. We make a light fresh-tasting sauce with the tomatoes from our garden.

for 4 servings (2-3 cups):
1 kg ripe red tomatoes
1 or 2 onions
2 Tbsp butter
basil, organum, thyme
1 tsp sugar
½ tsp salt
freshly ground pepper
hot pepper sauce

Pour hot water over the tomatoes, leave to stand for 20-30 seconds, or till you see the skins split, then drain and peel.

Chop the onion(s) finely and cook gently in the butter in a large non-stick pan, for 5 minutes, without browning. Add chopped tomatoes, herbs to taste, and remaining seasonings, and cook, uncovered, for 10-20 minutes, stirring often. Let mixture evaporate or thicken with about a tablespoon of cornflour mixed to a paste with cold water. Serve over freshly cooked pasta.

PASTA AND

This is a good recipe for a hungry family or flat. If you like the combination of pasta and cheese, stir in an extra cupful when you mix the cooked pasta and tomato.

for 4-6 servings:
500g pasta shells, macaroni, crests or spirals
3 medium-sized onions
2-3 cloves garlic

1 Tbsp butter or oil
1 (425 g) can tomato purée
1 tsp sugar
½ tsp salt
1 tsp basil
½ tsp marjoram
¼ tsp thyme
2 Tbsp chopped fresh parsley (or 1 Tbsp dried parsley)
black pepper
1 cup grated cheese
paprika

Cook the pasta according to directions on page 44 in a large pot of lightly salted water.

While the pasta cooks, dice and sauté the onion and garlic in the butter or oil. When the onion is soft and beginning to turn clear, reduce the heat and add the remaining ingredients, except for the cheese and paprika. Simmer gently over a low heat for a few minutes.

Drain the pasta, then combine with the tomato mixture in a large shallow casserole or soufflé dish. Sprinkle the cheese evenly over the top, then dust lightly with paprika.

At this stage you may either brown the top briefly under the grill for a few minutes to form a light crust, or, for a more solid product that can be sliced into squares and served more like a loaf, bake, uncovered, at 180°C for 40 minutes.

PEANUTTY PASTA SALAD

This is an interesting and different pasta recipe for peanut butter fans. It is good served warm, not hot, in summer.

FOR 2 SERVINGS:
100 g spaghetti
200 g of a mixture of carrots, celery and beans, sliced thinly
100 g bean sprouts (optional)
2 Tbsp crunchy peanut butter
1 Tbsp Kikkoman soya sauce
1 Tbsp wine vinegar
2 tsp sugar
1 tsp sesame oil

Break the spaghetti into 10 cm lengths. Cook in a litre of boiling salted water with a teaspoon of added oil. Trim the vegetables and cut them into long, thin matchsticks. Rinse the beansprouts.

Measure the remaining ingredients into a cup, and mix well until smooth. Thin down by adding 1 tablespoon each of water and oil, then repeat if necessary, until sauce is of pouring consistency.

When the spaghetti is almost cooked, add the vegetable matchsticks and cook for 2 minutes longer. Add the beansprouts and cook for 30 seconds more.

Drain, pour the peanut sauce over spaghetti and turn gently to coat everything with it. Serve warm, with cucumber and lettuce salads.

ZUCCHINI AND YOGHURT PASTA

This is a lovely light, summery pasta dish—although it tastes so good you may find yourself making variations all year round.

FOR 4 SERVINGS:
500 g zucchini
250 g pasta, ribbons or your favourite shape
3 cloves garlic, crushed
1 Tbsp butter
1½ cups yoghurt
½ cup sour cream
½-1 tsp salt to taste
½ tsp sugar
1 tsp paprika
2-3 Tbsp freshly chopped parsley
1 Tbsp lemon juice
freshly ground black pepper

Cut the zucchini into slices (or chunks depending on size), not more than 1 cm thick.

Put the pasta on to cook, using instructions on the

packet or those given on page 44.
Sauté the zucchini with the crushed and chopped garlic, until it has softened and is beginning to turn golden.

Remove from the heat and add the yoghurt, sour cream and seasonings. Stir gently until everything is well combined.

Stir into the cooked pasta and serve while hot. Sprinkle individual servings with grated parmesan if desired.

This makes a complete meal by itself but is even better when served with a mixed green salad.

LASAGNE

Lasagne is a popular casserole made up of different layers. Here pasta is alternated with a well-flavoured lentil and tomato mixture and a rich cheese sauce, which also forms an attractive topping.
Because this mixture uses dry pasta the lentil and tomato mixture needs to be fairly sloppy. The pasta absorbs any surplus liquid from this layer as it cooks. You may wish to cook your lasagne ahead and reheat it when needed, but remember that it should always be cooked as soon as you have assembled the layers, otherwise the pasta may disintegrate.

FOR 4-6 SERVINGS:
SAUCE:
1 quantity of lentil and tomato sauce (see above)

TOPPING:
3 Tbsp butter
3 Tbsp flour
2 cups milk
½ tsp salt
grated nutmeg
black pepper
2 cups (200 g) grated cheese—tasty cheddar, gruyère or Emmentaler
2 eggs
200-350 g lasagne noodles
paprika

Prepare the lentil and tomato sauce according to the recipe given above, then prepare the cheese sauce as follows.

Melt the butter in a medium-sized pot then stir in the flour. Cook for 30 seconds, stirring continuously.

Add about a third of the milk and bring to the boil, allowing the mixture to thicken. Add another third of the milk and bring to the boil again, stirring vigorously to ensure the sauce is smooth. Stir in the last of the milk, then bring to the boil again, remove from the heat, then stir in the seasonings and grated cheese.

(If you are cooking for a special occasion and/or feel like trying something a little different, use gruyère or Emmentaler cheese instead of tasty cheddar—they give a deliciously rich flavour.)

Reheat to melt the cheese if necessary, but do not boil as the cheese will turn stringy, then remove from the heat again and beat in the eggs.

Select a large shallow casserole dish and spread a thin layer of the lentil sauce (about a quarter) over the bottom. Arrange half of the noodles in a layer over this, then spread half of the remaining lentil and tomato mixture on top. Pour over half of the cheese sauce, then arrange the remaining noodles in a layer over this. Spread over the remaining lentil mixture, then top with the remaining cheese sauce and sprinkle with paprika.

Bake at 150°C for 45 minutes, or until the top is firm when pressed in the centre.

SPINACH AND COTTAGE CHEESE

This is an exceedingly popular and delicious mixture, as suitable for dinner parties as it is for a family meal. You can cook the whole casserole ahead, and reheat it when you want to eat, or you can prepare the sauce and the filling ahead, but once the filling is put into the cannelloni tubes the casserole should be cooked promptly, or the pasta will disintegrate.

FOR 4-6 SERVINGS
1 packet cannelloni tubes (about 16)

Sauce:
2 medium-sized onions
4 cloves garlic
2 Tbsp oil
1 small green pepper
1 tsp basil
½ tsp thyme
½ tsp sugar
½ tsp salt
1 (300 g) can tomato purée
1 Tbsp wine vinegar
¼ cup water

Filling:
about 1 kg of fresh spinach
   (2 cups when lightly cooked)
1 cup cottage cheese
1 tsp dried oreganum
½ tsp salt
½ tsp sugar
¼ tsp grated nutmeg
black pepper to taste

Topping:
1 cup cream cheese
1 cup grated cheese

Chop the onions finely and peel and chop the garlic. Sauté in the oil, stirring occasionally. Stir in the chopped green pepper and continue to cook until everything has softened and the onion turns clear. Add the seasonings, then the can of tomato purée, vinegar and water. Bring to the boil, then reduce the heat and leave to simmer while you prepare the filling. Bring a large pot of water to the boil, then add the fresh spinach. Cook for a minute or two, just until the spinach has softened and wilted, then remove from the heat and drain well.

Coarsely chop the spinach, then return to the pot or a medium-sized bowl. Add the cottage cheese and remaining filling ingredients to the spinach, and mix everything together until evenly combined.

Select a shallow casserole dish that will hold all the cannelloni tubes comfortably, then butter it lightly.

Fill each cannelloni tube, then place in the casserole dish. (There is no neat and tidy way to do this—just use your hands. Don't stuff the tubes too full or they may break, or you might run out of filling. Look for 'instant' cannelloni tubes when shopping—these make life much easier as you don't have to cook them first.)

Once all the tubes are full and arranged in the casserole, pour over the sauce. (This should be no thicker than tomato sauce—if it is, add a little more water to thin it down.) Shake the casserole gently to ensure the sauce is evenly distributed and has reached all the little nooks and crannies.

Soften the cream cheese (microwave for about 30 seconds or stand the unopened container in hot water for a few minutes) and spread over the sauce-covered tubes. Sprinkle the grated cheese evenly over this, then bake at 180°C for 40 minutes, or until the top is nicely browned and the pasta is tender.

Serve with your favourite vegetables and/or a salad.

MIX AND MATCH

The fillings for cannelloni and lasagne are interchangeable. Try making lasagne with layers of pasta, the spinach cannelloni filling, the cannelloni sauce and the lasagne cheese sauce.

Alternatively, make cannelloni by stuffing the pasta tubes with the lentil and tomato mixture instead of the spinach and cottage cheese filling, without changing the sauce or topping.

PASTA BASED MEALS

LENTIL AND TOMATO SAUCE

You may not find the idea of a lentil sauce for pasta particularly appealing, but we hope you will try it. This is well flavoured and cheap with an interesting texture. It is also very versatile and may be used in a number of ways as described at the end of the recipe.

FOR 4-6 SERVINGS:

1 cup brown lentils
1 bay leaf
3 medium-sized onions
3 cloves garlic
1 Tbsp oil
100 g mushrooms (optional)
1 green pepper (optional)
1 (425 g) can tomato purée
1 tsp basil
1 tsp marjoram
1 tsp oreganum
¼ tsp thyme
¼ tsp sugar
½ tsp salt
black pepper
350-500 g spaghetti, wholemeal or plain

Rinse the lentils, and then cover with plenty of water and boil with the bay leaf until tender (*see page 175*).

While the lentils are cooking, finely chop the onions and saute with the crushed, chopped garlic in the oil until tender. Add the sliced mushrooms and diced green pepper (if desired) and continue to cook until the onion is soft and clear.

Pour in the tomato purée, then add the herbs, sugar, salt and pepper. Simmer for a few minutes over a low heat to allow the flavours to blend.

Stir in the cooked lentils and reheat to serve as desired. This mixture may be eaten immediately if you are in a hurry, but its flavour improves if it is allowed to stand for a while.

Serve over spaghetti, rice, or, use as the filling for lasagne or cannelloni.

ORIENTAL TOFU AND NOODLES

This is a very quick and simple recipe if you can buy ready-fried tofu. Deep-fried tofu is golden brown, crisp, and chewy—quite different in appearance and texture from plain tofu. To fry it yourself, cut firm or very firm tofu into 1-cm slices, pat it dry, then deep-fry it for about 10 minutes, or until it has a golden brown, crisp crust.

FOR 4 SERVINGS:

200 g quick-cooking Oriental noodles
3-4 spring onions
3 cups boiling water
2 Tbsp dark soya sauce
1 Tbsp dark sesame oil
½ tsp brown sugar
½ tsp salt
½ tsp garlic powder
about 300 g deep-fried tofu
1 (385 g) can whole mushrooms in brine
½ cup walnut pieces or roasted cashew nuts
1 Tbsp cornflour
2 Tbsp sherry
2 tsp dark soya sauce
1 tsp brown sugar
¼ tsp ground ginger
¼ tsp garlic powder
½ cup water
liquid from mushrooms

Break the blocks of noodles into a large saucepan. Chop the spring onions over them. Combine the next six ingredients in a jug or bowl, pour over the noodles, then heat the saucepan until the liquid boils again, and cook for 3 minutes. Cover, turn off the heat, and stir occasionally while preparing the rest of the recipe.

Cut the pre-fried tofu into slices about 1 cm thick. Open and drain the mushrooms, reserving the liquid, and halve or quarter the mushrooms. Mix together the tofu, mushrooms, and nuts. Combine the remaining ingredients in a small saucepan, then bring to the boil stirring constantly, to make a lightly thickened glaze.

Thin down with extra water if necessary, then gently stir in the tofu, mushrooms and nuts.

Arrange the prepared noodles (which should have absorbed all the liquid) in a shallow serving dish, top with the glazed tofu mixture, heat if necessary, and serve.

Variation:
Mix stir-fried beansprouts, celery, etc., through the noodles.

Note:
The noodles used in this recipe are available in stores supplying Asian foods. They do not have sachets of dried stock enclosed.

PEANUT AND SESAME PASTA SAUCE

This sauce has a nice nutty flavour and can be made from ingredients which you are likely to have in your cupboard.

for 4 servings:
1 large onion
1 Tbsp oil
¼ cup peanut butter
1 Tbsp tahini (optional)
1 Tbsp sweet chilli sauce
1½ cups water
light soya sauce or salt
2 Tbsp toasted sesame seeds
about 350 g of your favourite pasta

Cut the onion in half from top bottom, then cut in thin slices, to form half-rings. Cook these in the oil in a covered pan for about 5 minutes, stirring and turning several times until evenly and lightly browned.

Add the peanut butter, tahini, sweet chilli sauce and water, and stir over moderate heat until the lumps have dissolved. Add extra water, or cook for a little longer until sauce is of thin coating consistency, then season carefully, adding extra chilli sauce for extra sweetness or hotness, and enough light soya sauce or salt to bring out the flavour.

Stir sauce into the freshly cooked, drained pasta (*see page 60*), sprinkle with toasted sesame seeds, and serve hot or warm with a cucumber salad, marinated green beans or a crisp green salad.

Variation:
For extra richness, add cream cheese or sour cream to taste.

PASTA WITH 'INSTANT' SAUCE

This is a sauce which can be prepared while the pasta cooks. Choose a pasta shape with lots of convolutions and crevices since these hold more of the sauce, which is stirred in so that it coats and flavours each individual piece.

for 4-6 servings:
350-500 g uncooked pasta
75 g butter
¼ cup hot water
1 Tbsp instant vegetable stock
1 Tbsp pesto (or chopped fresh basil or 1 tsp dried basil)
1 tsp sugar
½ tsp salt (to taste)
¼ tsp garlic powder
black pepper to taste
dash of hot chilli sauce
¼ cup grated parmesan
Optional: ½ cup grated tasty cheese
3-4 tomatoes, diced
1-2 Tbsp chopped fresh herbs if available, such as basil, parsley or chives

Cook the pasta, following packet instructions, or recipe on *page 44*.

Melt the butter, and add the next eight ingredients, stirring to make sure no lumps remain.

Pour this mixture over the hot, cooked pasta. Add the grated parmesan and any of the optional additions if desired. Stir together, reheating over a low heat if necessary, and serve.

TOFU AND TOMATO PASTA SAUCE

The protein content of this pasta meal is boosted by the addition of the tofu. Don't worry if the packet of tofu that you buy is larger or smaller than our suggestion—it will not affect the flavour of the final product.

For 4-5 servings:

2-3 cloves garlic
1 large onion, diced
2 Tbsp oil
1 small green pepper, diced
300-500 g tofu
¼ cup red or white wine
1 (425 g) can tomato purée
2 tsp sugar
½ tsp salt
1 tsp dried basil
1 tsp dried marjoram
dash hot chilli sauce black pepper
2 Tbsp chopped parsley
400-500 g spaghetti or fettuccine

Crush and chop the garlic, and finely chop the onion. Sauté in the oil, in a large frypan.

When the onion is soft, add the green pepper and cook for a few minutes longer.

Crumble the tofu into 5 mm pieces, draining off any liquid, and add to the mixture in the frypan. Cook for 5 minutes, stirring occasionally.

Allow any liquid that appears to boil away, or if there is a lot, drain off instead.

Add the wine, tomato purée and seasonings, except the parsley, then reduce heat and simmer for 5 minutes.

Cook the pasta as described on page 44. Toss with butter or oil. Divide between plates and top with sauce. Sprinkle with chopped parsley and serve.

Variation:
Top with sliced green or black olives.

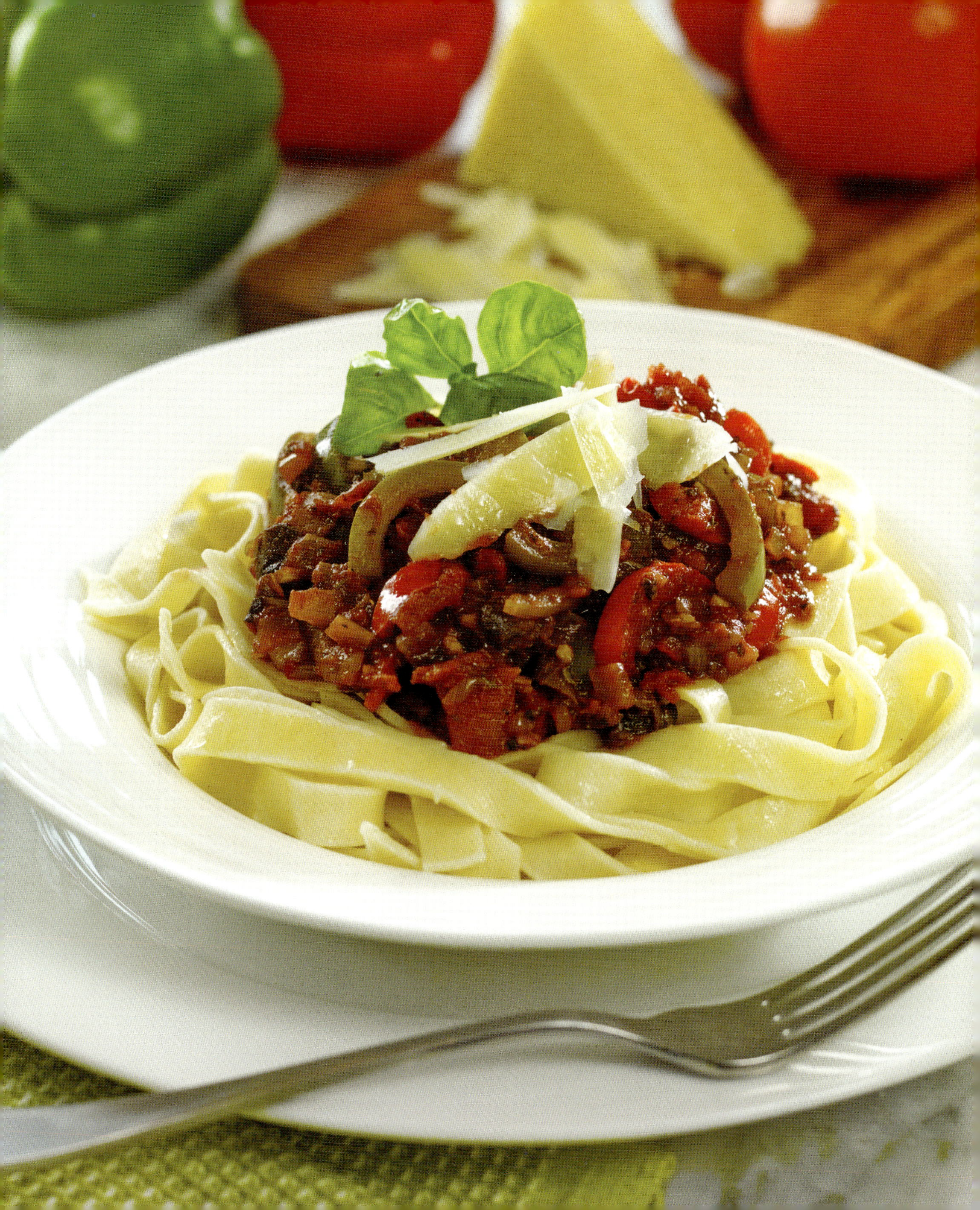

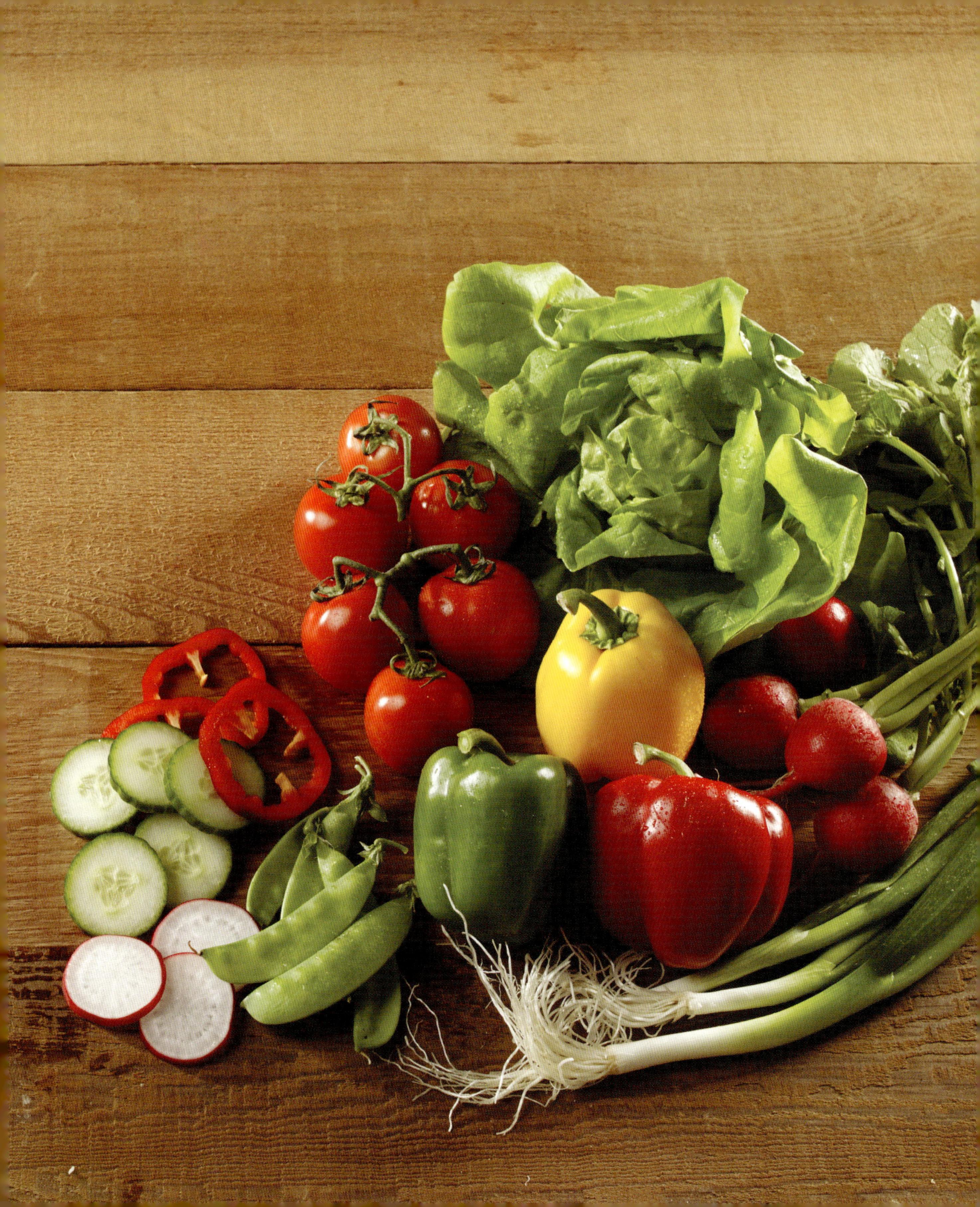

VEGETABLE MAIN COURSES

Try any of these interesting vegetable dishes for the main part of your dinner. You'll find some recipes which are just right for everyday family meals, others which are good for a quick meal for one or two, and a few that will suit you when you are having friends around. As a bonus, many will reheat well in a microwave oven, if you have leftovers.

STUFFED PEPPERS

No particular ethnic group would want to claim our stuffed peppers because we are so greedy! We like all the flavourings added to stuffed vegetables by different countries in the Middle East, so we put them all in, without restraint. Do not make this recipe unless you can get fleshy, plump peppers. Choose red rather than green, since they are sweeter, if you have the choice. If golden-yellow peppers are available try them too. A mixture of different coloured peppers is prettiest of all.

FOR 4 SERVINGS:
4 large or 8 small peppers (see above)
3 onions
2 cloves garlic
3 Tbsp oil
1 cup brown or white long-grain rice
½ cup pine nuts or chopped almonds
½ cup currants
½ cup chopped mint
½ cup chopped parsley
½ tsp ground allspice
½ tsp grated nutmeg
½ tsp cinnamon
1 tsp salt
1 (425 g) can savoury tomatoes or tomatoes in juice

First prepare the peppers. Cut across the tops, removing the stem portion, or cut large peppers in half lengthwise. Remove and discard seeds and pith, but chop trimmings from around the stem.

Chop two of the onions, and the garlic, finely. Heat in 1 tablespoon of the oil, in a large pan with a cover, until transparent. Add any chopped pepper, then the rice, and cook for a minute or two longer, then add 2 cups water, cover, and simmer until the rice is tender, about half an hour for brown rice, or about 15 minutes for white rice.

Soften the prepared peppers by putting them in a bowl, pouring boiling water over them, and leaving them to stand for 5 minutes. Drain, and discard the water.

Put the second tablespoon of oil in another pan and lightly brown the pine nuts or chopped almonds in it. Watch carefully so they do not darken. When evenly coloured, add the currants, and cook a little longer, until they have plumped up. Turn off the heat and remove from pan, mixing with the chopped mint and parsley.

Stir the allspice, nutmeg, cinnamon and salt into the almost-cooked rice. Watch rice carefully as it cooks, adding extra water if necessary. It should be tender and dry by the time it finishes. Stir most of the currant mixture into the cooked rice.

Lightly brown the last onion in the last tablespoon of oil, in the pot or pan in which the peppers will cook. Add the can of tomatoes chopping them into smaller pieces.

Pack the rice into the peppers, so that the tops are rounded, and all or most of the filling is used. Arrange peppers on the tomato, then cover the pot or pan and simmer very gently for 20-30 minutes, until the peppers are tender and the tomato mixture has thickened.

Serve two peppers or half peppers per serving, standing each on a spoonful of tomato mixture. Top with reserved currant mixture. Add a green salad and some sort of bread to complete the main course. Cooked green beans go well with these peppers, too.

CARROT AND MUSHROOM LOAF

Everybody likes this loaf! It is a good choice when you want to present a meal to rather conservative people. Team it with mashed potatoes, green beans or broccoli, and cubed pumpkin or baked tomatoes.

FOR 4 SERVINGS:
1 medium-sized onion
1-2 cloves garlic
2 Tbsp oil or butter
200 g mushrooms
1 tsp basil
¼ tsp thyme
½ tsp salt
black pepper
3 cups grated carrot (400 g)
½ cup dry breadcrumbs
½ cup grated cheese

½ cup milk
2 eggs
2 Tbsp dry breadcrumbs
2 Tbsp grated cheese
paprika

Finely chop the onion and garlic, then cook in the oil or butter until the onio is soft. Add the sliced mushrooms and continue to cook until these have softened.

Transfer the cooked onion-and- mushroom mixture to a medium-sized bowl and then add the next nine ingredients. Mix together well, then pour into a well-greased loaf tin. (Line long sides and bottom with a strip of baking paper, if you think it could stick.) Sprinkle with the remaining measures of breadcrumbs and cheese an dust lightly with paprika.

Cover pan with foil, and bake at 180°C for 30 minutes, then uncover am cook for a further 30 minutes or until the centre is firm when pressed.

ZUCCHINI AND MUSHROOM LOAF

This loaf has an excellent texture and an interesting flavour. It also provides a great way to disguise zucchini should you be cooking for those who would not otherwise enjoy such a treat!

for 4-6 servings:

1 medium-sized onion, diced
2 cloves garlic, crushed
2 Tbsp oil
200 g mushrooms, sliced
500 g zucchini, grated
2 cups fresh wholemeal breadcrumbs
2 eggs
1 cup grated cheese
1 tsp salt
1 tsp basil
¼ tsp thyme
black pepper
2 Tbsp dried breadcrumbs

Dice the onion and garlic, then sauté until soft in the oil. Add the sliced mushrooms and cook until soft and beginning to darken.

Grate the zucchini coarsely, and squeeze to remove as much liquid as possible.

Put the zucchini in a large bowl, and add the onion-mushroom mixture then the remaining ingredients, except ¼ cup of grated cheese and the dried breadcrumbs.

Transfer the mixture to a well-greased loaf tin, and top with the remaining cheese and the dried crumbs.

Bake at 180°C for 1 hour, or until the middle feels firm to touch, covering with foil during the first half of the cooking. Unmould and leave for 5 minutes before slicing.

CORN FRITTERS

Keep a can of corn in your storecupboard so that you can make corn fritters whenever you need a quick meal at short notice. The size of the tin you use in this recipe does not matter, so use a large tin if you want fritters for a lot of people, or a small tin if it is only for two or three.

for 2 large or 6 small servings:

1 egg
3-4 Tbsp liquid from corn
1 can whole-kernel corn, drained
1 cup self-raising flour

Put the egg into a mixing bowl. Drain the liquid from the can of corn. Put 3 tablespoonfuls of corn liquid in with the egg, and keep the rest aside in case you need to thin the batter later. Tip the drained corn into the bowl, add the flour, and stir with a fork, just until the mixture is dampened. Do not over-mix or the fritters won't be so nice. The dry ingredients should be just dampened.

Drop teaspoonfuls of fritter batter into a pan with hot oil, about 1 cm deep. (Heat an electric pan to 190°C.)

Turn the fritters with tongs as soon as they are brown on the bottom. Lift them from the pan as soon as the second side is cooked, and keep them warm on a plate lined with paper towels.

Note:
A large pile of little fritters is much nicer than a small pile of large fritters.

ZUCCHINI CAKES WITH RED PEPPER PURÉE

These little cakes, served in a luminous red-pepper sauce, are likely to convert those who are not excited about zucchini.

FOR 4 MAIN SERVINGS:
2 eggs
1 large garlic clove
½ tsp salt
3 cups shredded zucchini, unpeeled
¼ cup grated parmesan cheese about
½ cup self-raising flour
oil

In a medium-sized bowl beat the eggs to combine white and yolks. Crush the garlic clove into the salt, and add the paste to the eggs. Mix again.

Add the firmly packed shredded zucchini and the parmesan cheese, then stir in enough self-raising flour to make a batter of fritter consistency.

Drop batter into hot oil, 5 mm deep, a tablespoon at a time to make small cakes. Turn when golden brown Lower heat if necessary and cook until centres are firm. Serve with the following sauce.

Red pepper purée:
1 onion, finely chopped
1 clove garlic, chopped
1 large red pepper
1 Tbsp butter or oil
1 cup water

Finely chop onion, garlic and pepper. Saute in the butter or oil until transparent. Add water, cover, and cook for 10 minutes, until tender.

Purée, then press through a sieve. Boil down to thicken, if necessary, then season carefully and serve hot.

STUFFED MARROW (OR ZUCCHINI)

This recipe provides a good way to use large zucchini or 'teenage' marrows which are so plentiful and cheap towards the end of summer.

FOR 6-8 SERVINGS:
1 large marrow or eight 15 cm zucchini
2 medium-sized onions, diced
2 cloves garlic
2 Tbsp butter
200 g mushrooms, sliced
1 large tomato, peeled and chopped
1 egg
¼ cup white wine
¾ cup dry breadcrumbs
¼ tsp dried thyme
2 Tbsp chopped fresh parsley (or 1 Tbsp dried parsley)
2 Tbsp pesto (or 1 Tbsp dried basil)
1 tsp salt
1 tsp sugar
½ cup grated cheese
black pepper

Topping:
¼ cup grated cheese
¼ cup dry breadcrumbs
paprika

Halve the marrow or zucchini lengthwise, and scoop out the seeds and some of the flesh with a spoon, leaving a boat about 1 cm thick. Chop up the edible flesh that you scooped out and set it aside.

Sauté the onion and minced garlic in the butter until beginning to soften and then add the mushrooms and tomato.

When the mushrooms are soft, add the chopped marrow or zucchini pith and cook for a few minutes longer, until this softens also.

Remove from the heat and stir in the egg, wine, breadcrumbs and seasonings. Add the cheese and season with pepper to taste.

Preheat the oven to 180°C. While it heats, arrange

the 'shells' in a shallow baking dish. If they will not sit flat, take a thin slice off the bottom of each, forming a flat base to stand on. Fill the shells, heaping the filling up well in each.

Sprinkle each with breadcrumbs and a little cheese, then dust lightly with paprika. Cover with foil.

Bake for 30-60 minutes, until the cases are soft and the filling is set. The time will depend on the age and size of the marrows. Test flesh with a skewer to see if it is soft.

Variations:

Cut fairly large marrows into slices and fill the central round holes with the stuffing. Take care to butter well the dish in which these cook or stand them on nonstick Teflon liners.

Cook in a savoury tomato mixture, as in the Stuffed Pepper recipe.

VEGETABLE COMBO

This recipe makes a very pretty vegetable mixture. It isn't a stir-fried mixture, nor a long and slowly simmered one, nor is it a sauce—but it is somewhere between the three!

It is liquid enough to serve alongside any other food which needs a sauce, and it may be served on rice or on flat egg noodles, topped with grated cheese, as a complete meal.

You need a large frypan and a high heat to make this successful. If you have a non-stick pan, use it! You can alter proportions to suit yourself—you must alter seasonings to suit yourself. If you don't keep tasting, adding just the right amount of salt and sugar, you will not get an interesting flavour.

for 4 servings:

1 small-to-medium-sized (about 200 g) eggplant
¼ cup oil
1 medium-sized onion
2 cloves garlic
1 green pepper
1 red pepper
1 cup chopped marrow, zucchini or butternut
1 cup cauliflower pieces or
1 cup green beans
1 cup water
freshly ground pepper
1-2 tsp sugar
salt to taste
fresh herbs, chopped (optional)
2 tsp cornflour
¼-½ cup chopped parsley

For this recipe all the vegetables should be cut into 1 cm cubes—that is fingertip sized cubes. Of course the pieces don't have to be completely even or exact, but try to have everything cut that size.

Cut up the eggplant first, without peeling or salting it. Heat the pan, add the oil, and when hot, drop in the eggplant. Cook it on high heat, turning frequently, until it is golden brown on some surfaces. While it cooks add the chopped onion and garlic.

Chop the remaining vegetables while the first three cook. When the eggplant is evenly coloured, add the remaining vegetables, and stir to coat with oil. Keep the heat high, and put the lid on the pan. Cook for 3-4 minutes until all vegetables are wilted and brightly coloured, then add the water, cover, and cook on high heat for 3-4 minutes longer. By this stage the vegetables should be tender-crisp, and quite a lot of the added water should have evaporated.

Remove the lid and add the seasonings in the order given. Keep tasting. After adding the sugar add enough salt to bring out all the other flavours. Add fresh herbs at this stage, too. Mix the cornflour to a paste with cold water. Add enough of this to thicken the mixture. Sprinkle generously with parsley, stir it through briefly, then serve immediately.

PAKORA VEGETABLES

The batter on these vegetables gives them much more substance—as well as added protein. They are best eaten very soon after they are cooked, rather than reheated. If you have an electric wok or deep frier, you might like to try cooking these at the table.

FOR 4-6 SERVINGS:

500 g assorted vegetable pieces, such as cauliflower florets, thinly sliced potato, kumara and/or pumpkin, broccoli, small whole mushrooms, strips of peppers, etc.
1½ cups pea flour
1 tsp salt
½ tsp chilli powder
1 tsp turmeric
1 tsp ground cumin
1 tsp ground coriander
1 tsp garam masala
1 cup water
1-1½ cups water
oil to deep fry

Prepare the vegetables, cutting them into thin slices. In a bowl, mix together the dry ingredients. Add half the water, and whisk, getting rid of as many lumps as you can.
Add the remaining water, plus a little more if necessary, to form a thin coating batter.
Heat oil about 2 cm deep in a suitable container to about 200°C. Dip the vegetable pieces one at a time into the batter to coat them completely, then drop gently into the oil. At first they will sink, but they will rise to the surface again as they cook. Fry for about 5 minutes or until brown, turning occasionally.
These coated vegetables are delicious served with chilli mayonnaise or minted yoghurt for dipping. Serve with an interesting rice mixture, a tomato salad, and other curry-style side dishes if you are entertaining.

CHEESE AND PUMPKIN BALLS

We liked these so much when we ate them in a restaurant that we decided we should make them for ourselves. The combination of a crisp coating and soft smooth inside is very appealing.
If you want to prepare the cheese and pumpkin balls ahead, reheat them under a grill so that they do not lose their crispness.

FOR 12 BALLS, 4-6 SERVINGS:

500g peeled and seeded pumpkin (about ½ a small pumpkin)
2 cloves garlic
1 medium-sized onion
1 Tbsp oil
1 tsp dried parsley
½ tsp salt
½ cup grated cheese
½ cup dry breadcrumbs
black pepper

COATING:
flour
1 lightly beaten egg
breadcrumb-sesame seed mix

Peel the pumpkin, scoop out its seeds with a spoon, cut into 6-8 pieces and cook until barely tender. It is best steamed, or microwaved (5-6 minutes on High [100%] power) as you want it as dry as possible.
    Crush and chop the garlic, then sauté with the diced onion in the oil. When the onion is soft and clear, remove from the heat and transfer to a bowl (or food processor) with the cooked pumpkin. Mash (or process) until smooth and well mixed, and then add the remaining ingredients.
    The mixture should be thick enough to hold its shape when formed into balls. If not, add extra breadcrumbs.
    With wet hands, form the mixture into golf-ball-sized balls, and coat with flour.
    Next, coat each ball with the beaten egg and then with fine, dry breadcrumbs, or a mixture of equal parts breadcrumbs and toasted sesame seeds. Refrigerate for 15 minutes or longer if possible.
    Deep-fry, three or four at a time, for about 5 minutes, in oil heated to 180°C.
    These balls are delicious served with a peanut sauce. Serve with your favourite cooked vegetables or a mixed salad, and with a rice mixture.

EASY ZUCCHINI PIE

If you grow zucchini, or if you can buy 'teenage' zucchini at a reasonable price, I think you will find this recipe very useful! It is a variation of an American recipe, and it makes a very good weekend main meal or lunch, any time during the warmer months. It makes a good addition to an outdoor buffet, too. If you like this sort of easy, crustless pie, spend the time and money to find and buy some fairly heavy, non-stick, dark coloured metal pieplates, flan tins, cake tins or roasting pans. I make this recipe in a heavy non-stick 23 X 25 cm roasting pan, but it looks more elegant when made in two 23 cm cake or flan tins.

FOR **6-8 SERVINGS**

3 cups (500 g) grated zucchini
1 onion, grated
4 eggs
1½ cups grated cheese
½ tsp salt
¾ cup self-raising flour
pepper
herbs and tomato slices (optional)

Grate the zucchini and onion, and place in a fairly large mixing bowl, with the eggs, cheese and salt. Mix well with a fork.

Add the flour and as much pepper as you like, and chop in any fresh herbs you have and like.

Pour the mixture into a pan or pans which have been well sprayed or buttered. Because it rises quite a lot as it cooks, do not fill any pan more than two thirds full. Even though it may look skimpy, it does not matter if a pan is only filled to half its depth.

If you like, and if you have them, top the pies with sliced tomatoes.

Again, if you like, sprinkle the top of the pie or tomatoes with more grated cheese, or with grated parmesan cheese.

Bake at 200°C for 25-40 minutes, until the centre feels firm, and the top has browned slightly.

Leave to stand for at least 5 minutes before cutting into pieces.

TEMPURA VEGETABLES

It is always interesting to sit around a communal cooking container, and to let your friends prepare and cook their own food. Try this using an electric wok or deep frier. If you do not have a suitably presentable cooking container, someone should resign themself to cooking in the kitchen while the rest of the party eats, as these are best eaten as soon as they are cooked!

FOR **4-6 SERVINGS:**

500 g assorted vegetable pieces such as cauliflower florets, thinly sliced potato, kumara and/or pumpkin, broccoli, small whole mushrooms, strips of peppers, zucchini, etc.
1 egg
1 cup cold water
1 cup plain white flour
¼ tsp baking soda
¼ tsp salt
oil for deep frying

Prepare the vegetables cutting them into pieces about 5 mm thick, and arrange attractively on plates. Using a fork, lightly beat the egg and the cold water. Sift the dry ingredients into this mixture while you stir. Mix enough to combine everything. Thin batter with extra water, so that it lightly coats a piece of prepared vegetable.

Heat the oil to about 200°C. Dip the vegetables in the batter, and fry, a few pieces at a time, until golden brown and puffed up. Raise heat if necessary.

Serve with commercially made tempura sauce or make the following dipping sauce:

¼ cup water
¼ cup Kikkoman soya sauce
1 Tbsp dry sherry
2 tsp brown sugar
2 tsp grated fresh ginger
juice of ½ lemon
1 clove garlic, crushed and chopped
1 tsp dark sesame oil

Mix together all the ingredients and allow to stand for about 10 minutes.

Serve with brown or white rice, or before Oriental Tofu and Noodles.

Note:
Use leftover sauce as a marinade for tofu or other vegetables, at a later time.

SAVOURY CRÊPES

These thin, delicate, tender pancakes are made in a small pan. As long as they are kept from drying out, they may be made ahead and refrigerated or frozen until required. Crêpes make wonderful wrappers for many vegetable mixtures which might seen uninteresting if served alone.

Don't be discouraged if the first crêpes you make are not perfect. Once you get the hang of it, you will find you can turn put a pile of crêpes remarkably quickly and easily.

for 12-20 small crêpes, each about 15 cm in diameter:
2 eggs
¾ cup milk
½ cup flour
½ tsp salt

Combine ingredients in order given, in a food processor or blender. If mixing in a bowl, add egg then milk to dry ingredients and beat until smooth. Pour a measured quantity (e.g. 2 tablespoons) into a small, smooth-surfaced, well-sprayed or buttered preheated pan.

Immediately tilt pan so batter covers bottom in a thin film. If batter does not spread thinly, add more milk to thin it before making the next crêpe. Do not worry if pancakes are not evenly shaped circles.

When batter no longer looks wet in the centre, ease edges of crêpe from pan. Lift and turn carefully. Dry second side, without necessarily browning it. Remove from pan. Stack crêpes until required. Place them on a plate in a plastic bag to prevent drying out.

Note:
If freezing or refrigerating crêpes, place a piece of plastic between each, for easy removal later.

Use the following suggestions as a guide to make your own 'creative crêpes'. Use whatever quantities suit you.

Asparagus Crêpes
Roll cooked asparagus spears in crêpes which have been spread with cream cheese, or cheese sauce. Top with more cheese sauce and/or grated parmesan. Heat in microwave oven, or brown under a grill.

Savoury Apple Crêpes
Sauté sliced onions in butter until tender, then add sliced apple and brown lightly. Add a little white wine and chopped sage if available. Cook until tender. Taste and season. Spread on cooked crêpes. Fold or roll the filled crêpes, sprinkle with parmesan cheese if desired, and reheat if necessary. Serve with maple syrup.

Oriental Crêpes
Fill with lightly sautéed bean sprouts, sliced tofu (if desired), mushrooms and spring onions. Season with sweet chilli sauce. Roll or fold in parcels.

Cheesy Mushroom Crêpes
Fill with sautéed mushrooms in cheese and white wine sauce, with or without herbs. Roll. Sprinkle with parmesan cheese and brown under grill.

Creamy Vegetable Crêpes
Mix lightly cooked vegetables, such as broccoli, corn, sweet peppers, mushrooms. Bind lightly with cheese or curry-flavoured sauce, or sour cream and cottage cheese. Add herbs. Sprinkle with parmesan cheese, or top with extra cheese sauce. Brown under a grill or in a hot oven.

Chilli Bean Crêpes
Spread crêpes with refried beans. Roll up around several strips of sautéed red and green pepper, or a wedge of avocado. Brush surface with chilli mayonnaise and heat in microwave oven, or brown under a grill. Serve with more chilli mayonnaise or tomato salsa.

SPINACH AND CHEESE CRÊPES

For really successful spinach crêpes, you need to thicken the spinach and season it very carefully.

FOR 4-6 SERVINGS:
1 recipe crêpe batter
1-2 cups cooked, drained, chopped spinach
3 Tbsp butter
3 Tbsp flour
½ tsp salt
1 tsp grated nutmeg
1½ cups milk
1½ cups grated cheese
pakrika or parmesan cheese

Prepare batter and make crêpes, according to recipe given above, using a small pan.

Cook, drain, squeeze and chop spinach.

Make the sauce. Melt the butter, add the flour, salt and nutmeg.

Add the milk, ½ cup at a time, boiling and stirring between additions. After the last boiling, add the cheese.

Mix a third of the cheese sauce with the spinach. Spread spinach mixture over the crêpes and roll up. Place the filled crêpes in a well-sprayed ovenware pan. Pour sauce (thinned a little if necessary) over crêpes. Sprinkle with paprika or parmesan cheese. Bake at 200°C for 20 minutes or until bubbly. Brown surface under grill before serving, if desired.

EGGPLANT CASSEROLE

Kirsten sent this recipe with the note 'Absolutely delicious—even the most suspicious people ask for more.' This says it all, really. Eggplant has a very meaty texture and colour, and is often used in casseroles where a meaty appearance is an advantage.

This is a casserole which can be served as part of a buffet meal for a group of people which includes meat-eaters and vegetarians. It is great when served as the main part of a dinner, with other vegetables.

FOR ABOUT 4 MAIN SERVINGS:
1 large eggplant (about 750 g)
1 egg
1 Tbsp water
½ cup dry breadcrumbs
2 Tbsp oil
2 onions, quartered and sliced
1 Tbsp oil
8 large tomatoes, sliced
fresh basil or 1 tsp dried basil
½ cup water
1 tsp salt
2 tsp sugar
freshly ground pepper
1 cup grated tasty cheese

In this recipe you prepare two mixtures. For speed, brown the eggplant slices while the tomato mixture simmers.

Cut the eggplant into slices about 1 cm thick. In a shallow dish big enough to hold the slices, beat the egg with the water, just enough to combine. Dip the eggplant slices first in the egg, then in the crumbs, coating both sides.

Fry slices in a little hot oil until brown on both sides. Leave to drain on paper towels.

In another pan, sauté the sliced onions in 1 tablespoon of oil until lightly browned. Add the tomatoes, basil, water, salt, sugar and pepper, and simmer until the onion is tender.

Coat a large, shallow casserole dish (about 23x30 cm) with non-stick spray or butter, then put half the browned eggplant slices into the dish, cutting them to fit, if necessary. Pour half the tomato mixture over this layer, top with remaining eggplant, then spread the remaining tomato mixture on top. Top with the grated cheese.

Bake, uncovered, at 180°C for 45 minutes, or until the top browns and the eggplant is very tender. Do not hurry the cooking. Leave to stand for at least 10 minutes before serving, or reheat later, preferably in a microwave oven.

VARIATIONS:
Put a layer of grated cheese between the two layers of eggplant, as well as above the top layer.

PEANUT-SAUCED VEGETABLE PLATE

A plate of vegetables can be turned into an interesting, filling and delicious main course when you serve peanut sauce to pour over all or some of the vegetables. This platter is a modification of Gadogado salad, where the vegetables are served at room temperature. Decide for yourself whether you want your vegetables hot, warm, or somewhere in between.

Choose from this vegetable selection:
- Boiled or microwaved new or maincrop potatoes
- Green beans, whole or halved, lightly cooked
- Carrots, halved or quartered lengthwise, cooked until tender-crisp
- Cauli-florets, cooked
- Cabbage, thickly sliced, lightly cooked
- Red and green peppers, raw or blanched
- Beansprouts, raw or blanched
- Jerusalem artichokes, lightly cooked, in thick slices
- Celery, raw or blanched
- Choko, lightly cooked
- Zucchini sticks, raw or lightly cooked
- Brussels sprouts, halved and lightly cooked
- Cucumber strips
- Radishes
- Kumara, cooked and sliced
- Mushrooms, raw or lightly sautéed
- Spring onions, in 4 cm lengths
- Red onion rings
- Swede strips, lightly cooked
- Young white turnips, quartered, raw
- Witloof leaves
- Yams, boiled and halved
- Shredded lettuce

Arrange the vegetables you have chosen, prepared and cooked, on individual plates, on shredded lettuce or lettuce leaves if you like, in a sunburst pattern, or serve a large central platter and let everybody help themselves. Serve jugs of thinned, or bowls of thicker peanut sauce, and let your friends pour it over their vegetables.

Make sure that you have extra seasonings such as:
- lemon wedges
- black pepper (in grinder)
- salt (in grinder)
- hot pepper sauce
- Kikkoman soya sauce

Peanut Sauce:
2 Tbsp oil
1 large onion, chopped
2 tsp chopped garlic
¼ tsp chilli powder
1 Tbsp dark soya sauce
1 Tbsp lemon juice
½ cup peanut butter
1-2 Tbsp soft brown sugar
¼ tsp salt
about 1 cup (or ½ can) coconut cream
water

Heat the oil in a small pan, add the finely chopped onion, garlic and chilli powder, cover and cook gently without browning, until the onion is tender.

Add the soya sauce, lemon juice and smooth or chunky peanut butter, then 1 tablespoon of brown sugar. Add the salt and coconut cream, and bring to the boil, stirring constantly.

Taste, and add the extra sugar if required, (most people like it sweeter) more coconut cream if you like it bland, or water if you want it thinner. Add other seasonings as desired.

Bring to the boil again, purée in a food processor if you want it smooth and serve immediately, or reheat when needed.

Note:
Don't worry about leftover sauce. You can refrigerate it, freeze it, spread it on crackers or serve it on spaghetti or rice.

Variation:
Add quartered hard-boiled eggs to your vegetable platter, if you like.

RATATOUILLE

This vegetable stew is tasty and substantial, and should be carefully seasoned just before it finishes cooking to bring out its flavour.

FOR 8 SERVINGS:
2 large onions, sliced
2 cloves garlic
2 Tbsp cooking oil
2-3 cups sliced zucchini
1-2 green peppers, seeded and sliced
2-3 cups diced eggplant
¼ cup cooking oil
3 cups chopped and peeled tomatoes
fresh or dried basil or oregano to taste salt, pepper and sugar
cornflour
chopped parsley

In a large frying pan fry the onions and sliced garlic in the oil, allowing them to colour very slightly. Add the zucchini and peppers. Cook over moderate heat, turning vegetables occasionally, for 5-10 minutes. Remove vegetables from pan and brown the eggplant in the second amount of oil. Add the partly cooked vegetable mixture and the tomatoes. Cover and add a little basil and oregano. Cook over low heat for about 30 minutes, then season carefully with salt, pepper and sugar to taste.

Adjust heat and lid of pan so that vegetables cook in a small amount of liquid (from the vegetables). If too much liquid forms, remove lid and raise heat. If mixture dries out, lower heat and add a little water. If serving hot, thicken with a little cornflour paste and sprinkle with chopped parsley. If serving at room temperature, do not thicken.

NOTE:
Quantities of vegetables may vary and zucchini or peppers or eggplant may be omitted.

STUFFED LEAVES

Various leaves may be folded and rolled around savoury fillings to make attractive and tasty main courses. Work out your own recipe, using the following guidelines.

Suitable leaves include cabbage, lettuce, spinach, silver beet and grape leaves. These are wilted in boiling water to allow easy folding. Place the filling in the centre of the leaf, on whatever side of the leaf you like. Sometimes the package will look nicer, and roll more easily, if a particular side is uppermost. Fold the stem end of the leaf over the filling first, then the sides, and last the tip. Sometimes it is necessary to cut out a V containing the thickest part of the rib, so that the leaf will fold easily.

Fillings are well-seasoned mixtures, often based on cooked rice (see Stuffed Peppers, page 52), beans, pasta, or breadcrumbs. Raw egg in the stuffing gives extra firmness after cooking.

The leaf packages are simmered or casseroled in a covered container in a well-flavoured liquid which is often served as a sauce. Such sauces are often based on tomato, mushroom and sautéed onion. Simmering time is about 30 minutes. Baking time is 30-45 minutes at 180°C.

Leaf packages may be topped with sour cream when serving.

VEGETABLE MAIN COURSES

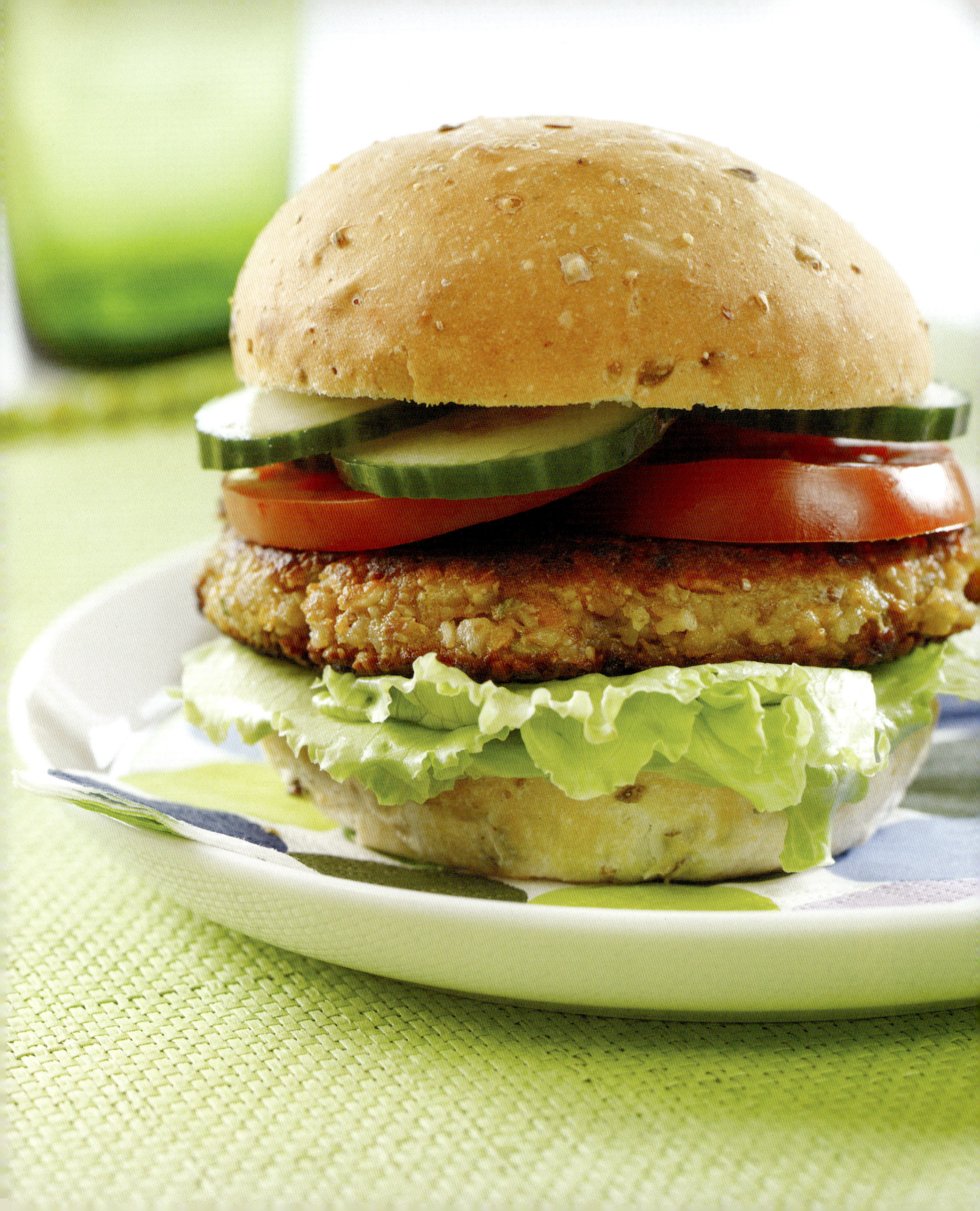

BURGERS

Burgers seem to be everlastingly popular. They are a quick and convenient addition to the repertoire of any cook. Some of the recipes in this section are doubly useful as they may be served to (and enjoyed by) both staunch meat-eaters and vegans alike! Small children will often eat and enjoy food that they would otherwise refuse if it is shaped and cooked as 'burgers'. This same principle may sometimes be successfully applied to those suspicious or conservative non-vegetarians among us, who will often enjoy new foods if given the reassurance of a familiar shape and texture.

Entice (but do not force) your family and friends to try something new and different by making any one of these delicious burgers. They are sure to enjoy them! We find that they have wide appeal and disappear very fast when placed on a buffet table for a mixed group. All of these burgers cook quickly, and make a mouth-watering focal point for any meal. They may be served on a plate with vegetables, or in a bun with your favourite toppings, in the same way as the ever-popular hamburger.

BEAN BURGERS

Most recipes using dried beans require long cooking. This is an exception to the rule. It seems unbelievable that dried beans can be soaked and cooked so quickly, but it works! What's more, the burgers have a very good flavour, much better than that of any of other commercial counterparts that we have tried. Keep a jar of this mixture on hand, since you can use it to produce very fast food when you are caught out.

Burger Mix:
½ cup chick peas
½ cup soybeans
½ cup peanuts (raw) or sunflower kernels
¼ cup toasted sesame seeds
½ cup rolled oats
¼ cup pea flour
1 Tbsp parsley
1 tsp salt
Optional: ¼ cup wheat germ
1 Tbsp nutritional yeast

Measure the first four ingredients into a bowl and mix together. Using a blender or food processor (we found the coffee- grinder attachment of our food processor to be the most effective) grind half a cup of this mixture at a time until it is the consistency of dry breadcrumbs. This process makes a terrible noise, but the convenience of the completed product makes it all worthwhile! Combine the freshly ground bean mixture with the remaining ingredients. Store in an air-tight jar until desired.

Making Burgers: for two 10 cm burgers:
1 cup burger mix (from above)
½ cup water
2 tsp dark soya sauce
1-2 Tbsp oil to cook

Mix everything except the cooking oil together and allow to stand for at least 15 minutes. For extra flavour add a clove of chopped garlic, or a few garlic granules, if desired.

Cook over a moderate heat for at least 5 minutes on each side, covering the pan with a suitable lid to collect steam and speed up the cooking.

Note:
Other bean varieties may be used in place of chick peas and soybeans, but kidney beans should be avoided.

TOFU BURGERS

Many people would like to try tofu but don't know what to make with this bland, white high-protein food. This recipe serves as a good way to introduce tofu to your diet.

for 8 burgers, to serve 4:
250 g tofu
1 medium-sized onion
2-3 cloves garlic
1 Tbsp dark soya sauce
1 Tbsp sherry
¼ tsp ground ginger
1 Tbsp nutritional yeast
¼ cup sunflower seeds
¼ cup wholemeal flour
black pepper to taste

Remove the tofu from its package and stand it on a sloping board for a few minutes, allowing any excess liquid to drain away.

Dice the onion and garlic very finely. Crumble the tofu into a bowl, add the onion and garlic, then the remaining ingredients. (If you don't have any sherry, add a little water and a dash of lemon juice instead.)

Mix together well, then working with wet hands, divide the mixture into quarters, then eighths. Shape each portion into a 7-10 cm pattie (so you have a total of 8 burgers).

Cook for 5 minutes per side, or until the burgers are golden brown.

Note:
If you have the choice, buy firm tofu for this recipe.

MUSHROOM BURGERS

These burgers are very popular with mushroom lovers. The recipe is especially good made with older mushrooms with dark gills, as these have a stronger flavour. Double the quantities for larger groups.

for 4 burgers, to serve 2:
1 medium-sized onion
1 clove garlic
1 Tbsp oil
150 g mushrooms
1 cup fresh wholemeal breadcrumbs
1 tsp cornflour
1 Tbsp fresh chopped parsley (or 1 tsp dried parsley)
1 tsp nutritional yeast
1 egg
1 Tbsp lemon juice (juice of ½ lemon)
1 tsp dark soya sauce

Chop the onion and garlic, then sauté in the oil until the onion begins to soften. Add the mushrooms and continue cooking until they turn soft and dark.

Tip the onion-and-mushroom mixture into a medium-sized bowl, and add the remaining ingredients. Mix well, using your hands if necesary. Add a few more breadcrumbs if the mixture seems too wet. Divide into four equal portions and then shape each quarter into a 10 cm pattie.

Cook in a little oil or butter, using a non-stick pan if you have one, until lightly browned on each side and firm when pressed in the middle.

Note:
A little fresh thyme is a nice addition to these burgers.

BROWN LENTIL BURGERS

These burgers take a little longer than some of the others to make, unless you have some cooked lentils on hand, but they have a definite firm texture, much like that of conventional burgers.

for 8-10 burgers, to serve 4-5:
½ cup brown lentils
1 bay leaf
2 medium-sized onions
2 cloves garlic
2 Tbsp oil or butter
1 Tbsp parsley
½ tsp basil
½ tsp marjoram
¼ tsp (a large pinch) thyme
1 tsp salt
black pepper to taste
½ cup fresh wholemeal breadcrumbs
2 eggs
2 Tbsp tomato paste
2 tsp dark soya sauce
½ cup flour

Cook the lentils with the bay leaf until they are tender (*see page 175*). Remove them from the heat, drain, and remove the bay leaf.

Finely chop the onions and garlic and sauté in the oil or butter until the onion is soft and clear. Add the herbs, salt and pepper.

Tip the cooked, drained lentils into a large bowl, add the onions and garlic, then mix in the remaining ingredients.

Divide the mixture into 8-10 evenly sized portions. Shape each portion into a 10-12 cm pattie, wetting your hands with cold water to prevent the mixture sticking. If the mixture won't hold its shape, add a few more breadcrumbs or a little more flour until it does.

Cook in a little oil until lightly browned on each side and firm when pressed in the middle.

BURGERS

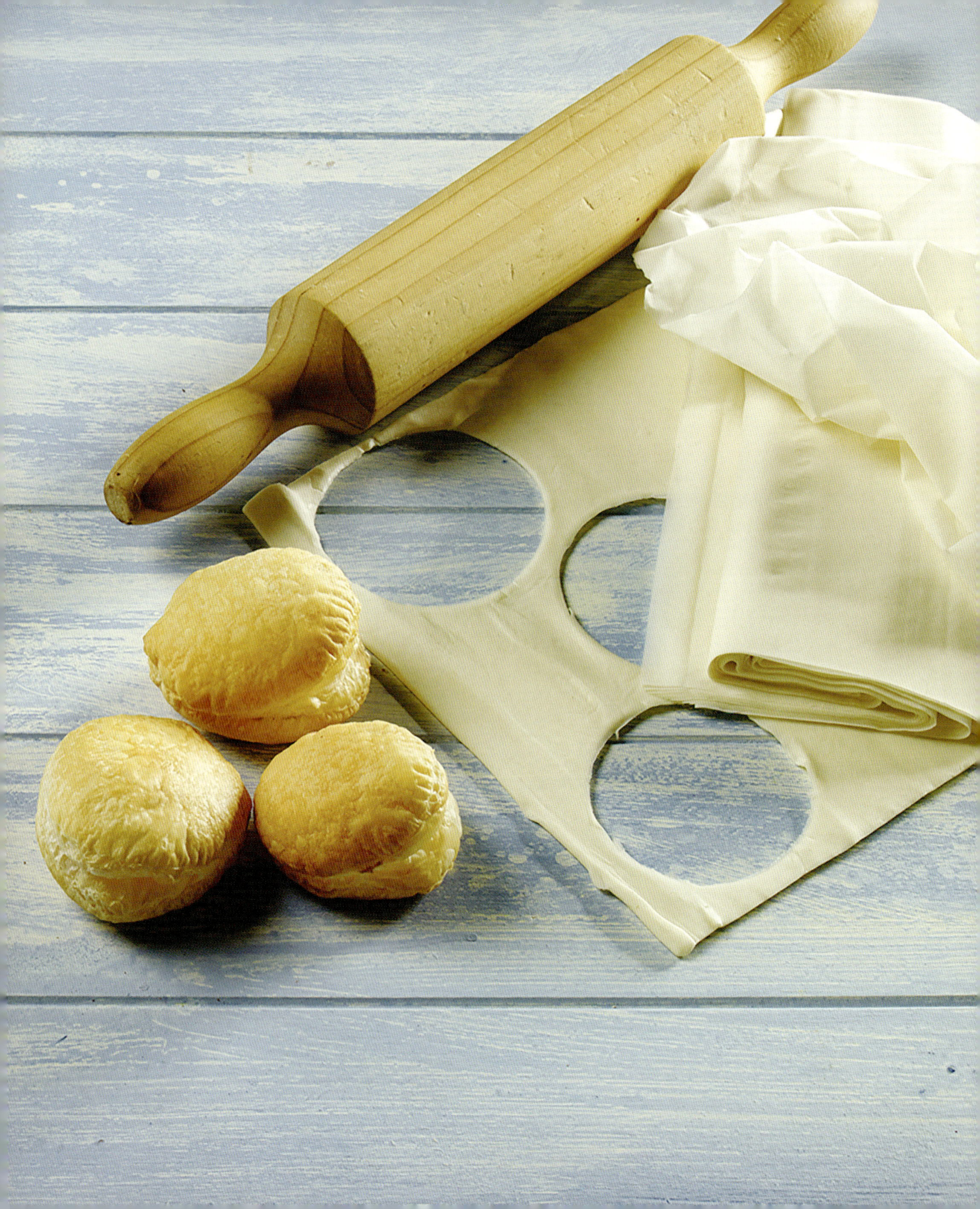

PIES & PASTRY

FILLO PASTRY

Fillo is fun! Although it costs more than regular bought pastry, it may be used for several different fillo-wrapped foods which will disintegrate in your mouth in a very satisfying way.

When you buy them, the sheets of fillo should be quite soft and flexible, and you should be able to roll and fold them without any cracking and breaking.

Always rewrap, seal, and refrigerate unused fillo promptly, to stop it drying out.

Use fillo pastry to replace bought pastry or home-made short pastry in other recipes in this or other books, if you like, following the cooking instructions for fillo pies given here.

Don't be heavy-handed with butter when brushing melted butter between layers of fillo. A few dabs over a sheet will do. You can try layering fillo without any butter between the sheets, if you like. The sheets will brown more quickly and be very crisp and light-textured.

PASTRY FOR PIES

Home-made short pastry contains less fat than bought flaky pastry. It is particularly good for flans and quiches (single-crust pies) and it is less likely to become soggy, and shrinks less during cooking. One cup of flour makes enough pastry for a large single-crust pie. Double these amounts for a pie with the filling enclosed in pastry (a double-crust pie).

SHORT PASTRY

Traditional Method:

Measure 1 cup plain or wholemeal flour no a mixing bowl. Cut or rub in 60-75g cold butter using a pastry blender, fingertips or two knives, until the butter is cut in small pieces and the mixture resembles rolled oats. Add about ¼ cup cold water, a few drops at a time, tossing the mixture with a fork until it will form a ball when pressed with fingers. Chill for 5-10 minutes before rolling out.

Food Processor Method:

Fit the food processor with its metal cutting blade. Add 1 cup plain or wholemeal flour and add 60-70 g cold butter, cut into about nine cubes. Do not process. Acidify ¼ cup cold water with 1-2 tsp lemon juice for extra tenderness if desired. Using the pulse button, add water in a thin stream while chopping butter through flour.

Test at intervals to see if the particles are moist enough to press together to form a ball. The mixture will still look crumbly at this stage. (If a ball of dough forms in the processor, the mixture is too wet.)

Note:

Overmixing or too much water makes tough pastry.

MUSHROOM STRUDEL

This recipe makes two long rolls of strudel. The completed rolls are not only attractive but delicious, too.

FOR 6-8 SERVINGS:

2 medium-sized onions
250 g mushrooms
2 Tbsp butter or oil
500 g cottage cheese
2 Tbsp fresh (or 1 Tbsp dried) parsley
½ tsp dried tarragon
½ tsp thyme
½ tsp salt
black pepper to taste
juice of 1 lemon
10 sheets fillo pastry
25 g melted butter

Finely chop the onions and slice the mushrooms into pieces' about 5 mm thick. Sauté the onion in the oil or butter over medium heat until tender then add the sliced mushrooms. Continue to cook until the mushrooms have heated through.

In a large bowl mix together the cottage cheese, seasonings and lemon juice. Add the mushroom-and-onion mixture and stir to combine.

Lay the first sheet of fillo on a dry surface and dot or brush very lightly with melted butter. Lay the next sheet directly on top. Repeat this process until you have a stack five sheets thick.

Spoon half the filling in a band across the pastry, about 5 cm from one of the short edges, then carefully roll up. Using a sharp (serrated) knife make diagonal slashes through several layers, three cm apart, across the top of the roll (to prevent the roll bursting during cooking).

Repeat this process with the remaining fillo and the rest of the filling. Stand the rolls on a buttered sponge roll tin. Bake at 225°C for 20-25 minutes or until the pastry is golden brown and crisp. Leave to stand for 5-10 minutes before serving.

Slice diagonally and serve with colourful vegetables and/or a mixed green salad.

Note:
If rolls split during cooking, slice them in the kitchen and serve, after reshaping them.

SILVER BEET AND CHEESE PIE

This is a delicious way to serve silver beet.

for 6-8 servings:
about 20 large silver beet leaves
500 g cottage cheese
1 cup grated tasty cheese
1 onion
3 eggs
1 tsp salt
½ tsp freshly grated nutmeg freshly ground black pepper
10 sheets fillo pastry
2 Tbsp melted butter

Discard the silver beet stalks. Wash the leaves carefully, then chop finely and cook until tender but still bright green (about 5 minutes) in a large pan with little or no added water. Press in a sieve to remove any surplus liquid.

Mix the cottage cheese, grated cheese, diced onion, eggs and seasonings together in a large bowl. Add the silver beet and stir until well combined.

Remove 10 sheets of fillo from the package. Lightly brush half of each sheet with melted butter then fold in half. Arrange five folded sheets in the bottom of a 23 X 30cm (or 25 cm square) roasting pan. The sheets should cover the bottom completely, although they need not cover each other exactly.

Spread the filling over the base, then top with the remaining folded fillo sheets. Brush the top with any remaining butter and bake at 180°C for 35-40 minutes, until the top is lightly browned and the filling set.

Cut in squares and serve hot or warm with cooked vegetables or a tomato salad.

BLUE CHEESE AND MUSHROOM PACKAGES

These little packages make very elegant dinner party food. Shape them into small triangular, or more conventional rectangular packages.

for 6-8 packages:
1 medium-sized onion
2 cloves garlic
2 Tbsp butter
200 g mushrooms, chopped
250 g cream cheese
50 g blue cheese
½ tsp sugar
¼ tsp thyme
spring onion, chopped
1 Tbsp sherry (optional)
6-8 sheets fillo pastry
100 g butter, melted

Sauté the finely chopped onion and crushed garlic in the butter. When soft add the mushrooms, and cook until they begin to soften.

Reduce the heat to very low, and then stir in the cream cheese. (If the cream cheese is cold or very

PIES & PASTRY

firm, it may pay to soften it by stirring or mashing first.) Crumble in the blue cheese while stirring, and add the remaining seasonings.

Remove the fillo sheets from the package. Lay one sheet on a dry surface, lightly brush with melted butter and then fold in half, lengthwise for triangles or crosswise for packages.

Place about ¼ cup of filling on the pastry and roll or fold it into the shape desired, completely enclosing the filling. Do not roll too tightly or packages may burst during cooking. Cut a slash on top as a further precaution against splitting. Repeat until you have used all the filling.

Place on a buttered oven tray, and bake for 15-20 minutes at 200°C or until golden brown.

One package per person is usually enough because of the rich filling.

LEEK FLAN

This flan, freshly baked or reheated, is a popular main course for lunch or dinner.

For a 20-23 cm quiche:
1 uncooked pastry pie crust
3 (about 500 g) small leeks
1 clove garlic
1 Tbsp butter
½ cup water
3 eggs
1 cup grated Emmentaler (or tasty) cheese
½ cup sour cream
¼ cup milk
¼ tsp salt

Roll bought or home-made pastry (page 66) thinly to line 20-23 cm flan tin or pie plate.

Slice the carefully washed leeks into 5 mm pieces. Cook the leeks and the diced garlic in the butter for 2-3 minutes without browning, then add the water and cook until tender. Raise the heat and let the rest of the liquid evaporate.

Beat the eggs, grated cheese, sour cream, milk and salt together.

Remove the leeks from the heat then stir into the egg mixture. Pour the filling carefully into the prepared crust.

Bake at 220°C for about 30 minutes or until the filling has set in the centre. Sprinkle with chopped herbs and/or paprika before serving if desired.

Variation:
Double the filling ingredients if using a 23 cm flan tin with high sides and increase cooking time until filling sets.

VEGETABLE FLAN

You can use this recipe to make a flan from any cooked vegetable that you have on hand. It will make a deep 17cm flan or a thin 23 cm flan with a shorter cooking time. Make it in a pie plate if you do not have a flan tin.

1 uncooked pastry pie crust
3 eggs
½ cup cream, sour cream or cream cheese
¼ cup milk
1½ cups grated cheese
1-1½ cups well drained, cooked vegetables

Roll out home-made or bought pastry thinly, to line a pie plate or flan tin.

Combine the eggs, cream or cream cheese, milk and a cup of the grated cheese, using a fork, beater, or food processor.

Put the well-drained, chopped cooked vegetable (or vegetable mixture) into the prepared, unbaked pastry shell, pour over the egg mixture, then top with the remaining grated cheese.

Bake at 220°C for 20 minutes, then at 180°C until the filling sets in the middle, about 10 minutes.

Note:
Suitable vegetables include asparagus, broccoli, corn, mushrooms, spinach, zucchini, etc.

CHEESE AND MUSHROOM QUICHE

This makes good lunch or dinner fare. Because it tastes almost as good cold as it does warm, a quiche like this is ideal if you want to turn a picnic into something really special.

1 uncooked 20-25 cm pastry pie crust
1 medium-sized onion
125 g mushrooms, sliced pinch of thyme
2 Tbsp butter
1½ cups grated cheddar or gruyère cheese
2 large eggs
½ cup sour cream
¼ cup milk
1 Tbsp flour
¼ tsp salt
½ tsp mustard powder black pepper paprika

This recipe makes a 20 cm fairly deep quiche, or a more thinly filled 25 cm quiche. Buy or make pastry (*see page 88*), and roll out to line a 20-25 cm flan tin or pie plate.

Sauté the onions, mushrooms and thyme in the butter until soft.

Cover the bottom of the uncooked crust with the grated cheese, then cover this layer with the onion-and-mushroom mixture.

Beat the remaining ingredients except paprika together, and pour into the crust.

Sprinkle with paprika, and bake at 220°C for about 30 minutes, or until the filling is set in the centre.

Serve with your favourite green vegetables and a potato salad.

HEARTY BEAN PIE

The filling for this pie consists of cooked beans (or lentils) in a rich and delicious brown-onion-and-mushroom sauce. Use canned beans when time is short, and add leftover cooked vegetables if you have them.

FOR 4-6 SERVINGS:
2 medium-sized onions
2-3 cloves garlic
1 Tbsp oil
100 g mushrooms
1 tsp sugar
½ tsp salt
½ tsp marjoram
¼ tsp thyme
black pepper to taste
1 Tbsp flour
1 cup water
2 Tbsp sour cream (optional)
about 2 cups cooked beans or lentils (see page 175)
200-300 g bought or home-made pastry

Sauté the finely chopped onion and garlic in the oil in a large frypan. Add the sliced mushrooms and sugar and cook until the onions are well browned. Stir in salt, herbs, pepper and flour.

Pour in the water slowly, stirring constantly, until the sauce is the consistency of thick gravy, remove from the heat and add the sour cream if desired.

Stir in the cooked, drained beans. Leave to stand and cool while preparing the pastry.

Roll out two-thirds of the pastry and use it to line a 20-25 cm pie dish. Spread the cooled filling evenly over the pastry. Dampen the exposed pastry with water.

Roll out the remaining pastry. Lay gently over the top, pressing onto the dampened edge. Trim, leaving a 1-2 cm overlap. Fold this under the sealed edge and decorate with a fork or by fluting the edge with your fingers if desired.

Bake at 220°C for 20 minutes, or until golden brown.

Serve with mashed potatoes and cooked vegetables for a main meal, or alone or with bread for lunch.

Variation:
Make several small pies or pastries if desired.

SAMOSAS

These little savouries are traditional Indian 'fast foods'. It is nice to shape samosas in the traditional way, but you can make them into small turnovers if you find this easier. The spiciness of the filling may be varied by adding more or less of the various seasonings.

FOR 16 SAMOSAS (4-8 SERVINGS):
Pastry:
1 cup wholemeal flour
1 cup plain white flour
¼ cup oil
4-6 Tbsp water
1 tsp salt

Filling:
4 medium-sized potatoes (500 g total), boiled and peeled
2 Tbsp oil
1 medium-sized onion, diced
1 cup peas, fresh or frozen
2-3 tsp curry powder
1 tsp garam masala
1 tsp ground coriander
1 tsp ground cumin
1-2 tsp salt, to taste
1 tsp sugar
¼ cup water
juice of 1 lemon

Make the pastry as usual (see page 88), using oil instead of butter. Be careful to add only enough water to form the 'crumbs' into one large ball.

Knead on a lightly floured surface for a few minutes, then oil the surface and allow the dough to stand while you prepare the filling.

Boil the potatoes. In a large frypan, Sauté the onion in the oil until soft. Add the potatoes (cut into 1.5 cm cubes), peas and seasonings. Cook together for a few minutes, until the peas are soft.

Stir in the water and lemon juice. There should be enough liquid to form everything into a very thick, lumpy paste. Taste and add more curry powder and/or salt if you wish.

Divide the pastry into eight balls. Keep one of these to work with but cover the rest. Roll the ball into a 20 cm circle. Cut this in half. Take one half and form it into a cone by overlapping the cut edges, using a little water to seal the join.

Place 1-2 tablespoons (or as much as you can fit) of the filling into the cone, then, as before, seal this edge with a little water. You may wish to decorate this edge by folding again and squashing with a fork.

Repeat with the other half of the circle, then with the other balls of pastry.

Cook three or four at a time, in oil heated to about 180°C, for about 5 minutes, or until golden brown. Serve warm, reheating in a microwave or conventional oven if necessary.

MUSHROOM-TOPPED SPINACH FLAN

FOR A 20 CM FLAN:
1 uncooked 20 cm pie crust
½ cup cream cheese
2 eggs
½ tsp salt
½ tsp grated nutmeg
black pepper
2 cups cooked spinach

Roll bought or home-made pastry (see page 88) thinly to line a 20 cm flan or pie dish.

In a large bowl mix together the cream cheese, eggs and seasonings. Fold in the chopped, drained spinach, then gently pour the filling mixture into the uncooked pie crust.

Bake at 220°C for 20 minutes or until the centre is firm. While the flan cooks, prepare the mushroom topping below.

200-300 g button mushrooms
2 Tbsp oil
1-2 cloves garlic, chopped

½ tsp cornflour
2 tsp light soya sauce
1 Tbsp water
2 Tbsp chopped parsley

Slice the mushrooms and Sauté in the oil with the crushed garlic. As soon as the mushrooms soften, stir in the cornflour dissolved in the soya sauce and water, then the chopped parsley.

Pile the mushroom mixture on top of the cooked flan. Leave to stand for about 5 minutes before serving.

EMPANADAS

If you like Spanish and/or Mexican food, you should really enjoy these cheesy savouries. They may be baked or deep fried, as you like. Try halving the size and making twice as many 'empanaditas' (little empanadas) to serve as pre-dinner starters or snacks.

for 6 empanadas or 12 empanaditas:
Pastry:

3 cups plain white flour
½ tsp salt
75 g melted butter
½ cup yoghurt
2-3 Tbsp water

Filling:

2 cups (200 g) grated cheese
2 hard-boiled eggs, chopped
1 large green or red pepper, or 1 small (130 g) can diced peppers
10-12 olives, chopped
1 Tbsp capers (optional)
½ tsp chilli powder
1 tsp ground cumin
½ tsp oreganum

Although this is an unusual pastry, it is made in the same way as normal pastry (*see page 88*). Be very careful not to add too much water or the pastry will be sticky and difficult to work with.

Once the pastry has been made, knead for a few minutes, then divide it into six equal-sized balls. Cover these and leave to stand while preparing the filling.

In a bowl combine all filling ingredients using liquid from canned peppers, if used.

Roll out the first ball of pastry until it is about 15-20 cm across. Place about ½ cup of filling just to one side of the middle, and then fold over until the edges meet (you should have a D-shape). Seal the seam using a little water, then press around the edge with a fork. Repeat to make six empanadas.

Deep fry in oil heated to 180°C for 5 minutes or until golden brown, or bake for 30 minutes at 180°C. Brush liberally with oil before putting in the oven, and again once or twice during cooking.

For a light meal or lunch, serve the empanadas alone or with a salad (they are surprisingly substantial), or, for a main meal, serve with brown rice and a salad.

Variation:
IIf you can't be bothered hard-boiling the eggs, just break the eggs straight in, and stir until combined.

SELF-CRUSTING QUICHES

Self-crusting quiches are made without pastry crusts but form their own fairly firm outer layers as they cook.

For best results you should remember these points:

- Use a metal pie plate or flan tin with a solid (not push-out) base.
- Use a non-stick finish for choice.
- Lightly oil or butter the dish before use, regardless of the finish.
- Take care not to overmix the egg mixture when you add the flour, or it may not form two layers as it cooks.
- Bake at a high temperature so the rust browns well.
- Leave to stand for 5 minutes after removing from the oven, before turning out.

SELF-CRUSTING POTATO AND VEGETABLE QUICHE

This quiche contains cooked potato for bulk and another vegetable for, flavour.

FOR 4-6 SERVINGS:
1 large onion, chopped
2 garlic cloves
1 Tbsp butter
3 eggs
¾ tsp salt
1 cup milk
½ cup self-raising flour
2 cooked potatoes
1 cup drained cooked asparagus or spinach or mushrooms or broccoli
1 cup grated tasty cheese

Cook the chopped onion and garlic in butter until tender. Cool. Stir in the eggs, salt and milk, and beat with fork until mixed. Pour this into a large bow containing the flour, and stir with the fork until just combined. Add the potatoes cut in 1 cm cubes, the chopped well-drained vegetables and cheese.

Pour into a prepared 20-23 cm pan (see above). Garnish with sliced tomato or thinly sliced red and green peppers if desired. Bake at 220°C for 20-30 minutes, until lightly browned and set in the centre.

SELF-CRUSTING HERBED MUSHROOM QUICHE

FOR 4-6 SERVINGS:
2 medium-sized onions
2 Tbsp oil or butter
200 g mushrooms
½ tsp dried basil
¼ tsp dried thyme
black pepper to taste
2 eggs
½ cup sour cream
¾ cup milk
½ tsp salt
½ cup self-raising flour
½ cup grated tasty cheese

Slice onions finely. Sauté in the oil or butter, and when soft add the mushrooms and cook until these soften too. Add the basil, thyme and black pepper, then remove from the heat and leave to stand while preparing the egg mixture.

In a medium-sized bowl lightly beat together the eggs, sour cream, milk and salt. Sprinkle the flour over this mixture and stir just enough to combine, then add the grated cheese, again stirring just enough to mix.

Butter a 25-30 cm flan or pie dish (see above). Tip in the onion-and-mushroom mixture, and spread it evenly over the bottom, then pour the batter evenly over this.

Three different versions of Self-Crusting Potato and Vegetable Quiche

Bake at 220°C for 20-30 minutes, until light brown and firm in the centre. Cool for 10-15 minutes before turning out.

Serve with baked potatoes or pasta, fresh tomatoes and a mixed green salad.

LOW-CAL SELF-CRUSTING QUICHE

This is lower in fat and calories than most other quiches, but it still tastes good!

FOR 4 SERVINGS:
1 (450 g) can whole kernel corn, drained
2-4 spring onions, chopped
½ cup self-raising flour
¾ cup Trim milk
2 eggs
2 Tbsp grated parmesan cheese black pepper to taste
3 firm tomatoes, sliced paprika

MEALS WITHOUT MEAT

Lightly oil or butter a 20-23 cm pie plate or flan tin. Arrange the drained corn and chopped spring onions in it.

In another bowl, mixing with a fork, combine the self-raising flour, milk, eggs, half of the cheese and black pepper.

Pour the egg mixture over the corn and spring onions, then slice the tomatoes, and arrange these over the surface of the quiche.

Sprinkle the remaining grated parmesan and a little paprika over the surface. Bake at 220°C for 20-30 minutes or until the centre is set and the top is golden brown.

Variations:
Replace the corn with 1 cup well-drained cooked spinach, 1½ cups cooked zucchini, 2 cups sliced mushrooms, or 2 cups chopped cooked broccoli.

SELF-CRUSTING LENTIL AND TOMATO QUICHE

This is a good way to introduce brown lentils to those who may have doubts about their virtues! The lentils give the quiche an interesting texture and make it quite substantial.

for 4-6 servings:
½ cup dry brown lentils
1 bay leaf
2 medium-sized onions
2 cloves garlic
1 Tbsp oil or butter
1 Tbsp lemon juice black pepper
3 eggs
1 cup milk
½ tsp salt
½ tsp basil
½ tsp oreganum
½ cup self-raising flour
½ cup grated tasty cheese
3 tomatoes, thinly sliced
2 Tbsp grated parmesan

Cook the lentils with the bay leaf until they are tender (*see page 175*).

Sauté sliced onions in the oil with the chopped garlic. When soft and clear, remove from the heat and add lemon juice and black pepper to taste.

In a large bowl, beat together the eggs, milk, salt and herbs. Stir in the flour and grated cheese, but do not overmix.

Combine drained lentils with the cooked onions. Stir into the batter. Pour into a prepared 23-30 cm flan tin or pie plate. Top with tomato slices, then sprinkle with the grated parmesan.

Bake for 25-30 minutes at 220°C, or until the centre is firm when pressed. Serve with salad or cooked vegetables.

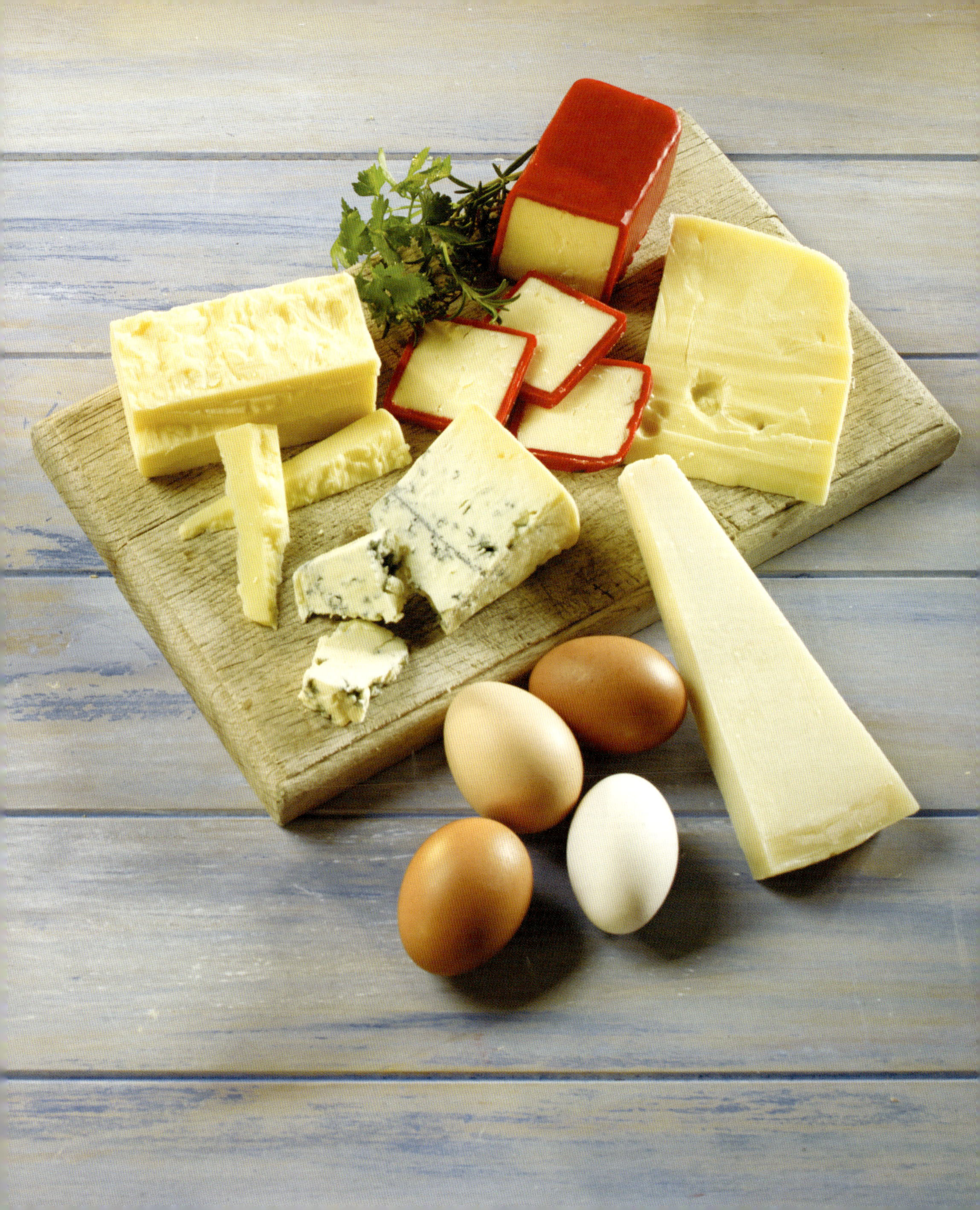

EGGS & CHEESE

SWISS EGGS

This is an interesting omelet variation.

for 1 large or 2 small servings:
2 thick slices bread
2 Tbsp butter
2 eggs
2 Tbsp milk
½ tsp salt
25 g cubed cheese

Cut the bread into small cubes. Heat half the butter in a small frying pan and toss the bread in it. Cook over moderate heat until the croutons are crisp and golden brown. Remove from pan.

Beat the eggs, milk and salt together with a fork. Heat the pan again. Heat the remaining butter in it until straw-coloured. Pour in the egg mixture. Cook, tilting pan and lifting the edge of the omelet to let the uncooked mixture run underneath.

Sprinkle the croutons and the cheese over half the omelet when it is barely set. Flip the other half of the omelet over the croutons and cheese. Serve immediately. The cheese should be warm but not melted, and the croutons still crunchy.

COTTAGE CHEESE OMELET

Always use small-curd cottage cheese for omelets, and do not add salt.

for 2 servings:
1 egg
2 Tbsp small-curd cottage cheese
1 spring onion, chopped
1 tsp butter

Stir together with a fork until barely mixed, the egg, cottage cheese, and spring onion (or other herbs). Heat the butter in a small pan until it bubbles and turns straw coloured, swirl to coat pan, and pour in the egg mixture.

Lift the edge to let the unset mixture run underneath, then fold in half and serve immediately.

FOR ONE

Scrambled eggs make a. really fast meal, cooked in a pan or the microwave oven.

1 tsp butter
1 egg
2 Tbsp milk
salt, pepper, and fresh herbs

To microwave:
Melt butter in a small bowl. Add remaining ingredients using little or no salt, beat with a fork to mix white and yolk, then microwave on High (100%) power for 60-80 seconds, or until mixture puffs, stirring after 30 seconds. Leave to stand for 30 seconds before eating.
To cook in a small pan:
Melt butter in pan. Stir in lightly mixed remaining ingredients. Cook over moderate heat, running a small fish slice along the bottom of the pan to push the cooked mixture aside. Remove from heat just before last bit sets. Serve on toast, etc.

SPAGHETTI SCRAMBLE

For a quick, satisfying meal, cook eggs in a pan with vegetables and spaghetti.

for 4 servings:
1 large onion
1 green pepper
1-2 Tbsp oil or butter
1 (450 g) can spaghetti
herbs, chopped (optional)
3 eggs
2 Tbsp milk
¼ tsp salt
pepper

MEALS WITHOUT MEAT

Chop the onion and green pepper, and cook in the butter or oil in a large pan until tender but not browned. Add the spaghetti and any herbs you like, and heat until bubbling.

Beat the eggs, milk and seasonings with a fork, and pour over the hot spaghetti. Without stirring, lift the spaghetti with a fish slice so the egg can run underneath.

Serve as soon as the egg has set, garnished with chopped parsley or spring onions. This is nice in split, toasted buns.

ASPARAGUS ROULADE

A roulade is a roll made of a soufflé-like mixture, enclosing a well-seasoned filling which usually contrasts in flavour and colour with the outside layer. Roulades may be made well ahead, then sliced, and served hot or cold, as a starter or main course.

for 4 lunch-sized servings:

50 g butter
¼ cup flour
¾ cup milk
3 Tbsp tomato paste
3 eggs
½ cup grated tasty cheese

Filling:

1 (about 400 g) can asparagus spears
¼ cup cream cheese
1 clove garlic, finely chopped
¼ cup finely chopped parsley

Melt the butter in a pan. Stir in the flour until it bubbles, for about 30 seconds. Add the milk gradually, stirring continuously, until the sauce boils and thickens. Stir in the tomato paste, and bring to the boil again. Remove from heat.

Separate the egg yolks and whites. Add the yolks to the hot sauce and quickly stir to combine. Stir in the grated cheese. Beat the egg whites until soft peaks form. Fold into the cheese mixture. Pour the mixture into a Teflon or baking-paper-lined sponge roll tin (about 20 cm×30 cm).

Bake at 200°C for 12-15 minutes or until puffed and golden brown. The roulade is cooked as soon as the centre springs back when lightly pressed with a finger. Remove from the oven and turn out onto a rack covered with a teatowel, or another Teflon sheet.

Carefully remove the lining paper or liner.

Make the filling while the roulade cooks. Drain the asparagus liquid into a pan. Chop the asparagus and press gently to remove more liquid. Boil the asparagus liquid and chopped garlic down to 1 tablespoon and stir into the chopped asparagus. Fold together the asparagus, cream cheese and parsley (or other herbs). Taste, and adjust seasoning. Spread evenly over the room- temperature roulade, leaving one long side uncovered. Holding the teatowel or Teflon with both hands gently roll the roulade, starting with the side nearest you, and finishing with the uncovered side.

Wrap the roll in plastic film, and refrigerate until needed, up to 24 hours. A short time before serving cold, cut carefully in 5 mm-1 cm straight or diagonal slices, using a sharp, serrated knife.

If serving warm, microwave carefully on a low power level; or cover in foil and reheat at 180°C until warm but not very hot right through, before or after slicing.

Serve with a salad, or salad garnish.

ASPARAGUS EGG AND CHEESE CASSEROLE

A cheese sauce will turn a few simple ingredients into an interesting meal. This casserole is always popular, and is good when you are entertaining, since it can be made ahead, and heated through when you want it.

for 4 servings:

2 Tbsp butter
3 Tbsp flour
1 tsp mixed mustard

½ tsp salt
1½ cups milk
½-1 cup grated cheese
1 bunch cooked fresh asparagus or 1 (340 g) can asparagus spears, drained
3 or 4 hard-boiled eggs, chopped
½ cup crushed potato crisps

Make a cheese sauce by melting the butter, adding the flour, mustard and salt, and stirring until blended. Add the milk, half a cup at a time, bringing to the boil between each addition, stirring constantly. Stir in the cheese, and remove from the heat.

In a buttered 20 cm casserole dish, layer the sauce, well-drained chopped asparagus and hard-boiled eggs, Starting and finishing with sauce. Top with the crushed potato crisps.

Reheat at 180°C until the sauce bubbles around the edges and the centre is hot.

Serve as is, or on noodles or brown rice if you are cooking for particularly hungry people. A salad is a nice accompaniment.

CHEESE STRATA

This is a popular recipe. The bread puffs up and browns slightly to produce a product that resembles a soufflé, but which has more body.

FOR 4-6 SERVINGS:
6 slices of sandwich bread
sliced cheese
mixed mustard
3 eggs
2 cups milk
1 tsp garlic salt

Make cheese sandwiches, using thick slices of cheese, mustard to taste, and no butter. Cut in quarters and stand, crusts down, in a buttered casserole dish.

Beat eggs, milk and garlic salt together and pour over sandwiches. Leave to stand for 30 minutes or longer, spooning the egg over the exposed bread at intervals.

Bake, uncovered, at 190°C for 30-45 minutes, or until the bread is puffed and golden brown, and the centre firm.

CHEESE SOUFFLÉ

Soufflés are not as complicated or temperamental as they are made out to be — but you would be wise to make one or two in private before serving them to impress guests!

Serve another course before your Soufflé, so diners are seated at the table when the Soufflé arrives from the oven.

FOR 3-4 SERVINGS:
3 Tbsp butter
½ tsp salt
1 tsp mixed mustard
¼ cup flour
1½ cups milk
1½ cups grated cheese
3 eggs, separated

Melt the butter in a medium-sized pot. Add the salt and mustard, then the flour. Stir over a low heat until the mixture bubbles. Add the milk, half a cup at a time, while stirring continuously and boiling between additions. Add the grated cheese, then remove from the heat and stir until smooth.

Separate eggs, putting the whites in a medium-sized bowl and adding the yolks to the cheese sauce (prepare to this stage in advance if desired).

Beat the whites until the peaks turn over at the tips when the beater is removed. Fold the whites into the sauce. Butter the bottom only of a 6 cup Soufflé dish and pour in the mixture. Run a knife through the mixture in a circle 2 cm inside the edge of the dish (this helps even splitting and rising).

Bake at 190°C for 40-45 minutes, or until a knife inserted in the middle comes out clean. Serve immediately, since Soufflés shrink on standing.

Variations:
For vegetable Soufflés add 1-2 cups of very well-drained, finely chopped, cooked broccoli, spinach, asparagus, or mushrooms to the cheese sauce after stirring in the egg yolks.

CHEDDAR CHEESE FONDUE

A cheese fondue is a companionable meal for a cold night. Children as well as adults enjoy dipping bread into the communal pot.

Microwave ovens make the cooking and reheating really easy, and do away with the need for table-top burners.

for 2 main or 4 starter servings:
2 cups grated cheddar cheese
2 Tbsp flour
1 tsp butter (for conventional cooking)
1 clove garlic, chopped finely
½ tsp nutmeg
1 cup flat or fresh beer

Microwave method:
Mix the grated cheese and flour in a bowl or flat-bottomed casserole dish. Add the garlic, nutmeg, and beer. Stir to mix. Microwave on High (100%) power for 2 minutes, stir with a whisk, then heat until the whole surface bubbles, stirring each minute.

Serve very hot, with chunks of crusty bread to dip, reheating the bowl of fondue if it cools down.

Conventional method:

Mix grated cheese and flour. Melt a teaspoon of butter in a small pot or pan, then add the garlic and nutmeg and cook gently for about a minute, without browning. Add the beer and heat until hot but not boiling. Stir in the floured cheese gradually, while stirring or whisking the mixture over low heat. Remove from the heat when the cheese has all melted, and the mixture is smooth.

Serve, keeping the fondue warm over a candle or low alcohol burner.

Note:
Although it is not traditional, some people like to dip cubes of raw apple, pear, cauliflower, etc.

Variation:
For special occasions, use other cheeses to replace half of the cheddar (or even all of it!). Try Raclette, Emmentaler or gruyère cheeses.

FRENCH TOAST

The most uninteresting, stale slices of bread take on new life if they are dipped in an eggy mixture, then browned in a hot pan containing a little butter.

Beat 1 egg with 1 tablespoon milk, orange juice, or white wine, until well mixed, but not frothy.

Dip sliced brown or white bread, or diagonally sliced French bread, into this mixture, turning to moisten both sides. Leave coated bread to stand on a flat plate or tray for several minutes before cooking in a moderately hot pan, allowing about half a teaspoon of butter for each side. Cook long enough to brown evenly on both sides.

Serve hot, with honey, maple or golden syrup, jam or jelly, and bananas, if you like sweet accompaniments.

For savoury accompaniments, serve sautéed sliced tomatoes, mushrooms, creamed corn, etc. with the French toast.

FRENCH OMELET

A French omelet for one person cooks in less than a minute. The mixture must be mixed, heated and worked with carefully, for good results. For a small omelet you need an 18-20 cm pan, preferably with a non-stick finish.

Combine in a bowl: 2 eggs, 2 Tbsp water, milk, or cream, ¼ teaspoon salt, and some finely chopped fresh herbs if desired.

Stir mixture for the first 5 seconds only. Tilt pan and lift the set edges to let uncooked egg run underneath.

Stir the ingredients together with a fork, only until the whites and yolks are combined. Do not overmix.

When egg is set but surface is still moist, omelet is ready to fold, or to fill with a precooked mixture.

Pour the mixture into a hot pan containing 1 teaspoon butter which has been heated until straw-coloured.

Spoon hot filling onto half the omelet. Fold the other half over the filling. Slide or flip onto plate.

SPANISH OMELET

Although you can add all sorts of things to this omelet, try it absolutely plain first, because it tastes so good.

FOR 2 SERVINGS:
2-3 potatoes
2 Tbsp oil
2-3 eggs
½ tsp salt

Scrub and cut the potatoes into 1cm cubes, then tip into hot oil in a small, preferably non-stick pan. Cover pan and cook over moderate heat until potatoes are tender, 5-10 minutes. It is nice but not essential if the potatoes brown slightly.

While potatoes cook, beat the eggs and the salt in a bowl with a fork, only until whites and yolks are combined. Tip the cooked potatoes into the egg, stir well, then tip back into the clean pan, containing a little extra oil.

Cook, uncovered, over moderate heat until middle is nearly cooked. Slide from pan onto lid or plate, flip back into pan with uncooked side down, and cook until lightly browned.

Slide out of pan, without folding. Cut in quarters or wedges to serve.

102   MEALS WITHOUT MEAT   FRENCH OMELET (FRONT), SPANISH OMELET (BACK)

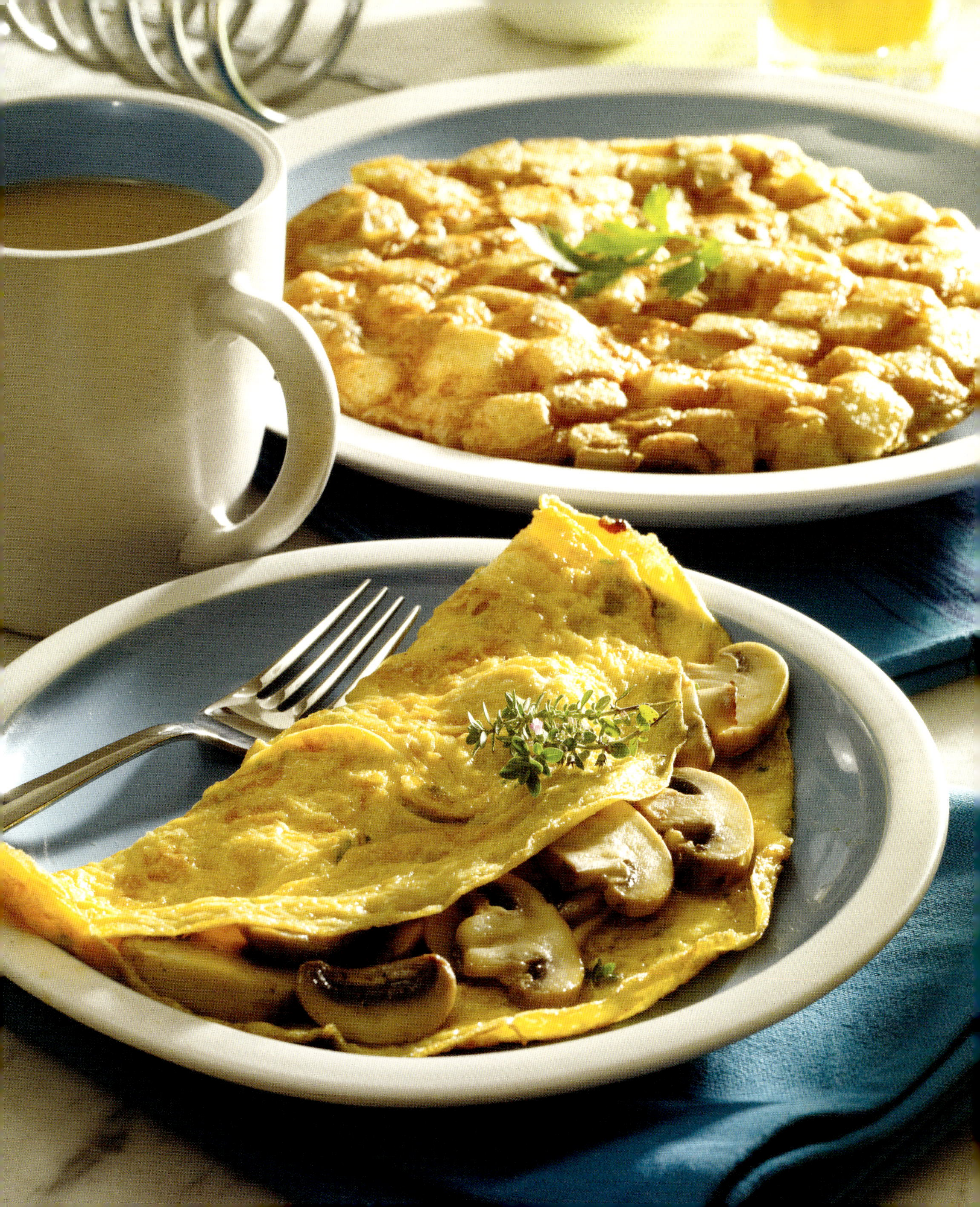

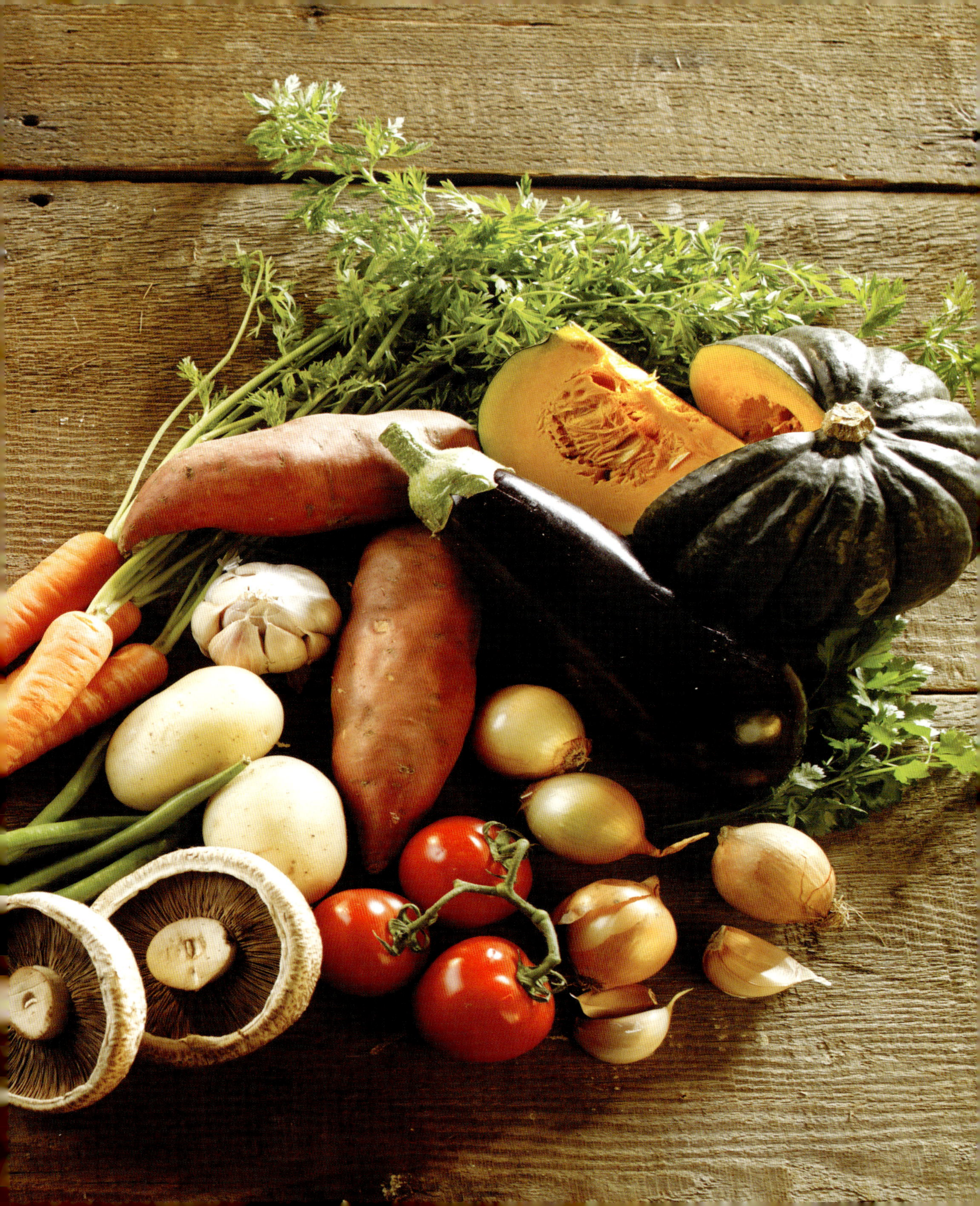

TOFU DISHES

If you are interested in specialist vegetarian products, you'll probably already know about tofu (or soya bean curd) which is now commonly found in the refrigerator cabinets of most supermarkets and health food shops.
Tofu is a high-quality vegetable protein, made by soaking, grinding, straining, heating and setting soya, beans. In some Asian countries it is produced, bought and eaten as commonly as we eat bread.
Tofu needs well-seasoned additions, either sweet or savoury, to make it interesting.

SWEET AND SOUR TOFU

Fast and colourful, this sweet-sour mixture is ready in less than the time it takes rice to cook.

FOR 2 SERVINGS:
200-300 g firm or very firm tofu, cubed
2 Tbsp oil
1 large onion
1 green and/or red pepper
1 Tbsp oil
1 Tbsp cornflour
¼ cup brown sugar
2 Tbsp wine vinegar
1½ tsp light soya sauce
½ cup water
red food colouring (optional)

Cut the tofu into 1 cm cubes (approx.) and brown evenly on all sides, in the first measure of oil, in a non-stick pan. This should take about 5 minutes.

In another pan, or after the tofu has cooked and been removed, sauté the onion and pepper, cut into pieces about the same size as the tofu, in the remaining measure of oil. When tender, but not browned (about 5 minutes), stir in the cornflour and brown sugar, then add the vinegar, soya sauce and water and bring to the boil, stirring constantly. Colour red with food colouring if desired. Stir the tofu into the sauce and serve over rice or noodles.

Variation:
Replace the water and half the sugar with pineapple juice. Stir pineapple cubes into the hot sauce before adding the tofu.

EGGY TOFU

In this recipe tofu is sautéed until crusted, mixed first with quick-cooking vegetables, then with an egg to hold it together, and finally coated with an interesting sauce. You finish up with a substantial meal for one person.

FOR 1 SERVING:
2 tsp oil
about 100 g tofu, drained and cubed
¼-½ cup sliced mushrooms
1-2 spring onions
1 egg
¼ cup water
2 tsp Kikkoman soya sauce
¼ tsp sesame oil
hot pepper sauce to taste
1 tsp cornflour

Buy firm or very firm tofu if you have a choice. Heat the oil in a non-stick frying pan. Cut tofu into cubes. Cook in the hot oil until all sides are golden brown. Add the mushrooms and spring onions. Stir-fry for 1-2 minutes until wilted.

Now prepare two separate mixtures. Beat the egg with a fork to combine the white and yolk, and mix the remaining ingredients in another container. Add the egg to the tofu mixture in the pan, stirring until the egg sets. Add the remaining ingredients which have been stirred together, and heat until this mixture thickens and turns transparent.

Sprinkle with chopped parsley or chives, and serve immediately on rice, toast or noodles.

Double or triple the recipe for 2 or 3 servings.

TOMATO TOFU TORTILLA STACK

This is a colourful and very popular casserole with a Mexican flavour. It contains uncooked tortillas, which are available from some delicatessens and Mexican restaurants. Make the sauce first.

Tomato and Chilli Sauce:
1 (425 g) can tomato purée
½ tsp chilli powder
1 tsp ground cumin
½ tsp oreganum
½ tsp ground coriander
½ tsp salt & 1 tsp sugar
½-1 tsp hot chilli sauce to taste & juice of ½ lemon

Combine all the ingredients in a medium-sized pot and simmer gently while preparing the remaining components of the stack as described below.

FOR 6 SERVINGS:
1 large onion
1 green pepper
2 Tbsp oil or butter
500 g (approx.) firm tofu
½ tsp chilli powder
1 tsp cumin
½ tsp oreganum
1 tsp salt black pepper
6 uncooked com tortillas
1 (425 g) can whole kernel corn tomato and chilli sauce (above)
½ cup grated cheese

Chop the onion and green pepper. In a large pan or pot sauté these in the oil or butter over a medium heat. While this cooks, drain and crumble the tofu. Tofu comes in a variety of different-sized blocks. Don't worry if you have 100 g more or less than the suggested amount.

Add the tofu and seasonings to the onion-and-pepper mixture, and continue to cook until they dry out a little.

To assemble the whole stack, lay two of the flat tortillas on the bottom of a medium-sized casserole dish so that they overlap as little as possible (an oval dish is probably the best shape if you have one). Spread one-third of the tofu mixture over these, then one-third of the drained corn over this. Complete the layer by pouring over one-third of the tomato chilli sauce. Repeat this process twice so that there are three layers of everything.

Sprinkle the grated cheese evenly over the top and bake, uncovered at 180°C, for 30-40 minutes, until hot.

MARINATED TOFU (FOR BURGERS AND KEBABS)

When left to stand in a well-flavoured marinade, tofu absorbs its flavour. Square slabs of the marinated tofu, sautéed in a teaspoon or so of oil, make good burgers or toasted sandwiches. Cubes, sautéed for a few minutes on all sides, may be threaded on sticks with vegetables, to make kebabs, which are then carefully grilled or barbecued. Although the outside will be quite firm and crusty, the inside will keep its original soft texture. Start with tofu which is firm, or extra-firm, or the tofu may fall apart when skewered.

about 500 g extra-firm tofu
¼ cup corn or soya oil
¼ cup lemon juice
¼ cup dark soya sauce
2 large cloves garlic, chopped
1 Tbsp sesame oil
1 tsp dried oreganum
hot pepper sauce to taste
Marinated Tofu Kebabs and Grilled Polenta Kebabs

Drain the tofu, cut into 15 mm thick, 10 cm square slices, or 2 cm cubes (approx.), and leave to stand while you prepare the marinade.

Measure the remaining ingredients into an unpunctured plastic bag, using enough hot pepper sauce to give the hotness you like.

Stand the bag in a shallow baking pan and place the tofu in it so that the slices or cubes lie flat. Suck out the air, so that the tofu is surrounded by the marinade, and fasten with a rubber band. Leave for at least 4 hours, or up to 48 hours turning occasionally.

Brown the drained tofu in a non-stick pan with a few drops of oil, over moderate to high heat. Give cubes 30-40 seconds per side, and give slices several minutes per side at lower heat, since the slices will not be grilled later.

For kebabs, thread the lightly sautéed cubes on skewers with mushrooms, little tomatoes, red and green pepper squares and cubes of zucchini or aubergine, all of which have been turned in the marinade. Grill about 5 cm from the heat, for about 5 minutes per side, turning once, and brushing with mayonnaise or with extra marinade if desired.

Serve the slices in toasted rolls or between slices of toasted bread, with tomato relish and other burger accompaniments. Serve the kebabs on rice, noodles, burgul, etc. They taste good with tomato sauce.

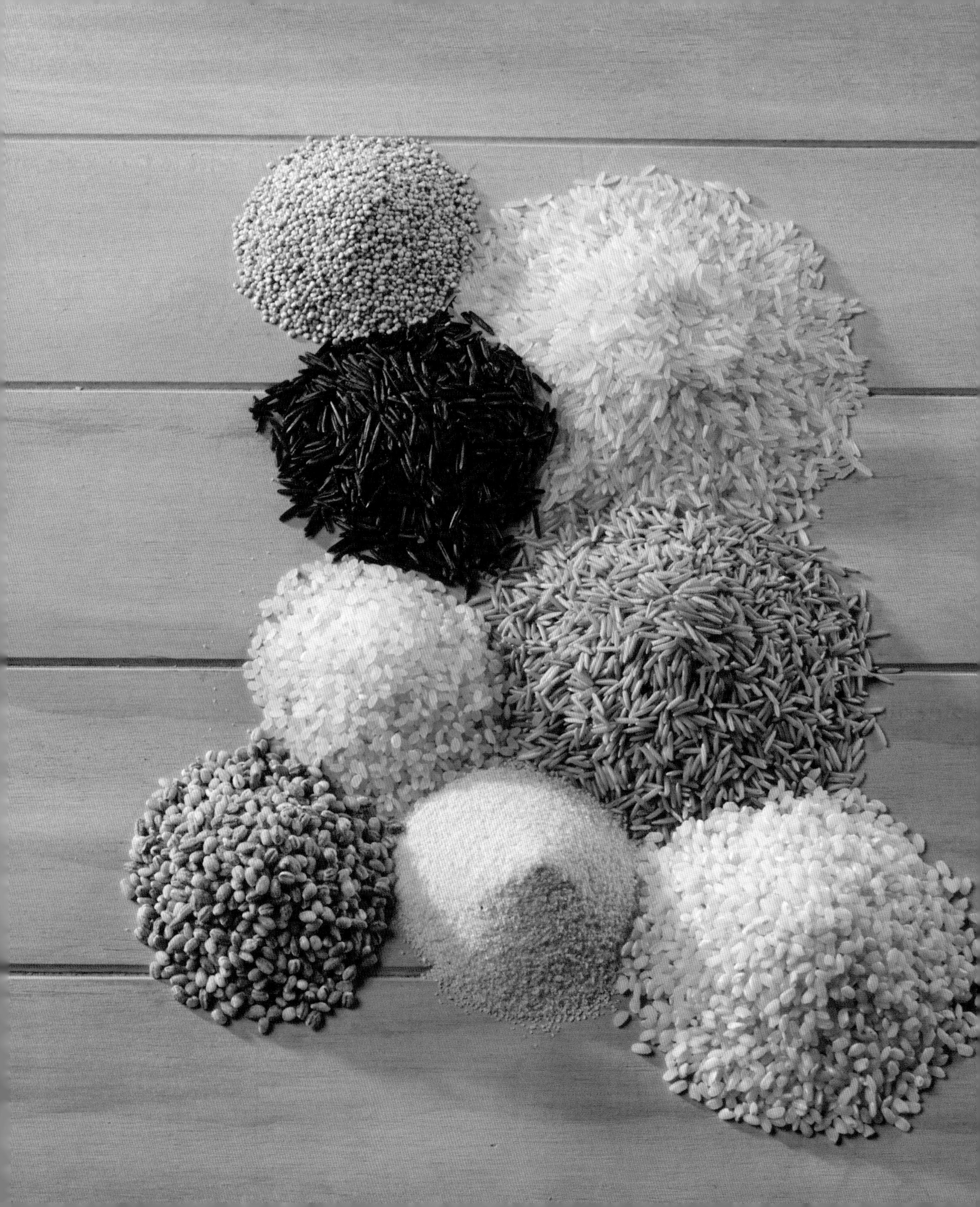

RICE & GRAINS

Grains, the seeds of grasses, are the most important staple foods in the world. Rice, wheat and corn are the most-used grains, but many others are grown in different parts of the world, according to climate.

Grains are processed in many ways; they may be left whole, flaked, chopped (kibbled), or ground coarsely or to fine powders. The outer layers of the grain are often removed during processing. As these layers contain valuable nutrients as well as dietary fibre, it is very important to include unprocessed or whole grains in your diet. Many grain products are now widely available and are worth trying for their interesting flavours and textures as well as their nutritional content.

1. SEMOLINA:
The coarsely ground heart of wheat kernels. In Indian cookery it is lightly browned before cooking, with interesting results.

2. COARSE CORN MEAL AND FINE CORN MEAL:
Corn kernels ground to different particle sizes. The finer types are usually used in baking, while the coarser types may be boiled with water to make a porridge-like mixture (polenta).

3. KIBBLED RYE:
Chopped rye grains. Boil or microwave, & serve instead of rice.

4. POPPING CORN:
Whole kernels of a special variety of corn. When heated with a little oil, the grains expand and pop violently. Without additions pop-corn is a low-calorie, low-fat snack.

6. FLAKED RYE:
If stirred during cooking, forms a chewy porridge-like mixture. If lightly browned in butter or oil, before cooking without stirring, the grains stay separate.

7. WHOLE GRAIN RYE:
Requires long cooking. Serve like brown rice. Sauté in butter or oil before cooking.

8. BURGHUL OR BULGAR:
Heat- treated, precooked chopped wheat which needs soaking or brief cooking in water, before being used in salads and savoury mixtures. Soaks up flavours of accompanying foods.

9. WHOLEMEAL FLOUR:
Made by milling the whole wheat grain. It contains the outer bran layer and the germ, which are high in fibre, vitamins and minerals, as well as the inner white part (or endosperm) of the grain. It gives a more solid texture to baked products. To include more in your diet, try replacing half, rather than all the flour in an existing recipe with wholemeal flour, and be prepared to add a slightly different amount of liquid to reach the usual consistency.

10. KIBBLED WHEAT:
Chopped wheat grains. Not cooked during manufacture, it needs more cooking than bulgar. Cook and serve as rice, include in porridge mixtures, or use in coarse-textured bread, after heating to boiling point in water, then draining.

11. WHEAT GERM:
A small part of the wheat grain, from which the new wheat plant grows. A concentrated food, especially high in protein, vitamins and minerals. Add it to baking, porridge, and other foods, to enrich them. Excellent value for money, nutritionally.

12. WHEAT GRAINS ():
Use as rice etc. Requires longer cooking than kibbled or flaked wheat.

13. WHEAT BRAN:
Made from the outer layers of wheat grains. Does not contain the wheat germ. High in fibre. Sometimes sold as baking bran. May be added to baking, porridge, etc.

14. FLAKED WHEAT:
STEAMED AND CRUSHED WHEAT.
If stirred as cooked, the flakes produce a porridgy mixture. If cooked without stirring, with a little oil or butter, they keep their shape. Use in place of rice, or in muesli mixtures.

15. MILLET:
Small, round grain (also sold for birdseed) which will grow in very hot and dry places.

16. FLAKED MILLET:
Flaked for quicker cooking in porridgy mixtures. Millet is gluten free.

17. SHORT-GRAIN, WHITE RICE:
The short, plump grains tend to break down during cooking, becoming sticky and thickening surrounding liquid. This is desirable in rice puddings, soups, and in sushi.

18. WHOLE GRAIN:
Oat grains which are steamed then flattened. Widely used in muesli, etc. Cook, without stirring, in mixtures to replace rice.

19. OAT BRAN:
Made from outer layers of oat grain; cooks with water to a much softer mixture than bran. Acclaimed as soluble fibre. If used to replace flour in baking, texture becomes drier.

20. FLAKED BARLEY:
Made from steamed, rolled barley grains. Use as you would other flaked grains.

21. BUCKWHEAT:
Often toasted before sale, to improve flavour. Cook in place of rice and in porridge mixtures. Ground for use in pancakes.

22. PEARL BARLEY:
Polished to remove the outside layers. Use in soups, as rice, or in salads etc.

23. LONG-GRAIN BROWN RICE and 26. SHORT-GRAIN BROWN RICE:
Retains its bran layers and germ, thus more vitamins, minerals and protein. Needs longer cooking, and often more water than white rice. It has firmer, more chewy texture and nutty flavour. Microwave or pressure cook to reduce cooking time. Little difference in behaviour of long and short grains. Serve in same way as cooked long-grain white rice. Pressure cooks in less than 10 minutes.

24. LONG-GRAIN WHITE RICE:
Grain shape and length vary slightly, but cooking and nutritional qualities are similar. The usual choice for plainly cooked rice to accompany other foods. Many different cooking methods are used. Methods where all water is absorbed give slightly more flavour. Overcooking causes stickiness. Microwaves well.

25. BLACK, GLUTINOUS RICE:
Novelty value. Cooking water is dark red, and cooked grains reddish-brown. When mixed with plain cooked rice, it looks interesting. Available in Asian food stores.

27. MIXED RICE:
Mixed long-grain rices, mainly brown and glutinous rices. Need long cooking time, as for brown rice. Looks attractive, and may be used to replace other cooked rice, in recipes.

28. HEAT-TREATED RICE:
Easily recognisable by its yellowish colour. Is heat-treated before outer layers are removed and is said to contain more nutrients than white rice because of this. Costs more than plain long-grain rice but cooks more easily and produces greater volume. Microwaves very well. When cooked, loses most of its yellowish colour. Usually sold under brand names.

29. WILD RICE:
Formerly expensive and rare because it was not cultivated, but is now grown commercially, so price has decreased, and availability increased. Nutty flavour; cooking time similar to that of brown rice. Sold in rice mixtures. A luxury item.

30. BASMATI RICE:
Aromatic rice, with appearance and nutritive value of long-grain white rice. Cooking smells are startling, and unusual. Flavour outstanding, stronger in some brands than others. More highly priced, understandably, than white rice.

COOKING RICE

FOOLPROOF WHITE RICE

If you coat rice grains with oil or butter before you cook them, there is much less chance that they will stick together.

Heat 1 tablespoon oil or butter in a heavy-bottomed saucepan with a tight-fitting lid. Add ½ teaspoon salt. Stir in 1 cup long-grain white rice. Add 2 cups boiling water. Put on a tight-fitting lid and cook gently, without lifting the lid or stirring, for about 15 minutes. Lift out a few grains of rice and test by squeezing them. (See Butterless White Rice below.) If it is not cooked, check if there is any water left in the pan. If not, add about ¼ cup more, cover again and cook for 3-4 minutes longer. Transfer to serving dish, forking it lightly to get a fluffy appearance.

FOOLPROOF HEAT-TREATED RICE

Cook as above, adding 2¼ cups water of any temperature to 1 cup of rice. Allow a little longer cooking time.

Note:
For softer-textured rice, add ¼-½ cup more water, and cook for about 5 minutes longer.

BUTTERLESS WHITE RICE

This is a good way to cook rice when you don't have a heavy pot with a tight-fitting lid, or when you don't want to add oil or butter.

Bring 8 cups water and 1 tablespoon salt to the boil in a large saucepan. Slowly shake 1 cup long-grain rice into the bubbling water, making sure water doesn't stop boiling. Boil gently with the pot lid ajar, or without a lid, for about 15 minutes.

Squeeze a grain of rice between your finger and thumb. If you can squeeze it completely in half, without having a hard core left, it is cooked. Drain, using a large sieve. If serving within an hour, rinsing is not necessary. If serving later, rinse with hot (or cold) water, leave to drain again, then store in a container in which the rice will not dry out.

BROWN RICE

Brown rice has a nutty flavour, an interesting, slightly chewy texture, and is nutritionally better than white rice. It is available in long-and short-grained varieties. Both may be cooked and served as long-grain white rice is served. All types of brown rice take longer to cook than white rice. Some brown rices absorb more liquid than others, and take longer to cook. You should always be prepared to add some extra water, and cook for longer, if the grains seem dry and hard.

Undercooked brown rice may put your friends and family off it forever. Brown rice is, in fact, easier to cook than white rice, because the outer coating on the grains stops them sticking together as they cook.

Make sure that you allow plenty of cooking time.

SIMMERED BROWN RICE

Turn 1 cup brown rice in 1 teaspoon of oil or melted butter.

Add 2½ cups water and ½ teaspoon salt. Cover tightly and simmer for about 45 minutes, adding extra water if rice dries out before it is tender.

MICROWAVED BROWN RICE

Microwave for 25 minutes, using same proportions as for simmered brown rice and general method as for white rice. Allow 15 minutes standing time.

PRESSURE-COOKED BROWN RICE

A pressure cooker revolutionises the cooking of brown rice. Our modern German pressure cooker cooks 1 cup of brown rice in 3 cups of water, with ½ teaspoon salt, at high pressure, in 9 minutes. We leave it to stand for 3-5 minutes after the pressure is lowered, before draining off any remaining water and serving it. Allow a little longer if pressure cooker is old, or is not working efficiently.

BUTTERLESS HEAT-TREATED RICE

Proceed as above for quantities, adding the rice to hot or cold water, but stirring until the water boils again, if necessary. Rice may be removed from heat, then heated again, if necessary, before cooking is completed. Cooking time is unlikely to be shorter than that of plain long-grain rice.

MICROWAVED WHITE RICE

The microwave oven cooks rice very well. Use heat-treated or plain long-grain rice. You do not need to attend to it at all during or after cooking so you can put in the rice, turn on the oven, and go away. When you come back later (any time after the cooking time plus the standing time), all you need to do is reheat the rice on High (100%) power, allowing 1-2 minutes per cup. It needs no draining, no stirring. It will not have stuck to the container, and will have a good flavour.

In a large microwave bowl, turn 1 cup long-grained or heat-treated rice in 1-2 teaspoons oil (or melted butter). Add 2¼ cups (preferably hot) water, and cover, folding back the edge 5 mm if you use plastic cling wrap.

For 1 cup, cook on High (100%) power for 12-15 minutes. Allow 10 minutes standing time.

For 2 cups allow 20-25 minutes, with 15 minutes standing time.

If rice boils over, use a larger container, keep lid ajar, or lower power level (to 50% power) and increase cooking time by 5 minutes.

STORING AND REHEATING RICE

Cooked rice should be covered to prevent drying out, and refrigerated to prevent spoilage. Tough, heatproof plastic oven bags (without holes) make excellent containers for refrigerating and reheating rice. Stir with fork or toss in bag once or twice during reheating. Sprinkle with extra water if rice looks dry before or during heating.

- Reheat rice in microwave oven on High (100%) power for 1-2 minutes per cup, in its serving dish or in an oven bag (without a metal twist tie).

- In conventional oven, spread oven bag flat on a flat, shallow dish, e.g. a sponge-roll pan. Tie loosely. Reheat at whatever temperature oven is already heated to. Flip bag over once during reheating, so both sides heat.

- Reheat in a sieve or colander over a saucepan of boiling water. Cover with a lid so that the steam from the boiling water is prevented from escaping.

- For fastest reheating (without a microwave oven) but with some flavour loss, pour boiling water through cooked rice in colander or sieve, or add boiling water to rice in saucepan, then strain.

- Add rice to hot oil, or melted butter, or sautéed, finely chopped ingredients, in a preheated, preferably non-stick pan. Stir to heat evenly.

Flavour and store other cooked grains in the same way as you would rice.

ADDING FLAVOUR TO RICE

Add butter, or chopped fresh herbs, or parmesan cheese, or soya sauce, or sesame oil, or chopped, sautéed sesame or sunflower seeds or nuts (or a combination of several of these) to cooked rice.

Replace salt with vegetable stock powder when cooking. Use 1-2 level teaspoons to 1 cup rice. When using little butter, use the larger quantity.

Sauté onion, celery, peppers, or mushrooms in extra butter before stirring in uncooked rice. Add curry powder, paprika, etc., before water. Add raisins, sultanas, currants, orange or lemon rind to rice when it is about half cooked. It is important to season rice carefully. Add extra salt with herbs, butter, etc., after cooking, if rice tastes too bland.

SPECIAL SPICED RICE

When you cook rice with these spices, you raise it to 'special treat' status. With two additions the mixture made by this recipe may be transformed into a interesting dessert. If you don't have saffron or pine nuts, leave them out. The spiced rice will still be fairly special!

FOR 4-6 SERVINGS:

¼ tsp saffron strands
½ cup boiling water
1 Tbsp butter or oil
4 cardamom pods
4 whole cloves
1 small cinnamon stick
1 cup Basmati rice
1 bay leaf
a strip (20 cm) orange peel
a strip (10 cm) lime or lemon peel
1 tsp salt
2 cups boiling water
¼ cup currants
¼ cup pine nuts
1 Tbsp butter or oil

Soak saffron strands in first measure of boiling water. Melt butter or oil in microwave on High (100%) power or in frypan.

Add crushed cardamom pods, cloves and a broken cinnamon stick. Heat for 2 minutes.

Stir in rice and heat for 1 minute longer, then add bay leaf, orange and lemon peel, salt, the second measure of boiling water and the soaked saffron and liquid.

Cover and microwave on Medium (50 %) power for 15 minutes or simmer for 20 minutes. Leave to stand for 10 minutes. Meantime stir currants, pine nuts and second measure of butter or oil in a small pan, until pine nuts turn golden brown.

Sprinkle over, or stir into cooked rice and serve.

SPECIAL RICE PUDDING

To half the cooked mixture above, add about 1 cup coconut cream and 2-4 tablespoons soft brown sugar. Microwave or heat gently for 5-10 minutes. Serve warm.

BROWN RICE AND LENTIL LOAF

This grain-based loaf is surprisingly solid, satisfying and well-flavoured.

FOR 4-6 SERVINGS:

½ cup brown rice
½ cup brown lentils
1 large onion
2 cloves garlic
2 Tbsp oil
½ cup sunflower seeds
1 tsp basil
1 tsp marjoram
½ tsp thyme
1 tsp sugar
½ tsp salt
1 Tbsp dark soya sauce
black pepper
¼ cup wheatgerm
2 eggs
1 cup grated cheese
¼ cup sunflower seeds paprika

Cook the rice and lentils separately (*see pages 112 and 175*), or use 1-1 ½ cups each of pre-cooked rice or lentils if you have them on hand.

Chop the onion and garlic and sauté in the oil until lightly browned. Add the sunflower seeds and herbs, and continue to cook for a few minutes.

Combine the next six ingredients and half of the cheese in a large bowl. Stir in the cooked rice, lentils and onion mixture, and mix until well combined.

Transfer the mixture to a carefully oiled, or lined loaf tin. Sprinkle with the remaining cheese, sunflower seeds, and a little paprika.

Bake uncovered at 180°C for about 45 minutes, until the centre feels firm when pressed. Leave to stand for 5-10 minutes before turning out. Serve with a selection of cooked vegetables, or salad of your choice.

Note:
Leftovers taste good cold.

CURRIED RICE AND TOMATO CASSEROLE

Any leftovers from this casserole are good piled on toast, sprinkled with grated cheese, and browned under a grill.

for 4-6 servings:
1 cup long-grain rice
  (preferably heat-treated)
2 medium-sized onions, finely chopped
1 tsp salt
1 tsp curry powder
1 cup tomato purée
1½ cups water
25-50 g butter or 3 Tbsp oil,
2 firm tomatoes, cubed
1 green pepper, if available
1 red pepper, if available

Put the first six ingredients together in a medium-sized casserole. Cube the butter, using the smaller amount if the larger amount bothers you, and add it, or the oil, too. Leave until required.

Bake, tightly covered, at 180°C for 45 minutes, or until rice is tender and all liquid absorbed, stirring once after about 20 minutes if possible.

Add the tomato and cubed peppers and fold through the hot rice.

Bake for 5 minutes longer, then leave to stand for 10 minutes, before sprinkling with parsley and serving with a selection of vegetables and/or salads.

Variation:
Replace white rice with brown rice, add an extra ½ cup of water, and cook for 1½ hours, or until rice is tender, making sure mixture does not dry out.

BASIC PILAF

Try this recipe with kibbled or flaked wheat, rye, oats or barley. You will wonder why we so often ignore these grains in favour of rice!

for 4 servings:
2 Tbsp butter or oil
1 medium-sized onion
2 cloves garlic
¾ cup kibbled grain
  (or long-grain white rice),
  or 1 cup flaked grain
1 cup chopped celery
1 cups water
½ tsp salt
¼ cup chopped parsley (2 Tbsp dried)
freshly ground black pepper to taste

Melt the butter in a large non-stick frying pan with a close-fitting lid.

Add the chopped onion and garlic and cook gently for 3-4 minutes without browning.

Stir in the flaked or kibbled grain, or long-grain rice. Continue to stir until all the grains are evenly coated with the oil or butter and have browned lightly.

Add the finely chopped celery, water and salt. Cover and cook for 20-30 minutes, or until the water is absorbed and the grain tender.

Add a little more water (½ cup) if you think the mixture looks too dry and the grains are not tender.

Stir in the chopped parsley, pepper, and add a little more salt if desired, then serve.

RICE & GRAINS

EGG FRIED RICE

This is a useful and delicious way to use up small quantities of vegetables that you may have sitting around in your refrigerator.

FOR 4 SERVINGS:

4 cups cooked long-grain white rice,
   or cooked brown rice
2-3 eggs
½ tsp salt
6 spring onions
3-4 Tbsp oil or butter
1 cup sliced mushrooms
1-2 cups beansprouts, chopped peppers,
   celery, etc.
½-1 cup shredded lettuce
soya sauce
sesame oil

Use rice that has been cooked and left to cool for several hours (overcooked or soggy rice cannot be used for this dish).

Put the rice in a large bowl, break in the eggs and add the salt. Add the chopped spring onions and stir until the eggs evenly coat the rice.

Heat a large, non-stick frypan or wok. Heat the oil or butter and lightly cook the mushrooms and vegetables (but not the lettuce).

Add the rice, then lift: the mixture with a fish slice as it heats. The grains should separate as the mixture cooks.

When thoroughly heated through, add the shredded lettuce, stir briefly, and remove from the heat (the lettuce should still be slightly crisp when the rice is served).

Taste, and add a little soya sauce if desired.

Sprinkle with extra soya sauce and sesame oil just before eating.

GRILLED POLENTA

Polenta is a type of corn porridge. This thick, well-flavoured porridge is left to set, then cut into cubes and browned lightly in a non-stick pan. The browned cubes, threaded on skewers with vegetables, make good barbecue food for vegetarians, or can be heated on a tabletop grill, as in the photograph on page 77.

FOR 4 SERVINGS:

2 cups water
about 1 tsp salt
fresh or dried thyme, basil and oreganum
1 cup coarse yellow corn meal
½-1 cup grated cheese

Bring the water and salt to the boil. Add about ½ teaspoon each of dried herbs, or more fresh herbs.

Sprinkle the corn meal into the water while stirring thoroughly. Keep stirring, over low to moderate heat, for about 5 minutes, until very thick. Remove from the heat and stir in the grated cheese. (Polenta may seem salty at first, but saltiness diminishes on standing.)

Pour into a buttered or oiled 20 cm square pan, and leave to cool for about 30 minutes, then turn out and cut into cm cubes.

Brown on all sides in a non-stick pan with a little butter or oil, then thread on skewers, alternated with vegetables, and barbecue or grill when required.

Variation:

Pour into a round pan, then cut in wedges, brown, and serve with fried eggs, mushrooms, tomatoes, etc.

Make without cheese for vegan diets.

TAKEFUMI RICE

Spiced rice and eggs make an interesting quick meal.

FOR 4 SERVINGS:

3 cups water
1½ tsp salt
½ tsp cinnamon
8 whole cloves
3-4 drops hot chilli sauce
1½ cups long-gram rice
50 g butter
1 onion, sliced
¼ cup chopped celery
1-2 cloves garlic, chopped
3-4 eggs, lightly beaten

Heat the first five ingredients until boiling, in a tightly lidded pot.

Add the rice and simmer gently for 15 minutes, or until the rice is tender and the water absorbed.

Melt the butter in a large frying pan.

Sauté the onion, celery and garlic until tender but not browned.

Add the beaten eggs, stir for 30 seconds, then add the hot spiced rice.

Mix carefully but thoroughly, then serve with a salad.

RICE & GRAINS

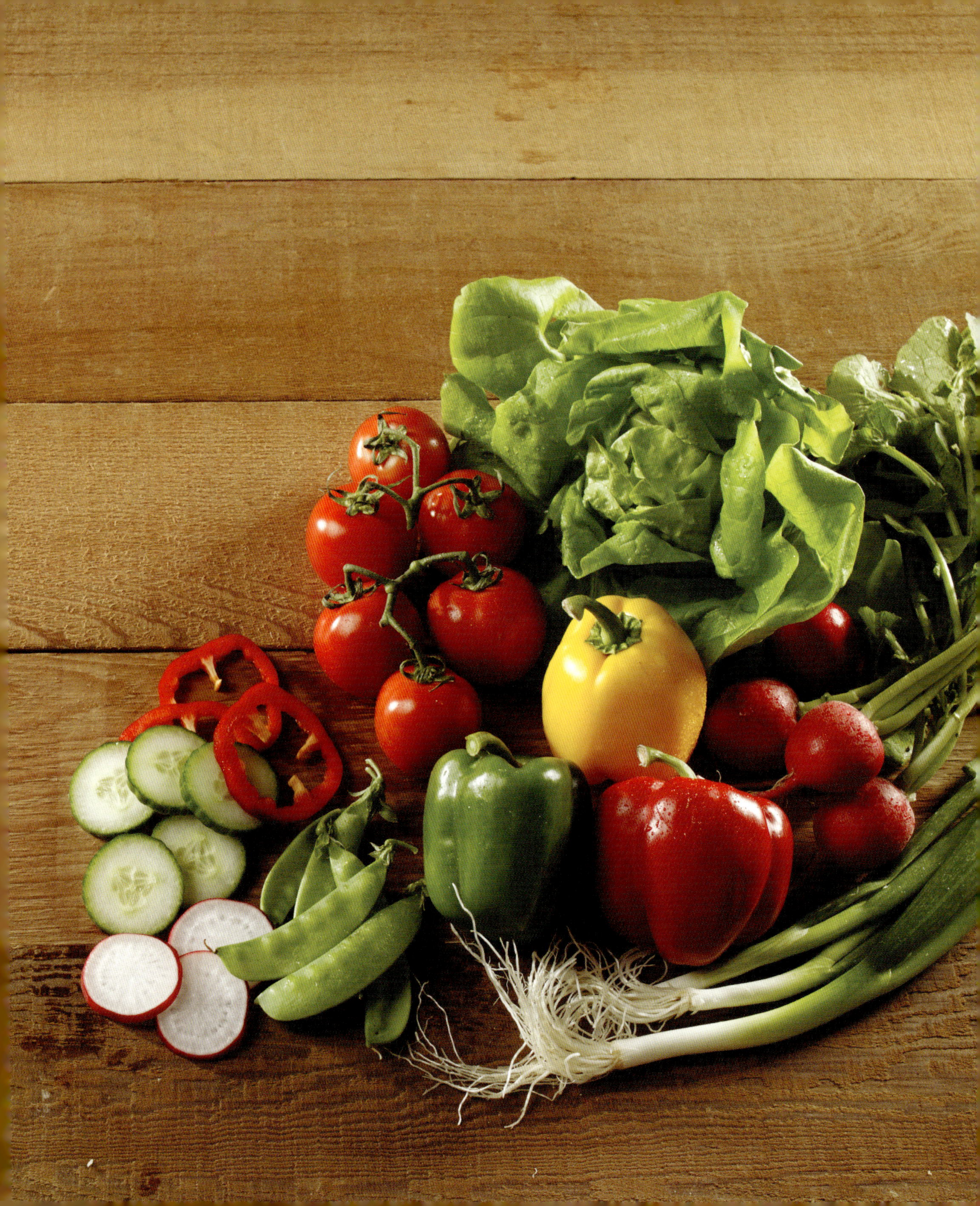

VEGETABLES & SALADS

When vegetables are an important part of your meal it is particularly important to serve them so that they retain their maximum flavour, colour, texture and food value.
There are so many inviting vegetables available that it is a pity to limit your choice to only a few varieties. Use different cooking and serving methods, remembering that many vegetables make good salads, when raw, or when cooked and cooled.

MAKING THE MOST OF VEGETABLES

ARTICHOKES (JERUSALEM):
Easily grown, lumpy tubers from plants related to sunflower. Scrub or peel, boil or steam to serve with sauce, purée for soup, or slice raw into salads for water-chestnut-like texture. Definite flavour, not universally popular.

ASPARAGUS:
Should be enjoyed during its short season. Early in the season try peeling the skin from the lower part of the stalk for more even cooking. Lie asparagus flat in a covered pan, add a little butter and water, and cook over a high heat until tender-crisp, for 3-5 minutes. Alternatively, slice diagonally and stir-fry-steam (makes a little go further). Fairly thick stalks of asparagus microwave well. Serve hot with butter or other sauce, or cold with French dressing or mayonnaise. Raw, tastes like young peas, good for dipping.

AVOCADO:
Usually eaten raw, in halves or wedges, or mashed or puréed for dips. Cut surface browns if not coated with lemon juice, vinegar, etc. Unripe avocados are horrible, so wait until flesh 'gives' when pressed gently. If over-ripe, delicate green flesh darkens,

BEETROOT:
Choose young, smallish roots. Naturally sweet. May be shredded raw for salad, but usually boiled before removing skin (for 15-60 minutes depending on size and maturity), then sliced or cubed, and served hot or cold in a sweet-sour sauce.

BEANS, BROAD:
If you grow your own, start eating sliced baby pods early, so that you don't get bogged down by over-mature beans. Pod and stir-fry-steam bigger beans using a little oil or butter, for 1-3 minutes, taking care not to overcook. Remove the outer skin as well as the pod if cooking over-mature beans. Young beans microwave well. Serve hot. Young beans are good raw.

BEANS, GREEN:
Buy or pick when young and tender. Remove tips and strings if necessary. Slice or cook whole, for 3-10 minutes depending on size and age. Stir-fry-steam. Serve when slightly crunchy. Beans do not microwave as well as peas. Serve hot, or cold after marinating. Really young beans are good raw.

BROCCOLI:
The stalks are as tender as the heads if you peel them first. Cut off the heads with a small amount of 'skin'. Peel stalks by pulling skin from bottom end. Slice stem and cook with heads (for about 5 minutes). Stir-fry-steam or microwave for 1 minute per serving. Good with cheese sauce.

CABBAGE:
Don't throw away all the dark green outer leaves, just shred them more finely than quicker-cooking inner leaves. Stir-fry-steam for 3-5 minutes, stir-fry or microwave for 1 minute per serving. Do not overcook. Stuff leaves, or slice finely for coleslaw. Different varieties available. Useful raw for salads which do not wilt easily.

BRUSSELS SPROUTS:
Like miniature cabbages. Heads should be tight. Halve, or cut deep crosses in stem ends for faster, more even cooking, (from 3-8 minutes). Marinate when cold and cooked, for salads.

CARROTS:
Very versatile, raw and cooked. Inexpensive, always in season. Shred, slice, cube, cut in sticks, serve whole, purée, juice. Naturally sweet. Good dipping sticks. Flavour and texture much nicer if not overcooked. Boil 3-10 minutes depending on age and size of pieces. Cook many ways, but not suitable for roasting, or stir-frying. Carrots microwave best in small pieces, about 1 minute per serving.

CAULIFLOWER:
Break or cut into florets. Excellent dipping food when raw. Stir fry, steam, microwave for about 1 minute per serving, coat and deep fry, only until tender-crisp in each case. Good plainly cooked (for 5-10 minutes), with sauce.

CELERY:
Pull the fibres from larger outer ribs, starting from the base. Slice stems diagonally or cut into julienne strips. Stir-fry, braise (for 15-20 minutes), or microwave. Use to flavour soups, cereals, etc. Good raw in salads or as dipping sticks.

CHOKOS:
Use when young if possible. Rub off outer prickles, peel only if mature. Halve lengthwise and slice. Simmer for 10-15 minutes. Seed is edible too. Add to stir-fries, or stir-fry- steam or microwave. Add garlic and herbs for extra flavour. Serve hot. Treatment and texture is that of firm zucchini.

CORN:
Enjoy on cob during fairly short season. Good processed corn available at all times. Corn on cob is best when not overmature. Don't choose largest. Best microwaved (allowing 3 minutes per cob, husk on) when on cobs. Can be boiled, barbecued, etc. Look for new varieties. Small whole cobs available canned.

CUCUMBER:
Usually eaten raw but can, be cooked like zucchini. Peel only if skin is tough. Salt, then rinse to remove excess water for some recipes. Make excellent pickles .

EGGPLANT (AUBERGINE):
During season, valued for dense, solid flesh, and attractive colour. Many different varieties, sizes, and colours grown in other countries. Sauté then simmer (about 15 minutes), bake, grill, barbecue, fry, microwave, purée for dips. Serve hot, warm, cold.

FLORENCE FENNEL:
Halve or quarter lengthwise, depending on size. Simmer (10-15 minutes) or braise until tender. Alternatively, slice crosswise and stir-fry-steam. Serve hot with butter or cold with French dressing. Serve sliced, raw, in salads, too.

KOHLRABI:
Pick or buy while small, young and tender. Peel, cut into strips or cubes and stir-fry, simmer (about 5 minutes), steam or microwave under tender-crisp. Serve with sauce after boiling. May be served raw in sticks or grated.

LEEKS:
Pick or buy when young before bases bulge. Wash carefully, then halve lengthwise to braise, e.g., for à la Grecque. Slice 5-10 mm thick to stir-fry-steam or simmer (for 5-10 minutes) and serve with sauce, or cold in dressing.

KUMARA:
Sweet-fleshed tubers, texture and flavour between potatoes and pumpkin, but more distinct flavour. Good baked in jackets, roasted, steamed or microwaved. Cooking times similar to potatoes.

LETTUCES AND SALAD GREENS:
Wide range of colours, textures and flavours available, to grow and buy. Store and prepare carefully to ensure crispness. Add dressing just before serving, or let diners add their own, so leaves do not wilt. Use different combinations and dressings.

MARROWS:
Use while young enough to have tender skins and edible seeds. Slice or shred coarsely and stir-fry-steam (about 5 minutes) or microwave. Stuff halves or slices. Add herbs or garlic for flavour.

MUSHROOMS:
Young, fleshy mushrooms are good raw, marinated or with dips. Cook older mushrooms briefly (3-5 minutes) with a little butter or oil, garlic and herbs. Add to other mixtures for extra body and flavour. Also good stuffed and baked or battered and fried. Look for other new types of edible fungi also.

ONIONS:
Widely used to intensify flavours of other foods. Flavours of browned onions, sautéed but not browned onions, and raw onions are different. Cook any of ways listed". Red onions have a short season, and are mild. Spring (young) onions are used raw or briefly cooked, for colour as well as flavour.

PEAS:
Unless you grow your own and pick them young, use frozen peas. Cook for a short time (2 minutes after boiling) in just enough water to stop them sticking, stir-fry-steam or microwave.

PEA PODS:
Flat pea pods, sugar peas or snow peas need very little or no cooking (about 1 minute). Remove ends and strings. Blanch, stir-fry or stir-fry- steam, for 1-2 minutes. Coat with tempura batter.

PEAS (SUGAR SNAP):
Look like ordinary peas in pods, but the pods are edible and even sweeter than the peas inside. Eat raw or stir-fry-steam for 1-4 minutes, depending on age.

PEPPERS (CAPSICUMS):
Slice and stir-fry until tender-crisp. Use in mixtures, add to stews, etc. Stuff. Very high in vitamin C. Brown under grill to char skin, peel, then serve with French dressing. Cut into strips or slices for dipping or salads.

PUMPKIN:
Available in a variety of shapes, sizes and colours. Mealy, sweet, bright orange flesh with a smooth texture. Steam (10-20 minutes), purée, microwave, roast, batter and deep fry, or stuff and bake.

PARSNIPS:
Creamish-coloured root vegetables, more distinctive flavour than carrots. Nice glazed with sugar mixture after cooking. Boil (15-20 minutes) or steam and mash, roast or deep-fry. Sweeter when harvested after frosts.

RADISHES:
Vary in size, colour and strength of flavour. Small red to large long white. Best when young. Nearly always served raw for colour and texture. Crisp in water if necessary.

SCALLOPINI & SUMMER SQUASH:
These belong to the marrow family. Cube or slice and stir-fry-steam, for about 10 minutes, with herbs, garlic and tomatoes for best flavour.

SILVER BEET & SPINACH BEET (SWISS CHARD):
Use while young if possible, using leaves as spinach. Slice older leaves, putting stems at the bottom of the pot, since these take longer to cook than the leaves. Cook until the whites are just tender, for 5-10 minutes depending on age. Thicken remaining cooking liquid adding butter, milk or cream for greater acceptability. Very young leaves may be added to salads.

SPINACH:
Wash very carefully, dunking in a large container of water to get rid of grit. Blanch, stir-fry or stir-fry-steam without adding any extra water (for 3-5 minutes). Do not overcook. Drain well, pressing out water, before combining with sauce for Soufflés, flans, etc. Microwaves well. Use raw in salads.

TOMATOES:
Enormously versatile. Best flavour in late summer, early autumn. Different varieties, shapes, sweetnesses, etc. available. Pear-shaped varieties tend to be more fleshy with fewer seeds. Small tomatoes are extra sweet. Use raw or cooked as sauces, purées, concentrates. Good commercially prepared cooked tomato products may be as good as you can make at home.

YAMS:
Usually small pink shiny tubers. Scrub and simmer (for about 10 minutes), stir-fry-steam or roast. Large sweet potatoes (not as sweet as kumara) may be called yams too.

ZUCCHINI (COURGETTES):
Do not peel. Slice, shred or cut in strips, stir-fry or stir-fry-steam with garlic and herbs for 3-5 minutes. Coat with batter and deep fry. Use in breads etc. Yellow varieties available.

— — — — — — — — — — — — — —

Here are some of the different ways you can cook vegetables. Don't drown them! You are throwing away a lot of flavour and vitamins when you boil vegetables in water to cover, or leave them to soak before cooking, or boil them until they discolour, or throw out lots of cooking liquid! Try to vary your cooking techniques, giving emphasis to methods using very little liquid.

BLANCHING:
Vegetables are immersed for a short time in a large pan of boiling water. They are often then dipped into cold water to halt the cooking process. This produces a very bright colour and is one of the steps in freezing. Opinions vary about flavour and nutrient losses by this method.

BOILING:
Add vegetables to boiling water in a saucepan which is then usually covered to keep in the steam formed. With this method it is best to use only a small amount of water.

STEAMING:
Place vegetables in steamer with perforated bottom, or in a basket resting above the water-level in a saucepan. The vegetables cook in steam instead of water, and lose fewer nutrients. Neither their flavour nor their food value is as good as that of stir-fried vegetables, however.

SAUTÉING:
This method is good for conserving flavour and nutrients. Cook sliced or chopped vegetables in a little oil, butter, margarine, etc., in a pan over a high heat, stirring at intervals. With a non¬stick pan very little oil etc. is required. Many vegetables can be sautéed before being cooked by another method.

STIR-FRYING:
One vegetable or a mixture may be cooked this way. Vegetables are usually sliced in varying sizes so they all take the same time to cook- Heat a little oil, sometimes with garlic and/or ginger, in a large pan or wok: Add the vegetables and toss and stir them to keep them moving, and to coat them. Pour in a little liquid and cover, so the steam formed cooks the vegetables until tender-crisp. Evaporate remaining liquid, or add extra flavourings mixed with cornflour to thicken juices. Toss so this coats the vegetables. Excellent for conserving flavour, texture and nutrients.

BARBECUING AND GRILLING:
Food is turned above hot embers or under a hot element. Pieces of pepper, aubergine, onion, tomato, mushrooms, zucchini, etc. may be threaded on skewers with other food. They require brushing with oil, butter, mayonnaise, French dressing, etc. to prevent them burning before they cook.

DEEP-FRYING:
Tender vegetables may be coated in a light batter, then cooked briefly in hot oil, as in Japanese tempura, (*see page 77*).

PRESSURE COOKING:
Vegetables are cooked in super-heated steam, resulting in a considerably shortened cooking time, and saved nutrients. Take care not to overcook green vegetables with this method, or colour and texture suffer.

BRAISING:
Turn the vegetable in hot butter or oil, then add flavoured liquid and cook slowly in a saucepan or in a covered ovenproof dish. Cooking liquid is often eaten with vegetables.

MICROWAVING:
The microwave oven cooks many vegetables very well in a short time, conserving colour, flavour and food value. In most cases green vegetables need very little or no added liquid. They should be cooked in a covered container which they nearly fill, and seasoned very lightly after cooking, if necessary.

STIR-FRY-STEAM:
This very good way of cooking vegetables falls into none of the foregoing categories, but is best described as the 'stir-fry-steam' method. Turn the prepared vegetable in a non¬stick pan containing a little butter, and sometimes garlic. Soon afterwards add a small amount of water, cover the pan tightly and cook over a fairly high heat, turning or stirring occasionally. By the time the vegetable is cooked tender- crisp, the water should have disappeared completely. The vegetable is lightly glazed with the butter, and usually needs no other seasoning. The heat used is lower than that required for a real stir- fry, but hotter than that used in braising.

EASY ON THE SALT!

It is easy to add salt by habit rather than by taste. We now season most vegetables very lightly, after cooking. Vegetables cooked so that no liquid remains (in pan or microwave) require little or no salt. If a little butter is added at any stage, it is probable that no salt will be needed at all.

KEEP COOKING LIQUID:

Keep any vegetable cooking liquid that remains when vegetables are served. Refrigerate up to 2 days. Use this as liquid for sauces, soups and stocks.

MARINATED ARTICHOKES

Serve 1 cold artichoke per person as a starter course, or as a light lunch.

Place artichokes in a large saucepan and cover with lightly salted water. Add the juice of 1 or 2 lemons, several crushed garlic cloves, a few peppercorns, a bay leaf, some basil and oreganum, and a few tablespoons of oil.

Cover the saucepan and simmer the artichokes for 30 minutes or more, until the outer petals pull away from the base easily. Leave to cool in the cooking liquid.

Serve each drained artichoke on a flat plate big enough to hold mayonnaise for dipping and a pile of discarded petals. To eat, pull off a petal at a time. Dip the stem end into the mayonnaise, then bite off the fleshy part of the petal and discard the fibrous core. You will find the inner petals are more fleshy and less fibrous. Eventually only the fleshy base, holding immature seeds, remains. Discard these if they are stringy, cut the base into quarters, and eat each piece with mayonnaise.

GRILLED OR BARBECUED AUBERGINE

Cut aubergines in 1 cm slices or in 2 cm cubes. Thread cubes loosely on skewers. Brush generously with Tomato Dressing, (*see page 138*) and cook about 12 cm from the heat, turning frequently, until tender, about 15 minutes.

SWEET-SOUR BEAN SALAD

This recipe has stood the test of time, for 8-10 servings:

*2 cups cooked green beans, in chunks,
  not thin slices
1-2 cups cooked kidney beans
1 onion, chopped
1 red or green pepper, chopped
¼ cup sugar
¼ cup wine vinegar
¼ cup bean liquid
¼ cup oil
1 tsp salt*

Put the prepared vegetables in a bowl. Add the remaining ingredients, stir gently to mix, cover, and refrigerate for at least 24 hours before serving.

BEANS À LA GRECQUE

Use this recipe to prepare a number of other vegetables in this way, too, if you find that you like it as much as we do! Replace beans with celery, fennel, leek chokos, peppers, scallopini or zucchini. It is usual to cut vegetables lengthwise, into strips.

FOR 4 SERVINGS:

*1 large onion
2 cloves garlic
¼ cup oil
½ tsp crushed coriander seeds
¼ cup wine vinegar
¼ cup water
1 tsp sugar
½ tsp salt
freshly ground pepper
400-500 g green beans
4 tomatoes, peeled, seeded and cubed
¼ cup chopped parsley
1 Tbsp lemon juice*

Chop onion and garlic. Cook in oil until transparent but not browned.

Add coriander, vinegar, water, sugar, salt and pepper to taste. Add topped and tailed beans (with strings removed necessary). Simmer for 2-3 minutes, then add the tomatoes. Cook until beans are tender-crisp. Cover and cool.

Just before serving (at room temperature) add the chopped parsley and lemon juice.

CUMIN BEAN SALAD

Use canned or freshly cooked dried beans for this salad. A combination of white haricot, pink pinto, tiger beans and red kidney beans with the add ion of some lightly cooked fresh beans makes a most attractive salad.

This salad may be kept in a covered container in the refrigerator for a week, and served whenever you want something quick and easy.

for 6 servings:
4 cups cooked, drained dried beans
1 cup chopped cooked green beans
½-1 cup diced green peppers
1 cup diced celery
about 1 cup diced tomato
cumin dressing (see page 137)

Put the drained beans, peppers and celery in a large, covered container. Add the dressing and mix to coat. Cover and refrigerate for at least 2 hours before serving. When required, bring to room temperature, add tomato to the amount you want to serve, and toss to mix.

Note:
Cook beans until you can squash them on the top of your mouth, following the guidelines on page 175.

SHREDDED BEETROOT

Beetroot does not have to be boiled whole before it is used in other ways.

for 4 servings:
300-400 g beetroot
1 garlic clove, chopped
2 tsp butter ¼ cup water
1 Tbsp orange or lemon juice
pepper, salt and sugar
fresh herbs (optional)

Thinly peel then shred the raw beetroot. Cook the garlic in the butter without browning. Add the beetroot, water and juice, cover and cook over moderate heat for 5-15 minutes, depending on the age of the beetroot. Try to have all liquid evaporated by the time the beetroot is tender.

Season, tasting to judge quantities required. Add a little sugar if the flavour is too bland. Add any fresh herbs you like, finely chopped. Serve hot.

BRAISED RED CABBAGE

for 8 servings:
1 large onion
2 cloves garlic
2 Tbsp butter
1 small red cabbage
2 apples
1 cup water
½ cup vinegar
1 tsp salt
1 Tbsp brown sugar
1 tsp cornflour
1 Tbsp vinegar

Chop onion and garlic finely. Melt butter in a large saucepan and add the onion and garlic. Cook over medium heat while you slice the cabbage thinly. Add it to

VEGETABLES & SALADS

the saucepan, with the grated apples and water. Pour first measure of vinegar over the vegetables in the pot, cover and simmer for 30 minutes, removing the lid for the last 5 minutes, to evaporate most of the liquid.

Add salt and brown sugar, mix well. Mix the cornflour with the second measure of vinegar, and add just before serving. Taste—you may need to add more salt. Serve hot or reheated. This mixture refrigerates and freezes well.

JOANNA'S CABBAGE

This is a delicious way to use late summer cabbage.

FOR 4 SERVINGS:
2 Tbsp butter or oil
1 medium-sized onion, sliced thinly
½ medium-sized cabbage, shredded
2 Tbsp wine vinegar
1 Tbsp sugar
1 tsp salt
black pepper to taste
1 cup tomatoes, skinned and chopped

Heat the butter or oil in a medium-to- large frying pan. Add the onion and cabbage, toss to coat, then add remaining ingredients.

Mix well, cover pan and cook over fairly high heat for 5-10 minutes, then remove the lid. Cook, turning mixture frequently for 5 minutes more, or until the cooking liquid has evaporated and the cabbage is tender but still crisp.

COLESLAW

Coleslaw is a useful salad since it is usually based on drumhead cabbage, which is available all year round, at a reasonable price.

Add one or more extra vegetables such as shredded carrot, sliced celery, chopped cauliflower.

Add toasted sunflower seeds, chopped peanuts, sultanas, etc. for extra flavour and texture.

Coleslaw dressings are usually sweeter and more acid than most other dressings. Modify any of the dressings on pages 94 and 95. One of our favourites is made by stirring together:

½ cup mayonnaise
1-2 Tbsp tomato ketchup
1 Tbsp lemon juice

Coleslaw is crisper and loses fewer vitamins if it is shredded and dressed shortly before it is eaten.

CARROT AND APPLE SALAD

These two flavours and textures complement each other to make a good winter salad.

FOR 2 SERVINGS:
1 carrot, grated
2 tart (preferably Sturmer) apples
2 Tbsp mayonnaise (see page 136)
lettuce cups

Grate the carrot and unpeeled apple into I long shreds. Coat with mayonnaise immediately to stop apple browning. Spoon into lettuce cups if available. Serve within 30 minutes, if possible.

SWEET-SOUR CARROT SALAD

This salad has definite character, and will 'lift' other bland foods.

FOR 4 SERVINGS:
1½ cups shredded raw carrot
1 Tbsp Dijon-type mustard
1 Tbsp honey
1 Tbsp lemon juice
1 tsp grated root ginger

Grate the carrot into long, even shreds, in a food processor if available.

126 MEALS WITHOUT MEAT

Measure the mustard and honey into a shallow serving bowl. Mix in the lemon juice. Grate the root ginger finely into a little pile, then pick this up and squeeze it, so its juice runs into the mustard mixture. Discard the fibres.

Turn the grated carrot in the dressing until it is evenly coated. Taste and season only if necessary.

Garnish with a few watercress leaves, or with chopped parsley.

VARIATION:
Mix ½-1 cup of chopped roasted peanuts through the salad a few minutes before serving it.

CELERY AND APPLE SALAD

This makes a good winter salad.

FOR 1 OR 2 SERVINGS:
1 stalk tender celery
1 firm apple
2 Tbsp mayonnaise (see page 136)
1 Tbsp chopped walnuts

Cut the celery and unpeeled apple into cubes. Mix immediately with the mayonnaise, and sprinkle with chopped walnuts. Serve in a lettuce cup available.

BRAISED CELERY

This recipe needs little attention while it cooks in the oven, or on the stovetop.

FOR 4 SERVINGS:
3 cups sliced celery
2 Tbsp butter
2 cloves garlic, finely chopped
1 cup water
1 tsp vegetable bouillon powder
1 tsp sugar
¼ tsp salt

cornflour
chopped parsley

Remove strings from celery and slice crosswise or diagonally. Melt butter in a pan. Add garlic, then celery. Transfer to ovenware dish if desired, or leave in pan. Add next four ingredients.

Either cover and bake at 180°C for 45-60 minutes, or simmer in covered pan for 20-30 minutes. Thicken liquid with cornflour paste and sprinkle with chopped parsley.

BARBECUED CORN COBS

Use small cobs of young tender corn. Soak in a bucket of water for 10 minutes, then barbecue over low heat, turning frequently, until the husks char. Cut bases from cobs, and peel off husks and silk. Eat with Chilli Mayonnaise (*see page 136*).

MICROWAVED CORN COBS

Microwave 1 or 2 cobs, as picked, in a microwave oven, without further coverings, allowing 3 minutes per cob. Cut off base, peel off husk and silk, and serve with Chilli Mayonnaise (*see page 136*).

CROUTONS

Croutons are useful items to keep on hand. Use them to add interest to soups, when serving; sprinkle over green leafy salads; top casseroles instead of browning a crumb topping; eat as snacks.

Cut any leftover bread (or crusts) into 5 mm cubes with a sharp serrated knife. Melt 1 tablespoon butter for every 2 cups of cubed bread. Toss cubes in hot butter. Add a sprinkling of garlic, celery or onion salt if you like. Spread in a roasting pan and grill, about 15 cm from the heat, until croutons are golden, crisp and dry, turning or shaking pan often. Use immediately, or store in airtight containers.

GLAZED ROOT VEGETABLES

Coat cooked kumara, parsnips, carrots or yams with this glaze.

FOR 4 SERVINGS:
cooked root vegetables for 4 servings
¼ cup brown sugar
25 g butter
½ cup orange juice

Drain the cooked vegetables. Heat the sugar, butter and orange juice until blended and bubbling. Add vegetables, turn to coat, and heat uncovered, stirring frequently, until glaze darkens slightly. Serve immediately.

KUMARA PURÉE WITH CORIANDER

Coriander makes kumara aromatic and gives a lovely flavour.

Scrub kumara thoroughly. Microwave on High (100%) power for 6-8 minutes per 250 g kumara or bake in a conventional oven, in an oven bag for 45-60 minutes.

Kumara is cooked when the flesh 'gives' when squeezed. Peel the cooked kumara without removing the coloured flesh under the skin.

Chop roughly and mash with a potato masher or purée in a food processor, adding a little butter and milk in equal quantities. Add pepper and salt to taste, then add freshly crushed coriander seed until the flavour suits you.

KUMARA OR PARSNIP PATTIES

FOR 3-4 SERVINGS:

1½-2 cups mashed cooked kumara or parsnip
1 egg
1 Tbsp brown sugar
¼ cup self-raising flour
pinch of ginger, cinnamon or mixed spice

Measure all ingredients into a mixing bowl, combine with a fork, and add a little extra self-raising flour to make a mixture firm enough to drop in spoonfuls into a pan containing 3 mm hot oil or melted butter.

Brown until evenly coloured on both sides, then serve immediately.

MUSHROOM SALAD

Firm, small button mushrooms make wonderful salads. Make about 15 minutes before serving, if possible. Slice or quarter cleaned mushrooms, and turn gently in any of the following dressings, using quantities to suit yourself:

French Dressing
Herb Dressing
Tomato Dressing
Herbed Creamy Vinaigrette
Cumin Dressing

See pages 137 and 138 for recipes.

MUSHROOMS

This is a very fast and easy mushroom recipe which is good as a side dish or as the main part of a light meal.

FOR 4 SERVINGS:
400 g mushrooms
2 cloves garlic, chopped
1 Tbsp butter
1 tsp light soya sauce
1 tsp cornflour
2 Tbsp chopped parsley or spring onion

Wipe mushrooms. Halve or slice if large. Chop garlic finely, and place with butter in a microwave casserole dish just large enough to hold mushrooms. Heat on High (100%) power for 30 seconds or until butter has melted. Stir in soya sauce and cornflour, then toss mushrooms in this mixture, coating them evenly and lightly.

Sprinkle with parsley or spring onion. Cover loosely and microwave for 3-4 minutes or until mushrooms have softened to the desired amount and are coated with lightly thickened sauce. Sprinkle with pepper. Serve on noodles, rice or toast.

SWEET AND SOUR ONIONS

These small onions are cooked in a tomato sauce with sultanas. Serve hot or at room temperature.

FOR 4-6 SERVINGS:

500 g small onions
2 Tbsp tomato paste
2 Tbsp wine vinegar
1 Tbsp olive or other oil
1 Tbsp sugar
1 tsp salt
1 cup water
¼ cup sultanas
1 bay leaf

Pour boiling water over the onions and leave to stand for 1 minute. Drain and cut off root and top sections, then lift off skins.

Combine next five ingredients in a microwave dish or saucepan big enough to hold the onions in one layer. Add water, sultanas and bay leaf then the onions.

Cover and microwave on High (100%) power for 6 minutes or until onions are tender, or simmer on the stovetop for 20-30 minutes. Serve immediately, reheat or serve warm.

SKILLET POTATOES

These take no longer than boiled potatoes, but they turn any meal into something special.

FOR 4 SERVINGS:

2 Tbsp butter
2 onions, sliced
4 potatoes, scrubbed
½ tsp salt
2-3 Tbsp parsley

Melt the butter, and cook the onions in it in a heavy pan, without browning, while you scrub and slice the potatoes. Rinse potatoes under a cold tap, then mix with the onions, cover and cook over low heat for 15 minutes, or until potatoes are tender, turning every 4 or 5 minutes.

Uncover, raise heat slightly and cook for 15 minutes longer, turning at intervals so potatoes brown evenly. Sprinkle with parsley and serve.

Variation:

Leave out onions, cut potatoes in 1 cm cubes, and cook the same way, letting them brown on all sides.

POTATO SALADS

You can make 101 versions of potato salad, all of which are likely to be popular!

Slice or cube cooked waxy or new potatoes, making sure that you allow up to twice as many as you allow for a normal serving.

Mix with chopped chives or spring onions, chopped parsley, basil and/or oreganum, or chopped dill leaf. Add chopped or sliced hard-boiled egg if you like.

For dressing, thin down mayonnaise, or mayonnaise variation, with more mild vinegar, or with French dressing, or another thin dressing. Or use French, Herb, Cumin, or Tomato Dressing, or Creamy Vinaigrette, alone.

Fold the dressing through the sliced potato, trying not to break up the pieces. Arrange in serving dish and leave to stand for at least 15 minutes. Garnish with more herbs, or egg, etc. Serve with extra dressing, if desired.

Note:

Never leave potato and pasta salads standing at room temperature in hot weather since they spoil easily.
From left: Potato Salad with French Dressing, Greek Salad, Mixed Salad Greens with Herb Dressing

VEGETABLES & SALADS

BAKED POTATOES

Scrub potatoes fairly large potatoes, rub with a little oil, and stand on oven racks, not a solid surface. Bake at 200°C for 45-60 minutes, until flesh 'gives' when pressed. Split or cut a cross in the top, press down between cuts to open them attractively, and top with a little butter, cheese, yoghurt, cottage cheese, cream cheese, fromage frais, Tofu Mayonnaise or Chilli Mayonnaise.

CHECKERBOARD POTATOES:

Scrub, and cut in half. Cut lines lengthwise then cross-wise in checkerboard design on cut side. Cut deeply, without piercing skin. Blot cut surface on paper towel then dip in melted butter or oil. Sprinkle with paprika, and bake, cut side up, as above. The cuts should open during cooking. No last minute attention is required for these attractively scored potatoes, nor is butter needed at the table.

HALF-BAKED POTATOES:

Scrub potatoes as for baking. Cut in half, and place cut surface down on a buttered or greased baking tray. Bake at 200°C for about 35-45 minutes until potatoes 'give' slightly when pressed. The cut surface of the cooked potato resembles that of a roast potato, while the rest is the same as a baked potato.

MICROWAVED BAKED POTATOTES:

Scrub potatoes, pierce in several places, arrange in a circle and microwave on High (100%) power, for 3-5 minutes per potato, until potato feels evenly cooked when pressed. Time required will depend on size. Turn potatoes over halfway through cooking.

NOTE:
For Stuffed Baked Potatoes *see page 52*.

VEGETABLE KEBABS

Thread 2 cm cubes of aubergine, red and green peppers and zucchini with squares of onion, blanched button mushrooms and quartered or whole small tomatoes. Brush liberally with Tomato or Cumin Dressing (*see page 137*), or Chilli Mayonnaise (*see page 136*), before and during cooking, and cook on a barbecue or under a grill, about 12 cm from the heat, turning frequently until tender. Thread only one type of vegetable on each skewer for more even cooking, if desired.

VARIATIONS:
Thread Marinated Tofu (*see page 107*) or pan-browned cubes of Polenta (*see page 116*) between the vegetables, if desired.

CONFETTI SALAD

This is a very pretty salad! I make to serve as part of a buffet meal, or when I want an interesting filling for pita bread.

FOR 4 SERVINGS:
½ cup uncooked brown lentils
1½ cups hot water
about 1 cup cooked rice
1 cup chopped celery
about ½ cup chopped red pepper
¼-¼ cup chopped spring onions
2 Tbsp wine vinegar
¼ cup oil
½ tsp salt
½ tsp sugar
¼ cup choppped parsley
black pepper

Cook the lentils in the water until very tender (*see page 175*), then drain.
    Add to the hot lentils the rice, celery, chopped pepper and onions. Mix the dressing ingredients (vinegar, oil, salt and sugar), sprinkle over the mixed salad, and mix again.

Stir in the parsley and as much black pepper as you like. Cover the salad and leave it to stand from 30-60 minutes before tasting it again, adjusting seasonings if necessary, and serving.

Note:
Vary the proportions of ingredients, or make additions or replacements. Suitable extras include cooked corn, barely cooked carrots or peas, firm cubed tomatoes, sunflower seeds or pine nuts, currants, chopped mint or other herbs, cubed cucumber, bean sprouts. Do not include too great a mixture, since this can spoil the flavour.

GREEN SALAD

Green salads are usually served as side dishes to provide texture and flavour contrast.
Use a variety of green leafy salad vegetables, with small amounts of thinly sliced spring onion, cucumber, bean sprouts, etc.

Make sure that leaves are washed, then dried and chilled before they are coated with a thin, tangy dressing just before serving. (To dry and chill them, spread washed leaves on a clean teatowel or paper towel, then roll up like a sponge roll, and store in the refrigerator, for up to 24 hours.)

Choose a thin dressing from *pages 137–138*, sprinkle it over the prepared leaves, and toss gently to coat leaves thinly, without bruising them.

SPINACH SALAD

This salad is addictive! Make more than you think you will need.

Wash carefully, then remove the stems from young spinach leaves in good condition. Spread over a dry teatowel, roll up like a sponge roll and chill until required.

Just before serving, toss in Herb, Tomato, or Cumin Dressing, or in Herbed Creamy Vinaigrette, and sprinkle with tiny croutons, finely chopped hard-boiled eggs, and thinly sliced mushrooms which have been tossed in the same dressing. (*See pages 137 and 138 for dressing recipes.*)

GREEK SALAD

This makes a good hot weather meal when served with crusty bread rolls. Use quantities to suit yourself. Arrange in individual dishes:

chunks of tender-skinned cucumber chunks or thick slices of tomato chopped onion, or sliced spring onion or thinly sliced red onion whole black olives crumbled dry or fresh Oreganum cubed feta cheese

Drizzle olive oil over the salads, and serve with lemon wedges if you like.

TABBOULEH

Make this salad when fresh, ripe tomatoes and fresh mint and parsley are plentiful.

for about 4 servings:
1 cup bulgar or kibbled wheat
2-3 cups water
¼ cup chopped spring onions
or ¼ cup chopped onion
¼ cup lemon juice
¼ cup olive or salad oil
½-1 cup chopped parsley
½ cup chopped mint
1-2 cups finely cubed tomato
salt and pepper to taste

Bring bulgar or kibbled wheat to the boil with the water. Simmer for 2-3 minutes then remove from heat and leave to stand for about an hour.

Squeeze the water out of it by lining a sieve with a clean tea towel, then squeezing the tea towel. Put the drained wheat mixture 1 a bowl with the remaining ingredients, toss to mix, and season carefully using enough salt to bring out the flavours. Serve in a bowl lined with lettuce leaves.

Note:
If you are making this salad several hours before it is to be eaten, stir the tomato into it in the last half hour

so the tomato does not make the wheat soggy. You can also make the salad with precooked brown rice. Alter proportions to suit your taste or make additions such as chopped red or green peppers, olives, celery, cucumber, radishes, garlic, etc.

MARINATED TOMATO SALAD

It's hard to beat a tomato salad, especially when you can pick ripe red tomatoes from your own garden.

FOR 4 SERVINGS:
5-6 medium-sized tomatoes
1 tsp sugar
¼-½ tsp salt
black pepper to taste
few drops hot pepper sauce
1 Tbsp wine vinegar
1 Tbsp chopped fresh basil, marjoram or parsley
1-2 Tbsp oil (optional)

Slice, quarter or cube the tomatoes into their serving dish.
   About 10-15 minutes before serving sprinkle the remaining ingredients, in the order given, over the tomatoes. Toss lightly and leave to stand at room temperature.

ZUCCHINI WITH HERB CREAM

This recipe revolutionises zucchini!

FOR 4 SERVINGS:
500 g sliced young zucchini
½ cup water
1 Tbsp butter
¼ cup cream
1 tsp chopped rosemary or thyme or sage
   or marjoram

Slice zucchini 5 mm thick. Cook in a covered frying pan over high heat, with the water and butter. When the liquid has evaporated, add the cream and herbs and cook uncovered, over high heat, until the cream thickens and coats the zucchini.

STIR-FRIED VEGETABLES

Slice a selection of quick-cooking vegetables such as cabbage, celery, cauliflower, broccoli, green beans, bean sprouts, mushrooms, pea pods, peppers, and zucchini, allowing about 200 g per serving.
   For two servings heat 1 tablespoon oil in a large pan or wok. Add a finely chopped garlic clove, then the prepared vegetables. Toss over high heat, then add 2 tablespoons water, cover, and leave to steam for 1-2 minutes, or until tender-crisp.

STIR TOGETHER IN A SMALL CONTAINER:
1 tsp cornflour
1 tsp brown sugar
1 tsp light soya sauce
¼ tsp salt
1 Tbsp sherry
½ tsp sesame oil (optional)

Stir quid into vegetable mixture to coat vegetables, and serve immediately over rice or noodles.
Microwave variation:
   Toss prepared vegetables in the preheated garlic and oil in a microwave dish, then cover and microwave on High (100%) power for about 3 minutes, or until tender-crisp. Stir in mixed liquid, then cook for about 30 seconds longer, or until glaze thickens.

NOTE:
Alter proportions to taste.

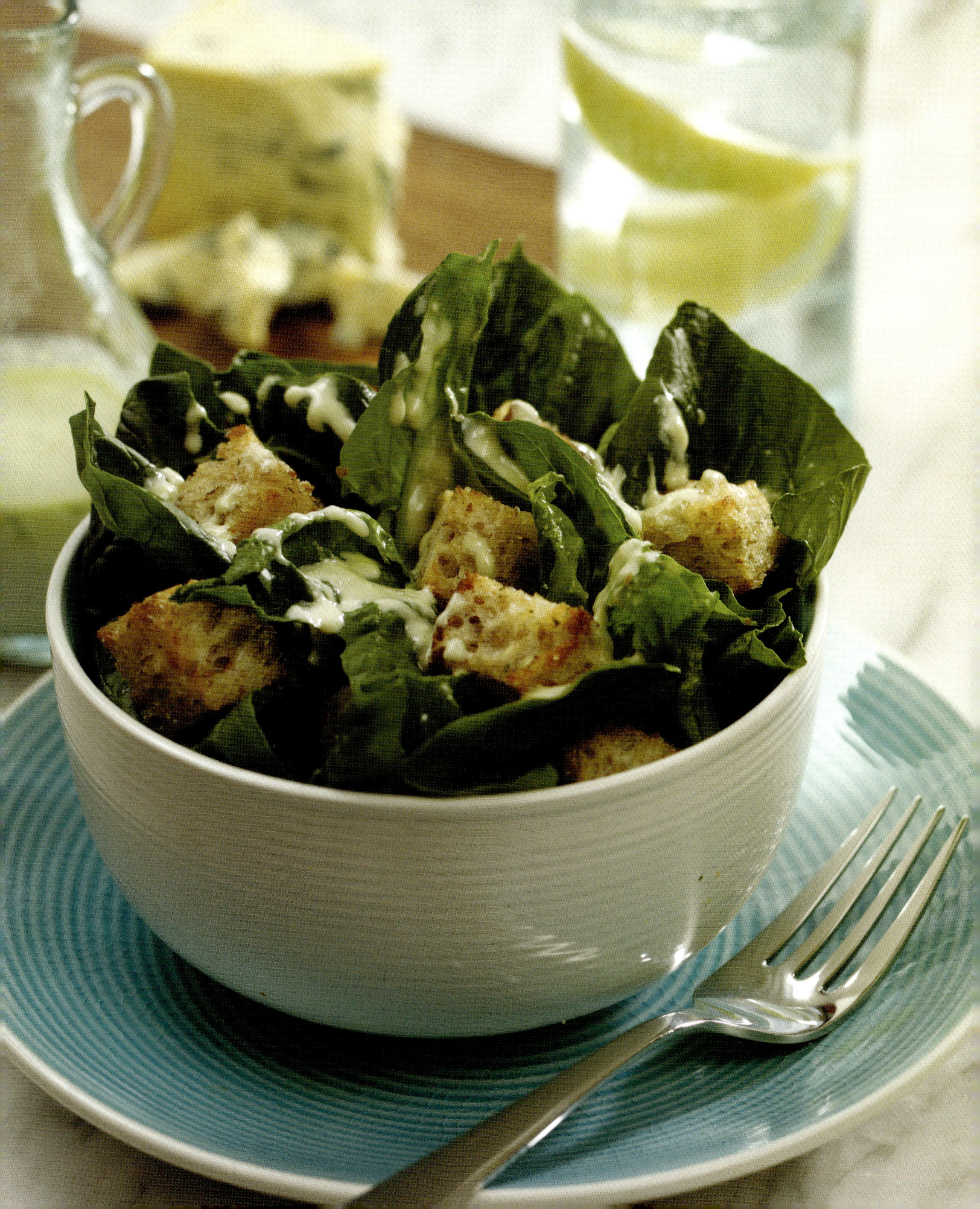

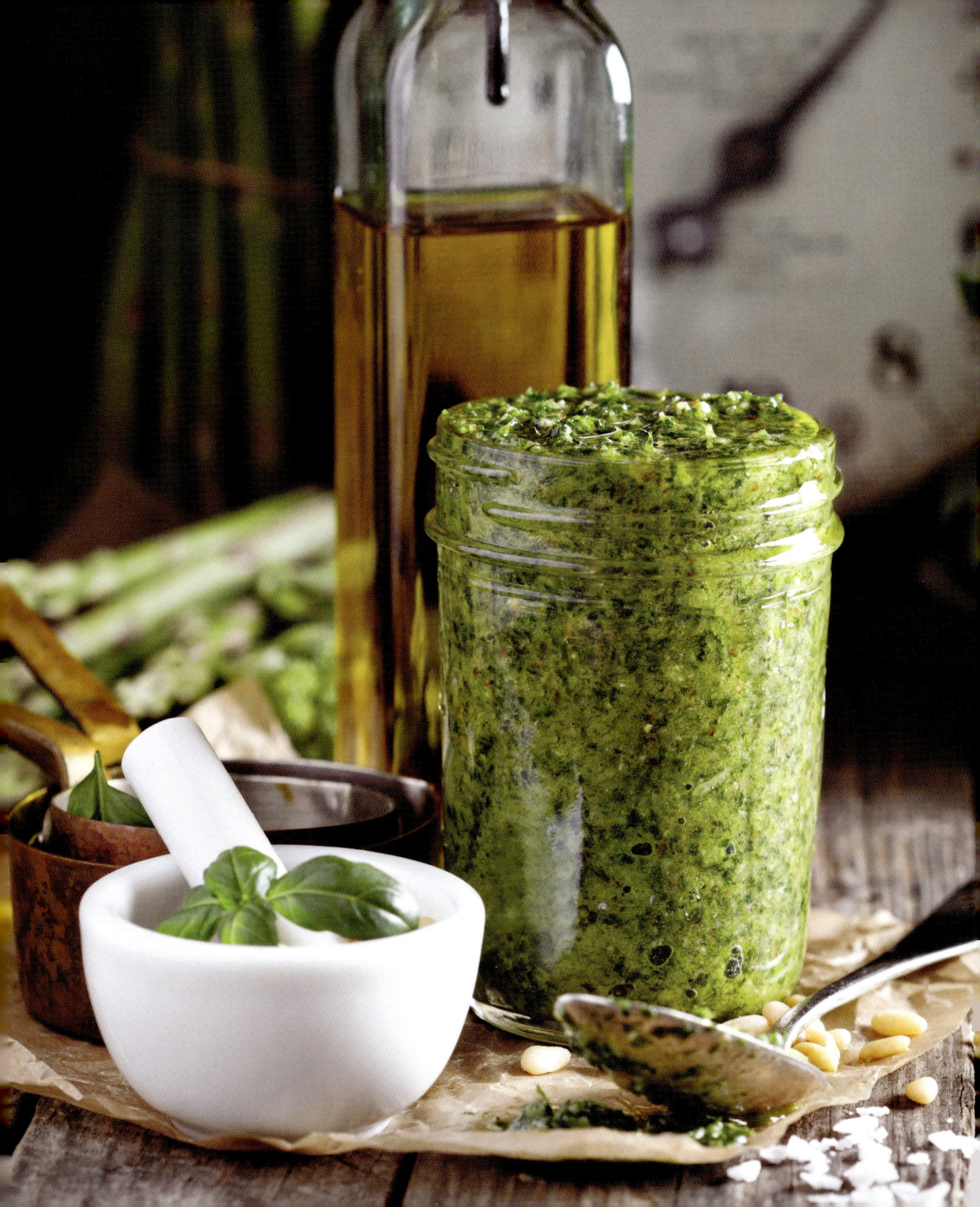

SAUCES & DRESSINGS

VEGETARIAN GRAVY

To many of us, gravy is 'comfort food'. Serve this gravy in a jug, and let your family and friends pour it over their main course, mashed potatoes, or whatever they like. You will probably be surprised by their pleasure!

2 medium-sized onions
2-3 cloves garlic
2 Tbsp oil or butter
1 tsp sugar
2 Tbsp flour
2 cups water
2 Tbsp dark soya sauce
black pepper to taste
¼-½ tsp salt

Finely chop or mince the onions and garlic. Heat the oil or butter in a large frypan or pot, add the onions and garlic, and cook, stirring occasionally until they brown. Stir in the sugar and flour and cook for about a minute longer.

Add half the water, stirring to remove any lumps, bring to the boil and allow to thicken before adding the remaining water and soya sauce. Bring to the boil again, season with black pepper and salt to taste, then serve!

CHEESE SAUCE

A good cheese sauce is all you need to turn a plainly cooked vegetable into a meal. Remember to use a standard, level measure or the sauce will be stodgy. A microwave oven makes wonderfully smooth sauce. Use it if available.

2 Tbsp butter
2 Tbsp flour
½ cup milk
½ cup milk, vegetable cooking liquid or other stock
1 tsp Dijon mustard (optional)
about ½ cup grated, well-flavoured cheese salt and pepper to taste

Melt the butter, then stir in the flour and cook over low heat, or microwave until it bubbles. Add the first measure of liquid and bring to the boil, stirring constantly, or bring to the boil in the microwave. Stir again. Add remaining liquid, and heat again, stirring until smooth and quite thick. Thin down with extra liquid and bring back to the boil if you like.

Stir in the grated cheese and heat only until the cheese melts. Taste, and adjust seasoning if necessary.

MAYONNAISE

This is an extremely useful and delicious sauce which is easy and quick to make in a food processor or blender.

1 egg
½ tsp salt
½ tsp sugar
1 tsp Dijon mustard
2 Tbsp wine vinegar
about 1 cup corn or olive oil

Measure the first five ingredients into a blender or food processor. Turn on, and pour in the oil in a thin stream until the mayonnaise is as thick as you like. Store in a covered container in the refrigerator for up to 2-3 weeks.

GARLIC MAYONNAISE:

Add one or two cloves of garlic before adding the oil. Leave to stand for an hour to soften the flavour, before using.

HERB MAYONNAISE:

Add about ¼ cup roughly chopped parsley, and 1-2 tsp each of one or more fresh or dried herbs such as basil, oreganum, thyme, dill, etc. before adding the oil.

CHILLI MAYONNAISE:

This is a particularly delicious variation. Add ½ tsp chilli powder, 1 tsp dried oreganum, 1-2 tsp ground cumin, and 1 clove of garlic before adding the oil. The flavour improves and becomes hotter after it stands for several hours.

TOFU 'MAYONNAISE' DRESSING

This low-fat, high-protein mayonnaise tastes remarkably good, due to careful seasoning. It contains no eggs and very little oil, and can be used in place of regular mayonnaise, where necessary.

FOR ABOUT 1 CUP:

2 small cloves garlic
2 Tbsp roughly chopped parsley
1 Tbsp roughly chopped chives
1 cup (300 g) crumbled firm tofu
¼ cup vegetable oil
1 Tbsp white wine vinegar
½ tsp mustard powder or 1 tsp Dijon mustard
½ tsp salt
¼ tsp sugar juice of
½ lemon
black pepper to taste

Chop the garlic and herbs in a blender or food processor. Don't be over-generous with the garlic or the dressing will taste of little else. Add the remaining ingredients and blend until the mixture is smooth and creamy. Refrigerate in a screw-topped jar for several weeks, if desired.

SESAME DRESSING

Sprinkle this on cucumber, avocado, or any salad you want to serve with Oriental food.

1 Tbsp Kikkoman soya sauce
1 Tbsp sesame oil
1 Tbsp lemon juice
1 tsp sugar

Shake all ingredients together in a small jar, and sprinkle over food in its serving dish or plate.

GREEN SAUCE

This substantial sauce turns many warm or room-temperature vegetables into a light meal.

1 egg yolk
1 Tbsp mild mixed mustard
1 tsp sugar
¼ tsp salt
2 cloves garlic
2 spring onions
3 Tbsp wine vinegar
½-1 cup mixed fresh herb leaves (e.g. parsley, chives, dill, tarragon)
½-¾ cup corn or soya oil
2 hard-boiled eggs, chopped

Combine first seven ingredients in food processor with metal chopping blade. Add herbs. (Use small amounts of strongly flavoured tarragon.)

Process while adding oil, stopping when thick. Add 1 hard-boiled egg. Chop remaining egg fairly finely and use to sprinkle over sauce when serving. Spoon over cooked cauliflower, asparagus, beans, new potatoes or raw halved avocados, tomatoes, etc. just before serving.

CUMIN DRESSING

½ cup corn or soya oil
¼ cup wine or cider vinegar
2 tsp ground cumin
1-2 tsp onion powder
¾ tsp salt
2 tsp dried oreganum
½-1 tsp garlic powder
black pepper and hot pepper sauce to taste

Place all the ingredients in a screw-topped jar. Shake well.

NOTE:
It is very important that the cumin is fresh and has a pungent, definite flavour.

SAUCES & DRESSINGS

FRENCH DRESSING

The name of this dressing is loosely given to dressings of oil and vinegar in proportions of two-three parts oil shaken with one part of mild vinegar. Mustard is added for extra flavour and to stop the two main ingredients from separating immediately.

We like to season this dressing fairly strongly, since we use it in very small amounts to coat salad greens. If you use a lot of dressing, reduce the amount of seasoning. You can mix small amounts of this dressing, by guesswork, in the bottom of a salad bowl, and combine it with a whisk or fork, before tossing it with the salad ingredients, or you can mix larger amounts and keep it in a jar, to be shaken and applied over a period of several days.

You can change the character of the dressing by adding one or more of the optional ingredients. It is worth experimenting with one at a time.

2 Tbsp olive or corn or soya oil
2 Tbsp corn or soya oil
2 Tbsp wine or cider vinegar
1-2 tsp Dijon mustard
¼-½ tsp salt freshly ground pepper
hot pepper sauce

Optional:
chopped capers
chopped fresh herbs
chopped spring onions
finely chopped garlic
about 1 Tbsp cream
1-2 tsp tomato paste
½-1 tsp sugar

Combine the ingredients of your choice in a screw-topped jar, or a blender or food processor. Shake or process, and use as required.

TOMATO DRESSING

This dressing is especially good with sliced or halved avocado, or with pasta salads.

1 Tbsp onion pulp
¼ cup tomato purée
3 Tbsp wine vinegar
1 Tbsp sugar
½ tsp salt
½ tsp celery salt
1 tsp mixed mustard
¾ cup corn or soya oil

Combine all ingredients in a blender, food processor or screw-topped jar. (For onion pulp, scrape a halved onion, cut crosswise, with the tip of a teaspoon.) Refrigerate in a screw-topped jar for up to a week.

HERB DRESSING

Toss with leafy salads just before serving, or pour over cooked vegetables and leave to cool to room temperature. Vary the herbs to suit the vegetable. Try new potatoes, young carrots, whole beans, sliced zucchini or cauliflower.

¼ cup corn, soya or olive oil
2 Tbsp wine vinegar
1-2 cloves garlic (optional)
½ tsp salt ½ tsp sugar
¼ cup finely chopped parsley small amounts of other fresh herbs, finely chopped

Combine all dressing ingredients in a food processor, blender or screw-topped jar. Mix thoroughly.

HERBED CREAMY VINAIGRETTE

There are times when you want a dressing which is sharper than mayonnaise but more solid than an oil and vinegar dressing. This dressing provides the answer. It is particularly good on vegetables which have been lightly cooked, cooled and well drained, e.g. carrots, beans and cauliflower. It makes a good potato salad too.

1 egg yolk
1 Tbsp Dijon-type mustard
¼ cup wine vinegar
1-1½ cups oil
2 spring onions, finely chopped
2 Tbsp finely chopped parsley
2 tsp finely chopped tarragon (optional)
salt and pepper

Beat the egg yolk, mustard and vinegar together with a wire whisk, then add the oil in a thin stream, beating all the time. Stop adding the oil when it gets to the thickness you want. Stir in the very finely chopped herbs, and add extra seasonings if you think they are needed. If you have a blender or food processor, use it to make the dressing, following the same order.

Refrigerate in a covered container, for up to a week.

PESTO

Fresh basil has a wonderful flavour but a short season. Make pesto so you can enjoy it all year, adding it to pasta, dressings, sauces, and many other dishes, as required.

3-4 cups lightly packed basil leaves
1 cup parsley
4 cloves garlic
¼-½ cup parmesan cheese
¼ cup pine nuts, almonds or walnuts
½-1 cup olive and/or corn oil
about 1 tsp salt

Put the basil and parsley leaves into a food processor with the peeled garlic cloves, the parmesan cheese and the nuts.

Using olive oil for preference, or some olive and some corn oil, process the leaves, adding up to half a cup of oil until they are finely chopped. Keep adding oil until you have a dark green paste, just liquid enough to pour.

Add salt to taste. Store in the refrigerator, in a lidded glass or plastic container, for use within 3 months. Freeze pesto for longer storage.

Note:
Pesto may darken at the top of jars where it is exposed to the air. Make sure there is a layer of oil at the top of each jar.

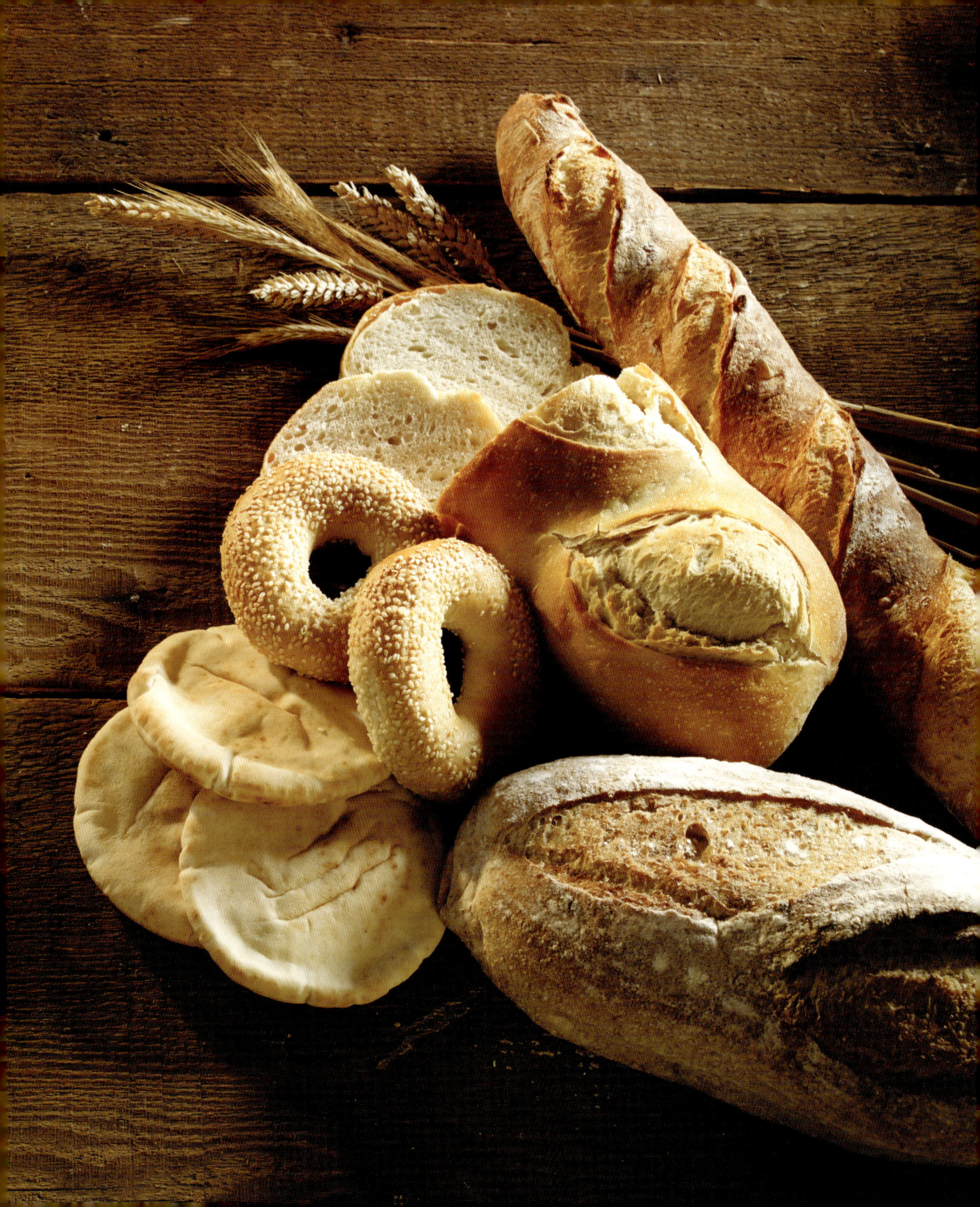

BREAD & BAKING

CHEESE MUFFINS

❄️

To make these savoury muffins easily and quickly, buy pre-grated tasty cheese.

FOR ABOUT 12 MUFFINS:
2 cups (200 g) grated tasty cheese
1½ cups self-raising flour
½ tsp salt
1 Tbsp sugar
pinch of cayenne pepper
1 egg
1 cup milk

Measure the grated cheese, self-raising flour, salt, sugar and cayenne pepper into a large bowl. Mix lightly with your fingertips to combine.

In a small container beat the egg and milk until evenly combined. Pour all the liquid onto the dry ingredients, then fold the two mixtures together, taking care not to overmix.

Spoon mixture carefully off a tablespoon, helping it off with another spoon, into well-sprayed or buttered deep muffin pans. Sprinkle with paprika if desired. Bake at 210°C for about 12 minutes, until muffins spring back when pressed in the middle and are golden brown. Cool before removing from pan.

CORN MUFFINS

❄️

These muffins make a good summer lunch when served with salads. If you like, replace the cornmeal with extra flour.

for 12-15 muffins:
50 g butter, melted
1 egg
½ cup creamed corn
½ cup yoghurt or milk
½ cup grated tasty cheese
¼ cup sugar
¼ tsp salt
½ cup yellow cornmeal (or flour)
1 cup white or wholemeal flour
3 tsp baking powder

Melt the butter in a fairly large mixing bowl. Add the egg and creamed corn and mix with a fork. Add plain yoghurt in preference to milk—it makes muffins more tender.

Add the cheese, sugar and salt and mix again. Stir in the cornmeal, if using it; otherwise sift, or fork lightly together, the flour and baking powder.

Fold the flour mixture into the wet ingredients, taking great care not to overmix.

Spoon into well-sprayed, deep muffin pans, half filling them. Bake at 210°C for 10-15 minutes, until quite crusty and nicely browned. Stand 5 minutes before removing from pans. Serve warm.

OATY MUFFINS

❄️

Make three dozen large muffins all at once and freeze them, or refrigerate the uncooked mixture for up to two weeks, cooking them as required.

½ cup treacle
2 cups rolled oats 1 cup baking bran
1 cup boiling water
1 cup brown sugar
2 Tbsp wine vinegar
1 tsp salt
2 eggs
2 cups milk
2 cups flour
1 cup oat bran
1½ tsp baking soda

Measure the treacle, rolled oats and baking bran in a large bowl.

Pour over boiling water and mix until treacle and oats are mixed. Leave to cool for 5 minutes, then add the next four ingredients and beat with a fork to combine eggs.

Add milk and then the last three ingredients, previously forked together. Stir only enough to combine. Spoon into well-buttered (or sprayed) muffin tins, filling each one half to three-quarters full. Bake at 220°C for 10 minutes or until firm or microwave half-filled microwave muffin moulds, 2 minutes on High (100%) power for 5 muffins. Always leave to stand for a few minutes before removing muffins from pans.

HONEY BRAN MUFFINS

These muffins have a lovely smell as they cook, because of the malty Allbran. Take care not to add fruit which is too moist since the mixture cannot take too much extra liquid. These muffins seem to stay moist for about 48 hours, but they are unlikely to last that long!

for 12 large muffins:
½ cup Allbran
¼ cup boiling water
100 g butter
2 Tbsp honey
1 egg
½ cup yoghurt
¾ cup baking bran
¾ cup flour
½ tsp baking soda
2 Tbsp sugar
1 banana, chopped

Pour boiling water over Allbran and leave to cool. In another container heat the butter and honey until the butter just melts and mixes easily with the softened honey. Add the egg and yoghurt and beat lightly with a fork, to combine.
   Fold together the dry ingredients, the soaked Allbran, the liquid ingredients and the finely chopped banana. Mix just enough to dampen the flour. Do not beat until smooth.
   Spoon the mixture into 12 oiled non-stick muffin pans. Bake at 200°C for 15 minutes, or until lightly browned and firm in the middle when pressed.
   Leave to cool for 5 minutes before carefully removing from the pans.

FRUITY MUFFINS

These muffins may be made right through the year, using different fruits and berries in season. Blueberries make especially good muffins because they are not sour when cooked. Use currants or sultanas in these muffins if fresh fruit is not available.

for about 12 muffins:
2 cups flour
4 tsp baking powder
½ tsp salt
½ cup castor sugar
100 g butter
1 cup milk
1 egg
1-1½ cups blackberries, blueberries, chopped
    banana, etc. or ¾ cup sultanas or ½ cup currants
about ¼ cup chopped walnuts (optional)
1 Tbsp sugar
½ tsp cinnamon

Sieve the first three dry ingredients into a fairly large bowl. Add the castor sugar. In another container melt the butter, remove from the heat and then add the milk and egg, and beat to combine these three.
   Prepare the fruit then tip the liquid, fruit, and nuts if used, into the bowl with the dry ingredients. Fold everything together, taking great care not to overmix. The flour should be dampened, but the mixture should not be smooth.
   Butter or oil 12 deep muffin pans thoroughly. Without stirring or extra mixing, place spoonfuls of mixture into pans, filling each half to three-quarters full.
   Combine the second measure of sugar with the cinnamon and sprinkle over the muffins before baking. Bake at 220°C for about 12-15 minutes, until muffins spring back when pressed in the centre.
   Remove from the oven, stand for 2-3 minutes, then twist muffins carefully to loosen before lifting them from their pans.

FLOUR TORTILLAS

Flour tortillas are quite different from their corn cousins. They are more substantial and remain flexible when cooked. Serve a pile with bowls of refried beans, shredded lettuce, grated cheese and sour cream and let everyone help themselves, or serve them as pre-filled buritos.

for 10-12 flour tortillas:
2½ cups white flour
1 tsp baking powder
1 tsp salt
¼ cup oil
about ¾ cup warm water

Combine the dry ingredients in a bowl. Add the oil and stir briefly through the flour, then gradually add the warm water. Use only enough water to form a kneadable dough.

Turn out onto a lightly floured surface and knead for about 5 minutes. Divide the dough into 10-12 pieces, form these into balls, then cover and leave to stand for 15-30 minutes.

Roll out each ball of dough until it forms a circle about 20 cm across. Stack these, separating each with a sheet of plastic.

Heat a lightly oiled heavy frypan and cook tortillas for 30-60 seconds per side (until they begin to brown and bubble). Stack tortillas together as they cook, and cover with a damp tea towel to keep them soft. Serve immediately, or wrap in foil and reheat when desired.

BROWN BREAD

This well-flavoured nutritious bread is quick and easy enough to make regularly, since it requires no kneading.

FOR 2 OR 3 LOAVES:
1 Tbsp dried yeast granules
1 cup warm water
2 tsp sugar
2 rounded household Tbsp malt
3 rounded household Tbsp treacle
2 cups hot water
1 Tbsp oil
2 tsp salt
1 cup wheatgerm
1 cup wheat bran (optional)
4-6 cups wholemeal flour
toasted sesame seeds (optional)

When you make bread you should keep the mixtures warm enough for the yeast to work to make the bread rise, but not let them get so hot that the yeast is killed.

Mix the yeast, lukewarm water, and sugar together in a food processor or bowl. (Yeast starts to work fast when food-processed.) Make sure the water is not too hot, or the yeast will be killed. Leave it to stand in a warm place while you prepare the rest of the mixture.

In a large bowl stir together the malt, treacle, hot water, oil and salt. The water should be as hot as a hot bath, to dissolve the (generous) spoonfuls of malt and treacle. Let the liquid cool to lukewarm.

Measure the wheatgerm and bran (if used) into the bowl of warm, malty liquid, and stir well. Measure 4 cups of the wholemeal flour onto this, make sure that the malty liquid is not too hot for the yeast, then tip in the yeast mixture, which by this time should be showing some signs of activity by bubbling or by fizzing when stirred.

Stir everything together thoroughly, using a large wooden spoon if possible. The mixture should be too thick to pour, but soft enough to spoon into pans and smooth the top surface. Add more flour as necessary. This amount of dough should rise to fill loaf tins which hold 12-15 cups altogether (depending on the amount of flour used). Butter the tins well, or spray thoroughly with non-stick spray. Spoon the mixture evenly into the tins, half filling each, sprinkle with toasted sesame seeds if desired, cover with plastic film, and leave in a warm place to rise, e.g., a warming oven which has been preheated then turned off, a sunny windowsill, a sink of warm water.

When the dough has risen to the tops of the tins or to twice its original volume, remove plastic film. Bake uncovered at 200°C for 30 minutes, or until the loaves sound hollow when tapped, or until a skewer comes out clean.

Turn out of the tins immediately, if they will fall out cleanly, otherwise leave to stand for 5 minutes, then remove, with the help of a knife if necessary.

Note:
Replace the malt with golden syrup, if desired. The colour and flavour will be good, but not malty.

SCONES, PLAIN OR FANCY

One of the easiest things to mix and bake, when you need something to serve with tea or coffee, is a batch of scones. If you feel that your scones leave a little to be desired, do not make plain scones, where every imperfection shows, but make an interesting variation.

Try twists or pinwheels, using fillings based on brown sugar, cinnamon and butter. Vary the fillings adding coconut, currants or sultanas, or nuts. The food processor is useful when it comes to making these scones, but do not actually mix the scone dough with it, because it is easy to overmix and toughen the dough.

Basic dough:
2 cups self-raising plain or wholemeal flour
25 g butter
about ¾ cup milk

Filling:
¼ cup brown sugar
1 tsp cinnamon
1 Tbsp cold butter
¼ cup coconut

Measure the flour into the bowl of a food processor. Add the butter, cut into cubes, and process until chopped into small pieces.

Tip into a bowl, and add the measured milk, all at once. Cut and stir the liquid into the dry ingredients. Add a little more milk or flour if the mixture seems too dry or too wet. The dough should be as soft as you can handle, to roll out on a floured bench. The scones will rise better if the mixture has been lightly kneaded with your fingertips before it is rolled out.

For plain scones pat or roll the scone dough out, 20-25 cm square. Cut into nine squares with a sharp, lightly floured knife. Place on a baking tray, about 1 cm apart.

For pinwheels or twists, roll the dough out to make a long thin rectangle, about 40x20 cm. Make the filling by combining the filling ingredients in the unwashed food processor bowl. Process just enough to combine the ingredients. (Overmixing turns them into a paste.)

To shape pinwheels: Spread the filling mixture evenly over the uncooked dough, leaving 1 cm clear on the long edge farthest away from you. Dampen this edge, then roll up the dough to form a long, thin sausage, rolling the dampened edge last. Cut the roll into pieces about 1 cm thick, and place each piece on a lightly buttered baking sheet, allowing space for spreading.

To shape twists: Spread the filling in a long strip on the half of the dough farthest away from you, leaving the outside 1 cm uncovered. Dampen the uncovered strip, then fold the uncovered half over the covered section. Press firmly together, then cut into 1 cm strips, crosswise. Twist each strip twice, then place on a lightly oiled baking tray and press the ends down firmly.

Bake at 200°C for 10-15 minutes, until lightly browned. Serve plain or buttered soon after cooking.

Variations:
For savoury scones add a little grated cheese (about ½ cup) and some fresh herbs to the dough. Try making savoury pinwheels or twists using this dough and 1-1½ cups of savoury filling. Some of our most successful fillings are grated cheese and tomato relish or grated cheese and chopped asparagus, but use your imagination and whatever you have on hand to create your own favourites.

QUICK YEAST BREAD/PIZZA BASE

This recipe seems to break all the bread-making rules. The resulting bread stales quickly and should be eaten the day it is made. Fast pizza bases can be made from scone dough (*see page 145*), but why bother when you can so easily make a yeast base like this in the same time.

1¼ cups warm water
3 Tbsp sugar
1 Tbsp dried yeast granules
1 Tbsp vegetable oil
1 tsp salt
3 cups wholemeal or white flour (or any combination of the two)
½ tsp baking powder

Dissolve the sugar in the warm (blood temperature) water, then sprinkle in the yeast granules. Add the oil and then stir gently for a few seconds. Leave to stand for at least five minutes to allow the yeast to begin acting.

Once the yeast mixture has begun to bubble and looks a little foamy, add the remaining ingredients. Sprinkle the baking powder in evenly to prevent it forming a single lump. Stir everything together until the dough begins to come away from the sides of the bowl and form one large ball.

With oiled hands, shape into rolls, or 2 loaves. Brush tops with milk or beaten egg. Top with grated cheese, poppy seeds, or toasted sesame seeds if desired. For a pizza, flatten the dough onto a well-oiled baking sheet or sponge roll tin (25x35 cm). If you have the time (or the patience) leave to rise for 5-15 mintes, although this is not strictly necessary. If you are going to make a pizza, use this time to assemble and prepare the toppings (see below).

Bake loaves at 200°C for 20-25 minutes. Bake rolls at 200°C for about 15 minutes. Bake pizzas at 230°C for 12-15 minutes, until the underside is brown and the toppings look cooked.

PIZZA TOPPINGS

Pizzas are best if assembled in a defined order. We suggest that you top the dough first with a tomato base, followed by the toppings of your choice, and finish with a layer of cheese.

Try spreading the uncooked base with a layer of tomato purée, tomato concentrate diluted to spreading consistency with water, or canned spaghetti or baked beans. Sprinkle this with fresh or dried basil and marjoram or oreganum.

Follow this with any combination of the following:
leftover refried beans
drained corn
plain, marinated or fried tofu
thinly sliced vegetarian sausage
red and green peppers
mushrooms
sliced tomatoes
mild onions
pesto
olives

Finally, add a layer of cheese. Grated or sliced Mozzarella is particularly good, but grated mild or tasty cheddar is just fine if this is what you have on hand.

Bake at 230°C for 12-15 minutes or until the edges and bottom are lightly browned.

Variation:
For something a little different, try sprinkling the unbaked pizza with a little Mexican Seasoning Mix (*see page 42*) or mild chilli powder.

BASIC BREAD ROLLS

When you ask friends to dinner, bake hot rolls to turn a simple meal into something exciting! Breadmaking does take a while from start to finish but you can do many other things while the bread looks after itself.

2 tsp dried yeast granules
1 Tbsp sugar
½ cup warm water
50 g butter
1 cup milk
1-1½ tsp salt
about 3 cups white or 1½ cups white and 1½ cups wholemeal flour

As soon as you think about making bread, mix the yeast, sugar and lukewarm water in a large mixing bowl. Leave in a warm place until frothy and bubbly, from 5-15 minutes.

Meantime, melt the butter, add the milk and salt, and warm to the same temperature as the yeast mixture. Add the milk mixture and 2½ cups of flour to the bubbly yeast, and beat well with a wooden spoon for about 30 seconds. Cover the bowl with plastic film or a plastic bag, and put it in a warm place until it rises to twice its original size.

Stir the mixture, then add just enough flour to make a dough which is soft enough to turn out onto the bench or a table to knead.

To knead, push the dough away from you with the heel of one hand, then collect it, and bring it back towards you with your other hand. Make sure you push the dough really hard.

Sprinkle just enough flour on the bench to stop the dough sticking. The longer you knead the dough the easier it will be to handle. It will become smooth and satiny, but should not stick to the bench.

Cut the kneaded dough into 12-16 pieces. Shape each piece as you like, making balls, or long pencil shapes which you can knot or twist or plait.

Place the shaped rolls on a lightly greased or sprayed oven tray or cake tin, leaving room for them to rise. Cover them loosely with oiled plastic, stand the tray over a sink of warm water if it is cold, and leave the rolls until they are 1½ times the size they were when you shaped them.

To make them shine, brush them very lightly with beaten egg. Sprinkle with poppy seeds, sesame seeds, or grated cheese, if you like, then bake in a hot oven, at 230°C for about 10 minutes, or until golden brown. Eat warm, or reheat, or freeze as soon as they are cold.

PITA BREAD (POCKET BREAD)

This bread is fun to cook, since each flat circle of dough puffs up like a balloon, in 1-2 minutes.

The cooled, deflated balls of bread are cut in half to form pockets which can be filled with anything you like (see suggestions below). They may also be frozen for later use.

1½ tsp dried yeast granules
2 tsp sugar
1 cup warm water
1 Tbsp corn or soya oil
2-3 cups flour
1 tsp salt

Mix the yeast, sugar and water and leave in a warm place to bubble.

Stir in the oil then enough flour to form a dough firm enough to knead. Use all white or 1½ cups wholemeal flour, with ½-1½ cups white flour.

Knead until smooth and springy then place in an oiled plastic bag, and leave to rise to about 1½ times its original size.

While the dough rises, turn the oven on to heat to its highest temperature. Put the oven-slide, on which the bread will cook, in the middle of the oven, and, if you have a cast-iron pan with a heat-resistant handle, put it on the rack underneath. Each circle of bread must be slid quickly onto a hot oven-slide to cook. A heavy-weight hot pan just underneath the oven-slide helps to keep it hot.

When the dough has risen, add the salt to it. Knead it again, then cut into pieces of golf ball size. Using just enough flour to prevent sticking, roll each piece out to form a circle the thickness of a 50-cent piece. By the time the last piece has been rolled out, the oven should be very hot, and the first bread ready to be cooked.

Slip the bottom of a loose-bottomed pan or a piece of cardboard, under the bread which was rolled out first, and, opening the oven for as short a time as possible, slide it onto the pre-heated tray. Within a

BREAD & BAKING   147

minute the bread should puff up, and within another minute the crust should be set. Remove it from the oven, and slide in another bread circle. Put the cooked bread into an ovenbag or plastic bag so it will not dry out. Cut each circle to make a pocket when cool.

NOTE:
If the first pita breads cooked do not puff, leave the rest to stand for 5 or 10 minutes longer, before cooking them. Cook two or three pita breads together if you want to.

Pita breads should be light in colour. If you leave them to brown, they become crisp, and lose their flexibility.

INDIVIDUAL PIZZAS:
Use the above recipe. Roll out circles of the dough as above, place on a cold, oiled oven-slide and top with pizza toppings (see page 146) as desired.

Bake at 200-220°C until browned underneath, and around edges.

PITA BREAD FILLINGS:
If possible fill the warmed bread just before eating it. Try warming the bread in a microwave oven, under a grill, or on a barbecue. Split the bread and open the pocket to fill, or, if this is difficult, arrange the filling on top.

If filling ahead, line the pocket with lettuce leaves before adding the other ingredients.

OUR FAVOURITE FILLINGS INCLUDE:
- cottage cheese
- marinated tofu
- sliced or cubed tomatoes
- chopped peppers
- bean sprouts
- alfalfa sprouts
- sprouted or cooked brown lentils or
- raisins or sultanas (especially nice with
- minty mixtures) brown or white rice hard-boiled eggs cheese
- salad greens and fresh herbs
- falafel and Sesame Cream Sauce (*see page 34*)
- tabbouleh (*see page 131*)
- natural yoghurt

PUMPKIN LOAF

This recipe makes a sweet, spicy loaf. It can be served warm with sauce or whipped cream as dessert the day it is baked.

1 cup pumpkin purée
100 g butter
1½ cups soft brown sugar
2 eggs
2 cups self-raising flour
½ tsp baking soda
1 tsp cinnamon
½ tsp grated nutmeg
½ tsp ginger
¼ tsp ground cloves

To make the pumpkin purée, microwave or boil the pumpkin pieces in lightly salted water, then purée in a food processor or press through a sieve.

Cream the butter and sugar, add the eggs and beat well, then stir in the puréed pumpkin. Sift the dry ingredients together. Fold in half of this sifted mixture to the pumpkin mixture, then mix in the remaining half until evenly combined, but do not beat.

Spoon the mixture into a lined 23 x 10 cm loaf tin. Bake at 180°C for 1 hour, or until a skewer poked into the middle of the loaf comes out clean.

Store in a loosely covered container or refrigerate in a plastic bag.

BROWN BANANA BREAD

This bread has a good banana flavour, and may be sliced like a cake when fresh. For special occasion it is good spread with cream cheese flavoured with finely grated orange rind.

100 g butter
¾ cup sugar 1 egg
1 cup mashed ripe banana

148 MEALS WITHOUT MEAT

1 cup wholemeal flour
¼ cup orange juice
¼–½ cup chopped walnuts (or sunflower seeds)
1 cup plain flour
1 tsp baking powder
1 tsp baking soda

Cream the butter and sugar together until light and fluffy. Add the egg and beat again. Mash the bananas (about 2 medium-sized bananas make one cup), and add them to the creamed mixture with the wholemeal flour, orange juice and walnuts (or sunflower seeds). Stir together until just combined. Sift in the plain flour, baking powder and baking soda. Mix until all the ingredients are just combined.

Line a 23 x 10 cm loaf tin with greaseproof paper, so that the paper covers the bottom and long sides, and spoor in the mixture.

Bake at 180°C for about an hour. When the loaf is cooked, the centre will spring back when pressed, and a skewer poked into the middle will come out clean. Stand for 5-10 minutes before removing from the tin. Store as for pumpkin loaf.

STEAMED HIGH-PROTEIN LOAF

Alison worked out this recipe for children who were refusing to eat other protein-rich foods. Try it!

FOR 2-4 CYLINDRICAL LOAVES:

1½ cups wholemeal flour
½ cup wheatgerm
1 cup soya flour
3 tsp baking powder
1 tsp salt
½ cup milk powder
½ cup chopped walnuts
3 Tbsp butter or oil
1 orange, grated rind and juice
½–¾ cup golden syrup
2 eggs
1 cup milk

Mix the first seven ingredients in a large bowl. Grate orange rind into a saucepan with the butter or oil. Warm to melt butter. Add the juice and syrup (the larger amount makes a sweeter, more orangey loaf), warm until liquid, then beat in the eggs. Tip this slightly warm liquid, and the milk into the bowl with the dry ingredients, and stir just enough to moisten.

Spoon into well-buttered empty fruit cans, filling each no more than two-thirds full. Cover cans with buttered foil, leaving plenty of foil folded down the sides in case loaves rise more than estimated. Stand in a pot containing about 5 cm boiling water, cover pot, and simmer for about 3 hours. Remove foil, cool for 5 minutes, then turn out onto a rack to finish cooling.

Slice and spread with butter or cream cheese. Freeze for long storage.

QUICK BRAN BREAD

Here is an old recipe for a quickly made loaf which makes a good lunch, served with cheese or honey, and peanut butter.

2 cups white or wholemeal flour
½ cup wheatgerm
½ cup baking bran
2 Tbsp baking powder
¼–½ tsp salt
1 Tbsp golden syrup
¼ cup hot water
½ cup milk

Stir the flour, wheatgerm, bran, baking powder and salt together in a fairly large bowl, until evenly mixed. Measure the golden syrup, using a household tablespoon, which has been preheated in hot water. The syrup should be rounded on the spoon, but if you use too much, the loaf will be rather sweet.

Stir the syrup and hot water together to dissolve the syrup, then add this, with about three-quarters of the measured milk into the dry ingredients. Stir with a fork or knife, to form the mixture into a ball of dough.

Add a little more flour, or more milk if necessary, to

BREAD & BAKING 149

make scone dough consistency.

Turn onto a lightly floured board and knead lightly four or five times.

Shape as desired—try one long loaf or two small round loaves. Cut a series of diagonal slashes into the long loaf, or a cross into each of the smaller loaves.

Bake loaves at 170°C for 15-30 minutes, until brown on top and bottom, and hollow-sounding when tapped.

Cool on a wire rack, then break or slice and serve while warm and fresh.

BOILED FRUIT LOAF

This low-fat, no egg, fruity loaf tastes so good that you do not even need to butter the slices.

1 cup hot water
¾ cup sugar
½ cup sultanas
¼ cup dried mixed fruit
25 g butter or ¼ cup oil
1 tsp cinnamon
1 tsp mixed spice
½ tsp ground cloves
1½ cups flour
1 tsp baking powder
½ tsp baking soda
½ tsp salt

Place water, sugar, sultanas, mixed fruit and butter or oil in a medium-sized saucepan. Bring to the boil, stirring occasionally, then simmer (uncovered) for 5 minutes. Stand the pot in cold water to cool contents to room temperature. Line a loaf tin with greaseproof paper while you wait.

Sift remaining ingredients into the cooled fruit mixture. Stir only enough to blend ingredients, as overmixing causes toughening and uneven rising.

Bake at 180°C for 45-60 minutes, until a skewer pushed into the centre comes out clean. This loaf is best left for 24 hours before eating.

COFFEE CAKE

This special occasion rich yet light cake is quite different from most made with wholemeal flour.

150 g soft butter
1 cup brown sugar
2 Tbsp instant coffee
2 eggs
2 tsp vanilla
2 cups wholemeal flour
1 tsp baking powder
1½ tsp baking soda
1 tsp ground cinnamon
1 tsp ground cardamon
½ tsp salt
250 g sour cream
¼ cup walnuts, chopped
juice of one lemon (2 Tbsp)

Cream the butter and sugar, then add the powdered or granular coffee and mix in well. Break in the eggs and add the vanilla, beat well, then transfer to a large bowl.

In another bowl, toss together the sifted dry ingredients. Add half of this to the creamed mixture, then mix in half the sour cream. Repeat with the other half of the dry ingredients and sour cream.

Stir in the walnuts and lemon juice, then tip into a large, well-oiled ring tin or a 23 cm paper-lined pan.

Bake at 180°C for 40-50 minutes, until a skewer poked into the middle comes out clean. Leave to stand in tin for a few minutes before turning out.

WALNUT TORTE

In this cake, ground nuts and biscuit crumbs replace flour. The resulting cake is rich and popular. It makes a wonderful snack or dinner party finale, served alone or with fresh berries. It is easy to chop the nuts and crumb the biscuits if you have a food processor.

150 MEALS WITHOUT MEAT

FOR 9-12 SERVINGS:
½ cup biscuit crumbs
125 g freshly shelled walnuts
1 cup sugar
3 large eggs

Thoroughly butter, or line, a round or square 23 cm cake tin, so it is ready as soon as the cake mixture is prepared. Heat the oven to 160°C.

Crumb maltmeal wafers or other biscuits, using a food processor or a plastic bag and rolling pin. Sieve crumbs to make sure they are evenly fine, before measuring them.

Chop the walnuts with half the sugar, in a food processor if possible, otherwise chop very finely, then mix with half the sugar. The nuts should be nearly as fine as ground almonds.

Beat the room-temperature eggs until thick, then add the remaining sugar and beat until very thick. (Beat yolks, then whites and sugar separately, if you have trouble getting really thick egg mixtures.)

Fold the three mixtures carefully together, pour into the prepared tin, and bake at 160°C for 30-40 minutes, or until the centre springs back when gently pressed. Leave for 10 minutes before removing carefully from pan.

Serve squares or wedges lightly dusted with icing sugar. Accompany with whipped cream or Fromage Frais, with extra nuts or berries.

APPLE AND WALNUT CAKE

This is a lovely moist, dense cake which is unlikely to sit around for long! Its generous size makes it useful when serving coffee and cake to a large group.

¾ cup corn or soya oil
1¾ cups soft brown sugar
2 eggs
1 tsp vanilla
1¾ cups wholemeal flour
1 tsp baking soda
2 tsp cinnamon
1 tsp grated nutmeg
1 tsp salt
½ cup chopped walnuts or lightly toasted sunflower seeds
4 cups grated apple (6 medium-sized apples)

In a smallish bowl or food processor combine the oil, sugar, eggs and vanilla until light coloured and creamy. In a large bowl, toss together all the dry ingredients and the nuts or seeds with a fork until they are lightly and evenly mixed.

Grate the unpeeled apples using a sharp grater (or food processor) so they are not too mushy and wet, press them lightly into a four-cup measure, then combine the three mixtures in the big bowl, stirring only until the dry ingredients are moistened.

Pour into a well-buttered roasting pan about 25 cm square, and bake at 180°C for 30-45 minutes, or until the centre springs back when pressed.
Cool in the tin, sprinkle with icing sugar, and cut into generous pieces.

ZUCCHINI CHOCOLATE CAKE

This combination of ingredients is unusual, but most successful. The resulting cake is one of our favourites.

125 g butter
1 cup brown sugar
½ cup white sugar
3 eggs
2½ cups flour
1 tsp vanilla
½ cup yoghurt
¼ cup cocoa
2 tsp baking soda
1 tsp cinnamon
½ tsp mixed spice
½ tsp salt
3 cups (350 g) grated zucchini
½-1 cup small pieces of chocolate (optional)

Prepare a 25 cm square pan or roasting pan by lining it with two crosswide strips of baking paper. Beat the butter with the sugars until light and creamy. Do not hurry this step. Use a mixer or food processor.

Add the eggs one at a time, with a spoonful of the measured flour to prevent the mixture curdling. Add the vanilla and yoghurt and mix well.

Sift the dry ingredients together. Stir in, with the grated zucchini. Turn into the prepared pan. Sprinkle surface with the small pieces of chocolate if desired. Bake at 170°C for 45 minutes, or until centre feels firm and a skewer comes out clean.

WHOLEMEAL CARROT CAKE

A good carrot cake is always popular—for dessert or with tea and coffee any time of the day.

FOR A 20-23 CM CAKE:

2 eggs
1 cup brown sugar
1 cup oil

2 tsp cinnamon
½ tsp salt
2 cups (250 g) grated carrot
1 tsp baking soda
1½ cups wholemeal flour

In a medium-sized bowl or food processor, combine eggs, sugar and oil. Beat until well combined and light in colour. Stir in the cinnamon, salt and grated carrot. Add the well-stirred baking soda and flour and mix until all flour is dampened.

Line the bottom of a 23 cm round or 20 cm square tin with greaseproof paper, then lightly oil the sides. Pour or spoon in the mixture.

Bake at 180°C for 45 minutes, or until the centre springs back when pushed, a skewer inserted in the centre comes out clean, and the side begin to pull away from the tin.

Leave to cool for 5 minutes in the tin, then invert onto a wire rack. When cool, ice with lemon butter icing (made by mixing 1½ cups icing sugar with 25 g soft butter and 1-2 Tbsp lemon juice).

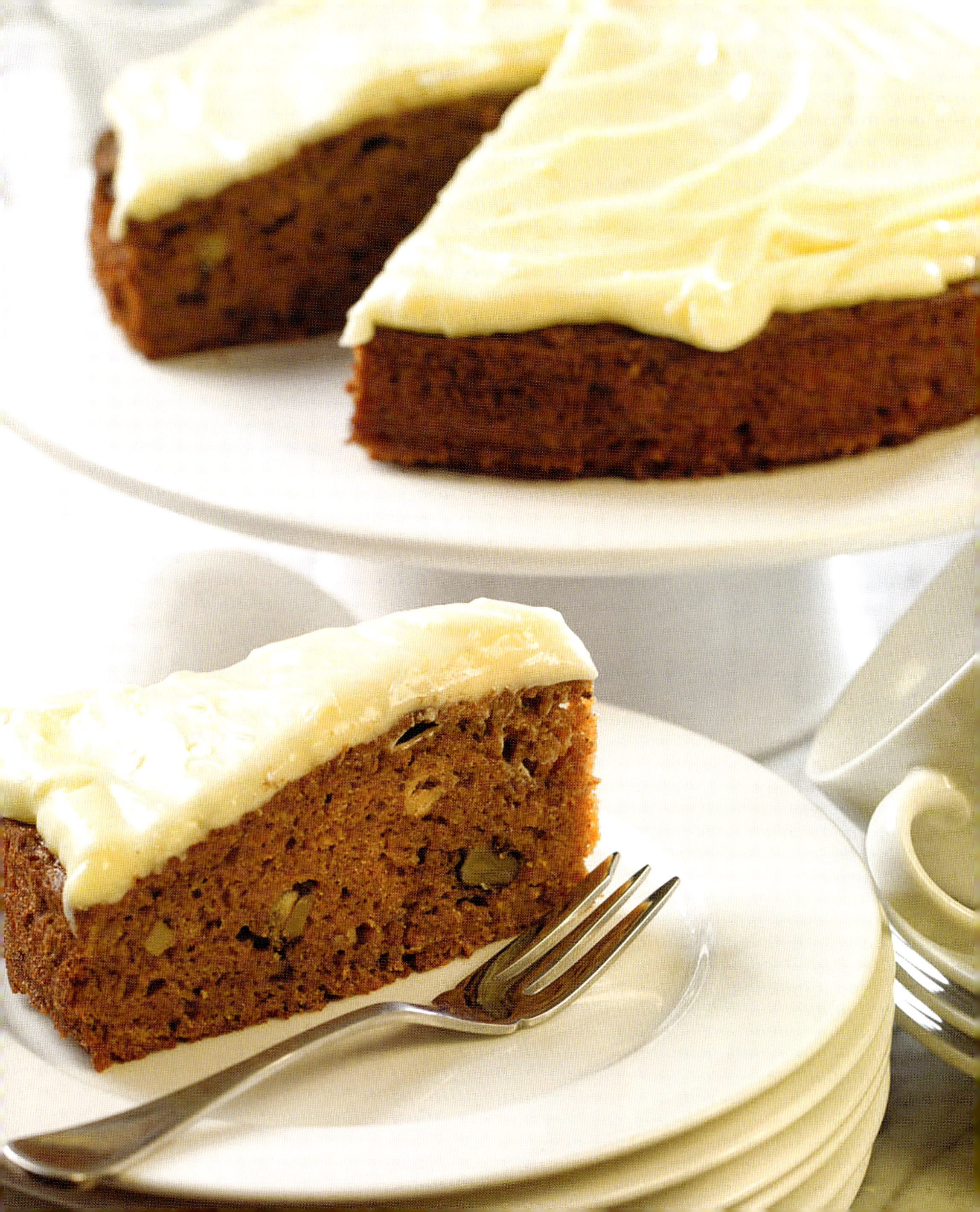

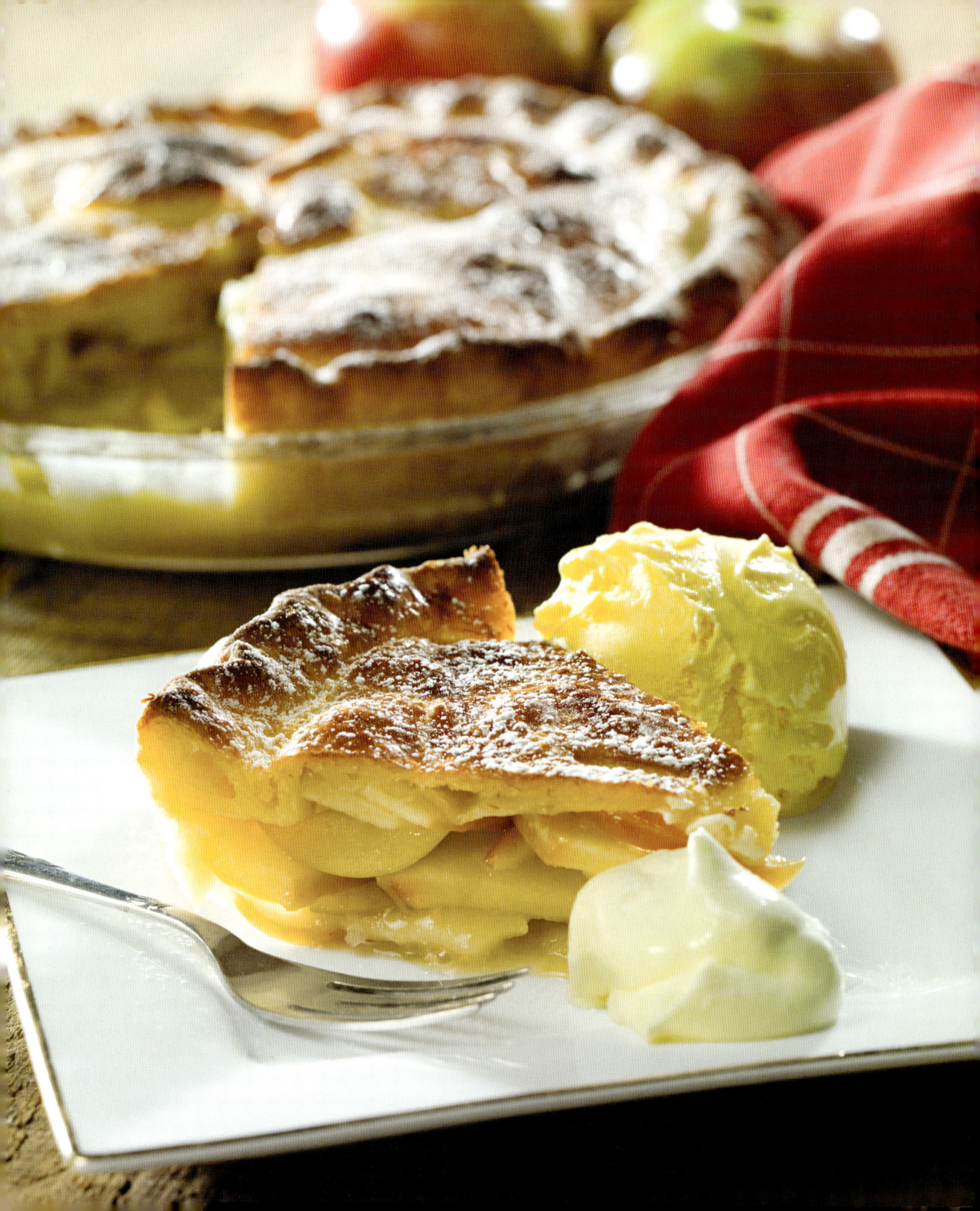

FAVOURITE DESSERTS

INSTANT ICE-CREAM

This ice-cream is ready to eat 1 minute after you start making it. Either freeze the fruit or berry of your choice in packets containing 2 cups, or buy frozen berries. Start with strawberry ice-cream, then experiment with cubed peaches and other berries.

for 3-4 servings:
2 cups frozen strawberries, etc.
½ cup icing sugar
about ½ cup chilled cream, milk, yoghurt,
*   or soya milk*

Chop frozen berries into smaller pieces if necesssary. Fruit must be frozen hard, free-flow and in 1-2 cm cubes. Tip into food processor bowl. Work quickly to keep fruit very cold.

Process with metal chopping blade until fruit is finely chopped (10-20 seconds). This is a noisy operation. Add icing sugar and process until mixed. Gradually add the chilled liquid of your choice through the feed-tube, using just enough to form a smooth cream. Stop as soon as mixture is evenly textured and creamy, cleaning the sides of processor bowl once or twice. Serve immediately.

APPLE CRUMBLE

It's much quicker to make a crumbled topping than to make pastry, and in our house the crumble rates nearly as high as a pie. Leftovers, warmed in the microwave oven, and eaten with yoghurt, make a good breakfast.

We grate the apples, skin and all, instead of peeling then slicing the fruit. It gives a 'fresher' flavour to the crumble

for 4 servings:
½ cup flour
½ tsp cinnamon
½ tsp mixed spice
¾ cup sugar
75 g butter
½ cup rolled oats
4 medium-sized apples, grated

Measure the flour, spices and sugar into a medium-sized bowl or food processor. Cut or rub in the butter until crumbly, then add the rolled oats. Grate the unpeeled apples into a shallow medium-sized ovenware dish.

Sprinkle the crumbly topping evenly over them.

Bake at 190°C for 45 minutes, until the topping is golden brown. Serve hot or warm with cream or ice-cream.

TOFU-FRUIT WHIP

When you mix puréed fruit and tofu, you get a thick, amazingly smooth and delicious, pudding-like mixture. Adjust the flavouring carefully, top with some toasted flaked almonds, and you have a popular, cholesterol-free, almost instant dessert.

for 2-4 servings:
175-250 g fresh apricots, strawberries, bananas
*   or drained, canned fruit*
250-300 g tofu
about 1 cup orange juice or white wine/water
*   mixture*
2 Tbsp brown sugar
¼-½ tsp vanilla

Chop the fruit into a food processor or blender. Process until it forms a fairly smooth purée. Crumble in the tofu and process for about a minute, until very smooth, before gradually adding enough orange juice or wine and water to thin the mixture to the consistency you want. Add sugar to taste. Add the vanilla.

Serve immediately, or refrigerate.

QUICK FLAKY PASTRY

This is an easy recipe for a pastry which is flakier and richer than the pastry on page 66.

FOR 1 THINLY ROLLED DOUBLE CRUST 20 CM PIE:
1¼ cups flour
1 tsp baking powder
125 g cold butter about
½ cup milk
1 tsp wine vinegar

Mix the flour and baking powder. Grate butter or cut it into about 25 small cubes, and rub or cut into the flour, by hand or with a food processor. (Pieces of butter should be visible when pastry is rolled out.) Mix liquids, and add slowly to flour mixture until it forms a fairly stiff dough. Roll out thinly, and use as required.

RHUBARB CREAM FLAN

Rhubarb in party dress!

FOR 4-6 SERVINGS:
Quick Flaky Pastry
3-4 cups thinly sliced rhubarb
3 eggs
½ cup sugar
½ cup sour cream

Make once the recipe of the pastry. Roll out pastry thinly and use to line a 20 cm pie plate or loose-bottomed flan tin. (There will be some pastry left over.) Fold pastry edges back for a pie, and cut pastry level with edge for a flan.

Cut rhubarb thinly, and arrange in uncooked crust. Combine eggs, sugar, and sour cream until well mixed, then pour over fruit.

Bake at 220°C for 20 minutes, or until golden brown, then at 180°C until filling is set in the middle. Serve warm.

VARIATION:
Replace rhubarb with other raw or cooked fruit.

APPLE PIE

Everybody seems to like apple pie, so it is worth learning how to make this old favourite.

FOR A 20-23 CM PIE:
Quick Flaky Pastry
½ cup sugar
2 Tbsp flour
4-6 apples
25 g butter, melted
6 cloves or ¼ tsp ground cloves

Make once the recipe of the pastry. Cut the pastry in half, then roll it out thinly and evenly on a lightly floured board, turning it often, to form two rounds a little bigger than a 20 or 23 cm pie plate. Put one piece in the plate, with its edge overhanging, stretching it as little as possible.

Put the sugar and flour in a bowl. Coarsely shred or slice the peeled or unpeeled apples, and toss them in the sugar and flour. Pour the melted butter over the apple, add the cloves if you like them, and toss to mix. Put the prepared apple into the pastry-lined pan, dampen the surface of the remaining pastry, and place on the apple, dampened side down. Press the two layers of pastry together, trim about 1 cm beyond the edge of the pie plate, then fold the overhanging pastry under, pinching the layers together. Flute or fork the edges if desired, make one central hole or several holes for steam to escape, and brush with lightly beaten egg if you want a glazed surface. Bake at 220°C until golden brown and the apple is tender when tested with a skewer, lowering the heat to 180°C if the pastry browns before the apple is cooked.

Serve warm, with cream, ice-cream, yoghurt, or fromage frais.

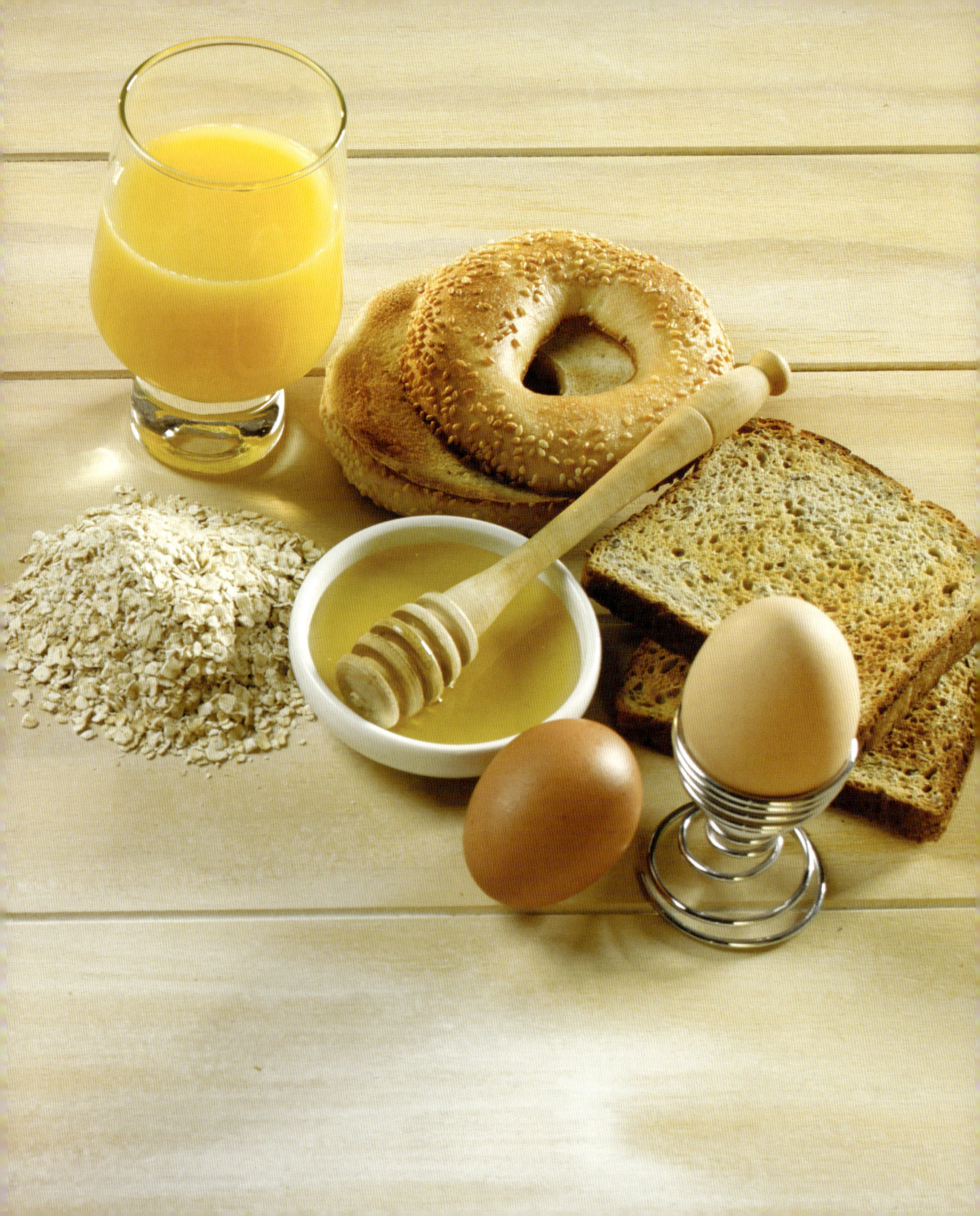

BREAKFAST TREATS

SWISS MUESLI

This mix-in-a-bowl combination makes a good easy meal at any time of the day.

FOR 1 SERVING:

3 Tbsp rolled oats
3 Tbsp boiling water
1 Tbsp lemon juice
1 Tbsp sweetened condensed milk
1-2 Tbsp chopped or flaked nuts
1 unpeeled grated apple or other fresh fruit, sliced or chopped.

Measure oats into a cereal bowl, and pour on the boiling water. Leave to stand while you prepare the other ingredients. Fold everything else into oats, and eat immediately.

Variation:
Replace condensed milk with runny honey and yoghurt, if desired.

MICROWAVE MUESLI

This is, without a doubt, the easiest muesli we make.

½ cup honey
¼ cup brown sugar
¼ cup oil
1 tsp cinnamon
1 tsp vanilla
½ tsp salt
3 cups whole grain oats
½ cup oat or wheat bran
½ cup coconut
½ cup wheatgerm
½ cup chopped nuts

Mix the first six ingredients in a bowl. Heat on High (100%) power until mixture bubbles, about 2 minutes. Meantime, combine remaining ingredients in a large, wide, shallow microwave dish. Stir in the hot mixture. Cook on High, stirring every minute after 4 minutes, until mixture turns golden brown and starts to firm up, from 6-10 minutes. Cool. Break up if necessary. Store in airtight jars when cold.

Variations:
Heat syrup until it bubbles, in a pan on the stove. Combine with dry ingredients and bake in a roasting pan at 150°C, stirring frequently until it browns lightly, in about 30 minutes, or brown in a large shallow dish under a grill, turning frequently.

Add chopped dried fruit to the cooked muesli.

HOT CEREAL MIX

Although you may not be particularly excited by porridge or boiled rice, you may find that you really enjoy mixtures of flaked and/or kibbled cereals which are simmered together in a bowl in the microwave oven, or in a pot on the stove.

It is easy to cook a different combination every day if you keep different cereals in jars near your cooking area.

Use one or more level measuring tablespoon(s) of each, and keep a count of the total number of tablespoons used. If you are going to microwave your cereal, add twice as many tablespoons of water. For stovetop cooking allow three times as many tablespoons of water.

Four tablespoons (¼ cup) cereal will need 8 tablespoons (½ cup) water if microwaved, and 12 tablespoons (¾ cup) water if boiled. This should be about one serving. Add a pinch of salt per serving.

Microwave 1 serving for about 5 minutes, and a two-serving container for about 10 minutes, both on 50% power. Or simmer in a pot for about 15 minutes. Alter times and amounts of liquid if necessary.

Top with sesame sugar, brown sugar, maple syrup, etc., add toasted sunflower seeds if you like, and serve with plenty of milk, yoghurt, soya milk or fromage frais.

Suitable cereals include

- flaked barley, oats, wheat, rye and millet
- kibbled wheat, rye and burghul
- corn meal and oatmeal
- wheatgerm, oatbran and wheat bran

Sesame sugar:

Grind together in a pestle and mortar or in an electric grinder, more or less equal volumes of toasted sesame seeds and sugar, and a pinch of salt. Store in an airtight container.

MOCK MAPLE SYRUP

1 cup soft brown sugar
½ cup water
1 tsp vanilla

Boil sugar and water until sugar is dissolved. Cool and add vanilla. This keeps well in a covered jar or jug in the refrigerator. It thickens on cooling and can be warmed by standing in a container of hot water before use.

OATY PANCAKES

We tasted these for the first time years ago in California, in a cabin surrounded by very deep snow. They have been favourites with our family, ever since.

for 4 servings:

¾ cup milk
¾ cup rolled oats
½ cup flour
2 tsp baking powder
½ tsp salt
2-3 Tbsp sugar
1 egg
2 Tbsp melted butter

Pour the milk onto the uncooked rolled oats and leave to stand for 5 minutes. Meanwhile, sift the flour, baking powder and salt into a medium-sized bowl. Add the sugar and egg to the milk mixture and beat with a fork to mix. Melt the butter, and pour the oat-milk mixture and butter into the dry ingredients. Stir until mixed but not smooth. Add a little more milk if necessary to make a batter slightly thinner than pikelet batter.

Spoon or pour the mixture onto a lightly greased, moderately hot frying pan. Turn when bubbles appear and when the underside is golden brown. Spread with a little softened butter and stack two or three pancakes together. Serve with golden syrup, honey, maple syrup or Mock Maple Syrup.

Note:

For speed and ease, measure all ingredients, without sifting, into a food processor bowl, and process very briefly.

ORANGE MILK SHAKE

This 'instant' breakfast is fat-free. It is quick, and a good start to a hot day for those who feel they can't face a solid breakfast.

for 1 serving:

½ cup orange juice
2-4 Tbsp non-fat dried milk powder
1-2 iceblocks, optional

Shake the orange juice, milk powder and ice together in a screw-topped jar, or process in a food processor, and drink immediately. Alter the proportions of milk powder to suit yourself. A spoonful of vanilla instant pudding mix may be added to the other ingredients before mixing. The orange and vanilla flavours go well together.

Variation:

Add an egg to the ingredients above, and mix in a food processor, a blender, or with an egg beater.

TOFU-SHAKES

Here's a nutritious meal in a glass that is almost as quick to make as it is to drink!

FOR 2 MEDIUM SHAKES:
about 125 g tofu
1 banana
2 Tbsp brown sugar
1 cup orange juice or milk
½ tsp vanilla essence

Put the tofu and pieces of banana in a blender or food processor and process until well mixed.

Add the sugar, orange juice or milk and vanilla. Process again until the mixture is smooth and creamy.

Pour into one very large, or two medium-sized glasses. Serve with thick straws and/or long handled spoons.

SUPER MUESLI BARS

This is not really a breakfast recipe, but it did not fit in anywhere else, and it is much too good to leave out. These bars are solid-packed with goodies. Their texture, chewy or firm, depends on the stage at which you cook the toffee-like mixture into which you stir the solids.

FOR 20 BARS (2x2x10 CM)
50 g butter or ¼ cup oil
½ cup honey
¼ cup peanut butter
1 cup rolled oats, toasted
½ cup wheatgerm, toasted
½ cup roasted sesame seeds
½ cup roasted sunflower seeds
¼ cup dried apricots, chopped, (optional)

Measure the butter or oil, the honey and peanut butter into a large frying pan. Bring to the boil, stirring to blend the ingredients, then turn the heat to very low, and lightly toast the rolled oats, then the wheatgerm, about 10 cm from a grill, stirring frequently, and watching carefully so neither burns. Mix these in a bowl with the previously roasted sesame seeds and sunflower seeds (*see page 35*). Chop the dried apricots finely, in a food processor if available, and mix with the other dry ingredients.

Cook the honey mixture gently until it forms a firm ball when a little is dropped into cold water and left for about 1 minute, then stir in the dry ingredients thoroughly. Press into a lightly buttered or oiled 20 cm square, loose-bottomed pan, and leave to cool until it is firm but still flexible. This is the time to turn it out and cut, with a serrated knife, into two pieces, then cut each piece into 10 fingers. Wrap individually in cling wrap, or store in a completely airtight container.

Oaty Pankcakes

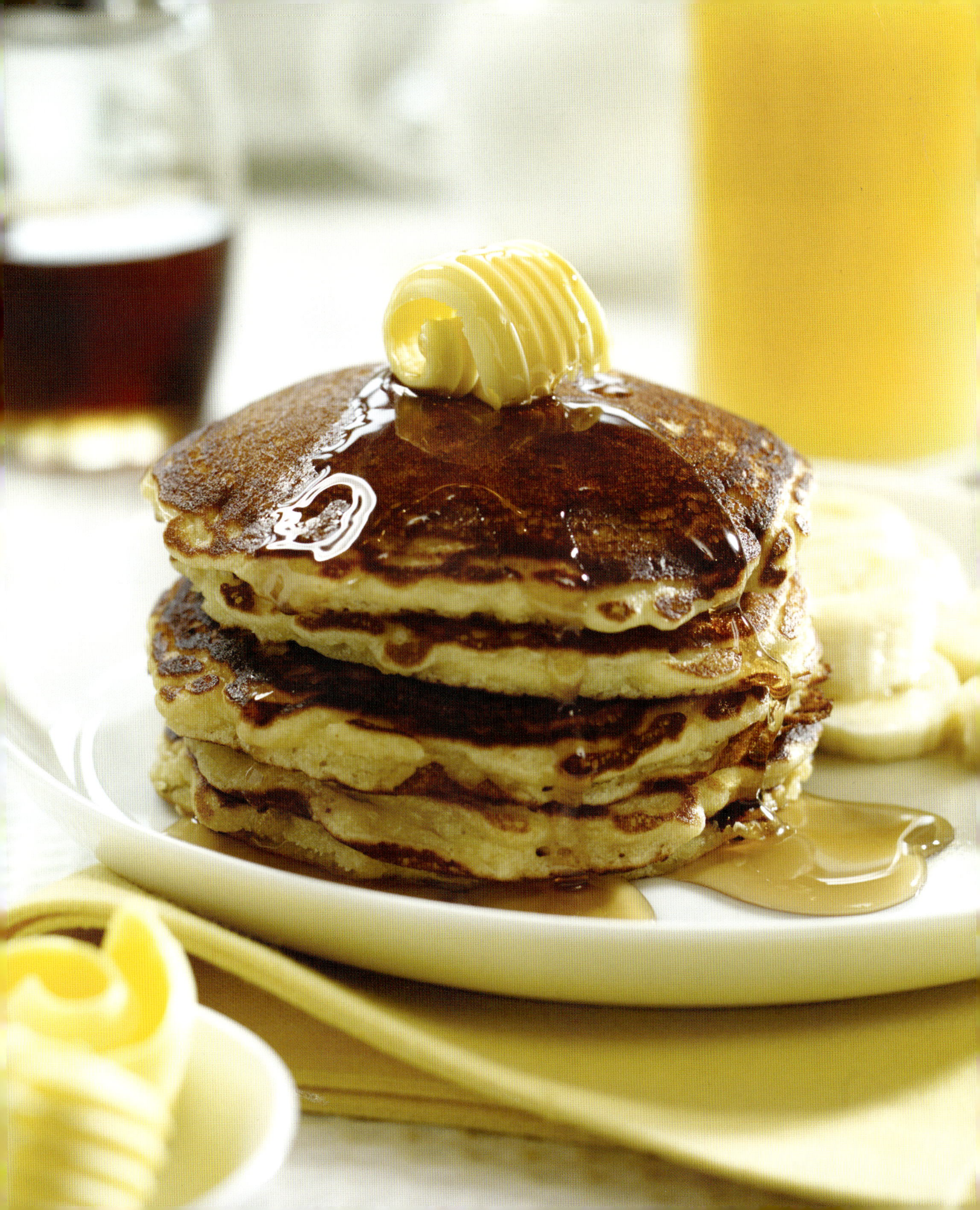

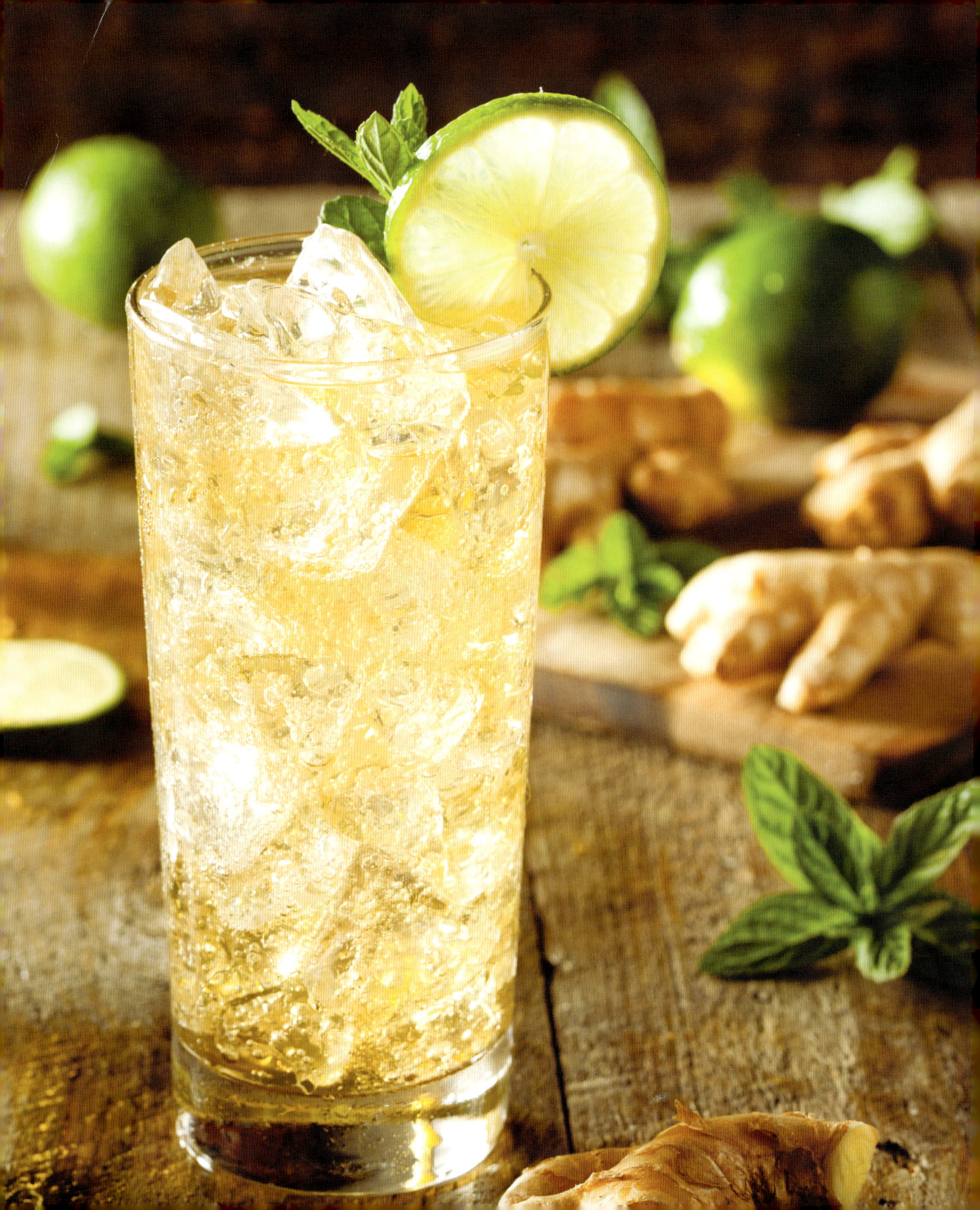

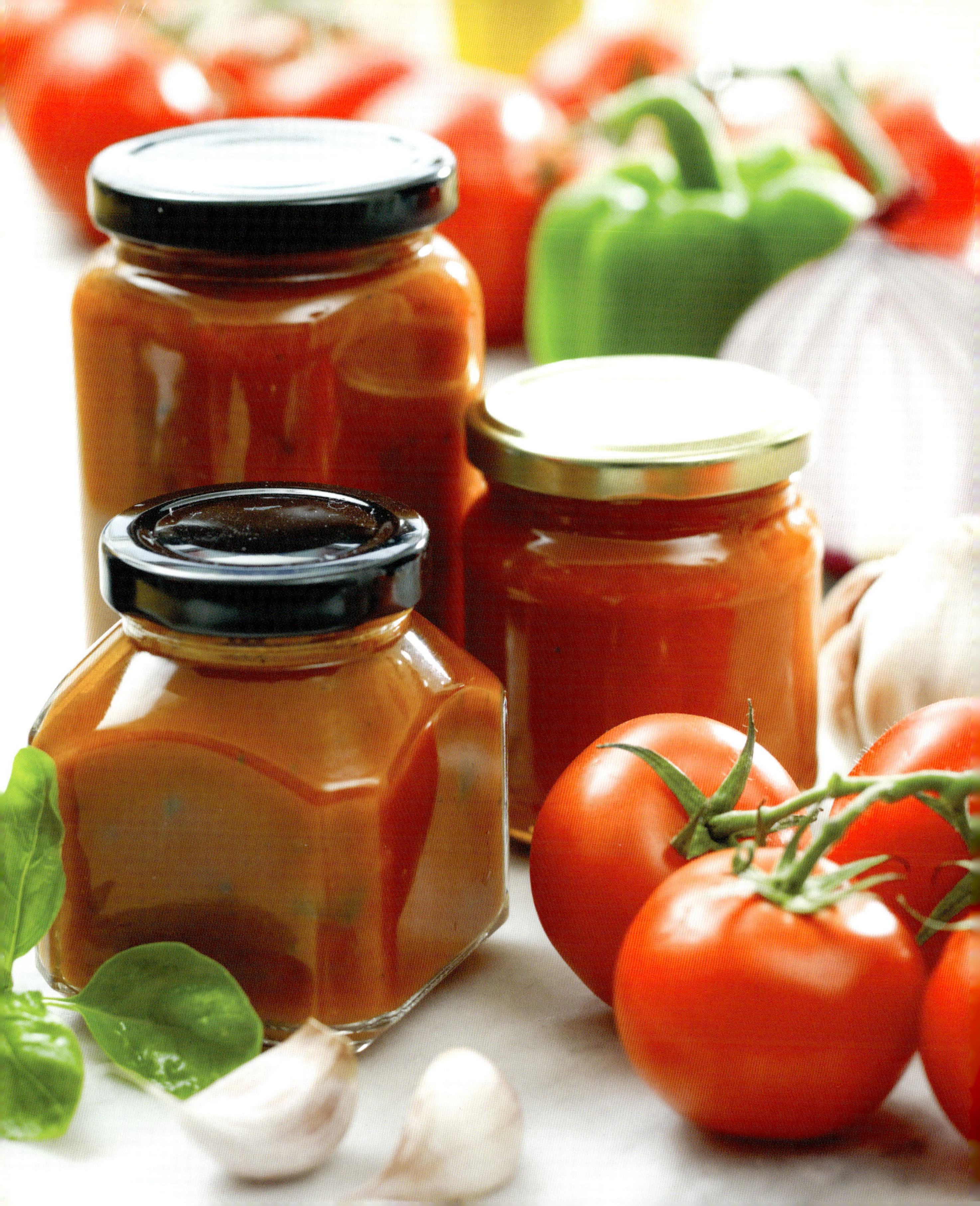

Combine the sugars, malt, and salts with 2 litres of boiling water. Strain into a 10-20 litre plastic container, then add 4 more litres of boiling water.

Simmer the hops in 5 litres of water for 30 minutes, then strain the liquid into the plastic container, too. Leave to cool to 30°C.

Mix the yeast with a cup of blood-temperature water and 2 teaspoons sugar, and leave to start working while the hot liquid cools.

Add the bubbling yeast mixture to the 30°C brew, cover the container loosely or fit with a water lock, and leave to ferment at a warm room temperature for about 10-14 days (longer in colder weather).

If desired, add finings, following the manufacturers' instructions. We don't usually bother and find that the beer is usually quite clear anyway.

While the beer ferments, organise your bottles (screw-top plastic soft-drink bottles are fine). Wash thoroughly, then dip into a mixture of 1 tablespoon of sodium metabisulphate dissolved in 10 litres of water, and leave to drain. If you are working in advance, cover the openings with lids or pieces of foil.

When the beer is clear, siphon off the clear liquid into a clean container. Pour 1 cupful into each 750 ml bottle, and a proportionate amount into bottles of other sizes, add ½ teaspoon sugar to each bottle, then nearly fill the bottles with cold water. Top with crown tops, or screw on the tops of the plastic bottles.

Leave for about 2 weeks before drinking. You can judge when the beer in plastic bottles is bubbly by squeezing. They are hard when ready. Refrigerate bottles before opening, taking care not to disturb any sediment in the bottom. When pouring, it is a good idea to decant the beer from the bottle into a glass jug, and to fill glasses from this.

For best results, drink your beer 1-3 months after making it.

GINGER BEER

What we like best about home-made ginger beer is that it has such a good flavour—quite unlike anything bought. The element of chance, as each batch will differ slightly, and the satisfaction from the savings made on each bottle, add to the enjoyment.

FOR 4x1.25 LITRE BOTTLES:

1 tsp dried yeast granules
2 tsp sugar
½ cup warm water
2 cups sugar
1 Tbsp ground ginger
1 tsp lemon essence
1 tsp tartaric acid
2 litres hot water
2 litres cold water

Stir the first three ingredients together in a glass and leave to stand in a warm place.

Measure the remaining sugar, ginger, lemon essence and tartaric acid into a clean bucket. Pour on the hot water and stir to dissolve the sugar. Add the cold water to cool the liquid down.

When you are sure the lemon syrup is no hotter than lukewarm, add the bubbling yeast. Leave in the lightly covered bucket for 24-36 hours, then strain into four thoroughly clean 1.25 litre plastic soft-drink bottles. Fill each bottle up to within 3 cm of the top with extra cold water. Put 1 teaspoon of sugar in each bottle, and screw on the washed tops. Shake to dissolve sugar.

Leave to stand in a warm place until the bottles feel absolutely rigid when you squeeze them. This should take from 1-5 days, depending on the temperature, type of yeast, etc.

Refrigerate bottles for at least 2 hours before removing the lids. If the bottles are very fizzy, loosen then tighten the lids several times, so that the gas is released slowly.

Plan to drink all of the brew within 3-4 weeks.

SOYA MILK

It is not difficult to make an inexpensive and nutritious 'milk' from soya beans. One cup of dried beans yields six cups of liquid which may be used for drinking 'straight', making flavoured cold drinks, hot chocolate drinks, in baking, and even for milk puddings.

The flavour is not the same as cows' milk, but it is acceptable to many people, and it is a great help to those who cannot drink, do not want to drink, or cannot afford cows' milk.

(Soya milk needs added calcium and vitamin B12 to give it a nutritive value similar to that of cows' milk. See the note at the end of the recipe.)

Follow the instructions exactly, since the milk will have a strong flavour if boiling water is not used during the grinding.

FOR ABOUT 6 CUPS:
1 cup dried soya beans
4 cups warm water
7 cups boiling water
flavourings:
2-3 Tbsp honey, malt or brown sugar
1 tsp vanilla
about ½ tsp salt

Pour the lukewarm water over the soya beans and leave to stand for 2-4 hours, or until the beans have softened right through. Change the water, and rub the beans to halve them, if you are in a hurry. Leave the beans to soak for longer, if this suits you.

When you are ready to grind the beans, drain them and pour 1 cup boiling water over them. Rinse out a food processor with hot water, then discard the bean water and the rinsing water.

Put half the drained beans in the food processor. Process to chop finely then add 2 cups boiling water and process until very finely chopped. Pour mixture into a large sieve lined with a clean cloth, over a large bowl. Repeat this with the remaining beans.

Tip the beans from the cloth back into the processor, process again, to chop as finely as possible, then add the remaining 2 cups of boiling water, and process about a minute longer. Pour into the cloth-lined sieve. Squeeze and twist the bag to get out as much liquid as possible, then heat all the strained liquid, in a microwave oven until liquid boils, or in a covered bowl over boiling water for 30 minutes. Remove from heat.

Add extra boiling water to make up to 6 cups, if necessary, then stir in flavourings, varying quantities to taste. Store in a covered container in the refrigerator for up to 4 days.

To fortify soya milk so that it is about the same composition as cows' milk, add to the warm liquid above, at the same time as the flavourings:

2 Tbsp oil
1 Tbsp (about 2 g) powdered calcium carbonate
1 (25 microgram) tablet Vitamin B12, crushed

Get the powdered calcium carbonate and vitamin B12 from a chemist. Shake the bottle of soya milk before using it.

HOME-BREWED BEER

Home brewing is fun, and can save you a considerable amount of money. The most important, and unfortunately most time-consuming aspect of successful beer making is hygiene, but with a little care the rewards are great! Always clean and rinse your brewing equipment and bottles before and after use, and you should have few problems.

TO MAKE ABOUT 40x750 ML BOTTLES:
1 kg white sugar
1 kg soft brown sugar
about 1.5 kg light malt extract
1 tsp Epsom salts
1 tsp common salt
150 g dried hops
1 (about 5 g) pkt Lager beer yeast or 2 tsp DYC granulated yeast
2 tsp extra sugar
brewers finings (optional)
sodium metabisulphate to clean bottles

DRINKS

TOMATOES

Tomatoes are called for in many recipes because of their flavour, colour and acidity. If you grow, or have access to a good supply of ripe red tomatoes, you may want to preserve some of them to use during the winter. Look in other books if you want to preserve large amounts of tomatoes in bulk. Try these recipes if you want to put aside a few kilograms at a time.

There are plenty of good ready-prepared tomato products around, and we use many of them, finding the following products especially useful.

- tomato juice
- tomato purée
- tomato paste (concentrate)
- whole peeled tomatoes in juice
- diced tomatoes
- savoury tomatoes

(s

For the following recipies you will need carefully prepared, completely clean jars. Thoroughly wash, then bring to the boil in a large pot, covered with water, the preserving jars or empty jars with metal screw tops which you will use. Boil gently for at least 5 minutes, with the preserving seals, or the screw-topped metal lids (with composition inserts).

The lids should be concave when the jars are cold. If any gas forms during storage, or if any off-flavours or odours develop, do not taste or eat the contents.

Any of the bottled recipes may be frozen in plastic bags or covered containers, if preferred.

'OVERFLOW' BOTTLED TOMATOES

Quarter or cube firm, ripe, red tomatoes, cutting off the white core at the stem end, and squeezing and shaking the tomatoes to remove extra juice and seeds. When you feel you have enough to fill the jar(s), bring to the boil, stirring often, pressing the tomatoes until liquid forms.
Add about ¼ teaspoon of salt and sugar and 1 tablespoon lemon juice for each cupful.

When the tomato mixture has been boiling fast for 3-4 minutes, spoon or ladle the very hot tomato pieces into the hot jar which has been removed from the pot in which it boiled. Work fast, and make sure that there are no pockets of air in the jars. Fill to the top of the jar, wipe around the rim with a clean paper towel, and top with the hot seal then screw on the band, or top with the cleaned metal lid, screwing it on tightly.

PRETTY PICKLE

This pickle is easy to make and turns the plainest snack into something special. Try it with bread and cheese, or in a baked potato. It makes a nice gift, too.

8 cups diced cucumber
¼ cup plain salt
4 onions, diced
2-3 red peppers, diced
1-2 green or gold peppers, diced
1 cup drained whole-kernel corn
3 cups sugar
1 tsp celery seed
1 tsp mustard seed
2 cups wine vinegar
3-3 Tbsp cornflour

Use long, thin-skinned cucumbers. Halve lengthwise then scoop out central, seedy part using a teaspoon. Without removing peel (unless it is very tough) cut cucumber flesh into small, evenly shaped cubes. Measure cucumber into a glass or plastic container. Sprinkle with salt and leave to stand for 30 minutes, stirring several times. Drain and rinse, discarding liquid. Put cucumber, onion, peppers, corn, sugar, seeds and vinegar in a large saucepan. Bring to the boil, stirring constantly. Mix cornflour with a little extra vinegar and stir into cucumber mixture.

Ladle into bottles with metal screw-topped lids, prepared as for tomatoes. Seal immediately.

THICK TOMATO SAVOURY

Prepare tomato purée as above using tomatoes only, and boil down to about half its original volume. Measure it and put it aside.

For two cups of purée, cut in small cubes 1 medium-sized onion, 1 red pepper, and 1 green pepper. Sauté these in 2 tablespoons oil (not butter) without

MEALS WITHOUT MEAT

browning, until onion is transparent, then add the tomato purée, ½ teaspoon each of dried basil, oreganum, and mustard seed and ¼ teaspoon celery seed. Cook over moderate heat for 5-10 minutes, until thick enough to spread on pizza, etc., add salt to taste, then spoon into small jars with metal screw tops heated as above. Fill jars to overflowing and seal as above.

DEHYDRATED TOMATOES

The easiest way to preserve tomatoes is to dry slices or 1 cm cubes, using a dehydrator. Spread the prepared tomatoes on the dehydrator trays and dry according to the instructions until they are crisp. Store in screw-topped jars, or chop to powder in the food processor, alone or mixed with dehydrated chopped peppers, onions and herbs, to use for salad and pizza toppings.

Use dried tomato cubes and slices as snacks (they are remarkably sweet) or add them to simmered mixtures, or microwave or simmer them with water, for 5-15 minutes.

TOMATO LEATHER

Make tomato purée as above, and pour it onto the solid dehydrator trays to make tomato leather. When you want it, rip pieces off the discs of dried tomato and reconstitute to instant juice, purée or paste in a food processor according to the amount of hot water you add. The discs of tomato leather may well all get eaten dry, as snacks! They are very light to carry, if tramping.

You can also make tomato leather from food-processed uncooked tomatoes, if you like.

TOMATO PURÉE AND PASTE

Chop ripe tomatoes into a microwave dish or saucepan. Add some finely chopped onion and red pepper, and fresh or dried oreganum and basil if you like. Microwave on High (100%) power, or boil until everything is soft, then push through a coarse sieve, discarding seeds and skin, etc.

Microwave or cook uncovered until boiled down to half or less of its original volume. Stir occasionally in the microwave oven, and stir frequently on the stovetop, until mixture is as thick as you want it. Season with salt and sugar to taste at this stage. Spoon into smaller jars which have been cleaned and boiled as above, and seal as above.

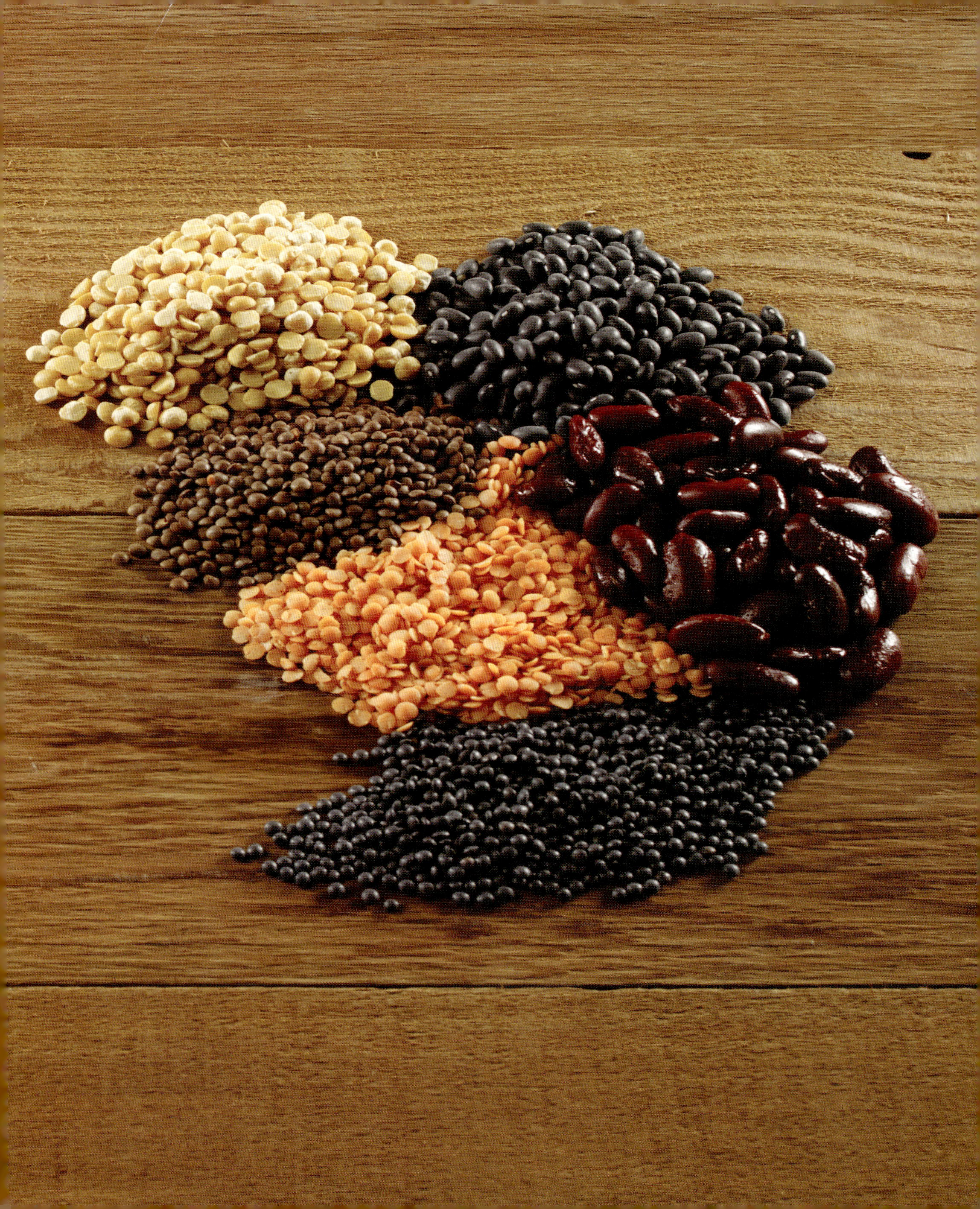

BEAN BASICS

The shapes and colours of dried pulses are so attractive that they are often stored in clear jars for decorative purposes, as well as for convenience. The term pulse covers peas, beans, and lentils, all of which are important foods in a vegetarian diet because of their high protein content, especially when they are eaten with other vegetable protein foods (see page 176).

As well as being a good source of cheap protein, dried beans, peas, and lentils are important for their high fibre content. It is also interesting to note that beans have a much lower fat content than other protein-rich foods.

We are lucky, these days, to have such a variety of pulses to choose from. Make a point of looking at the different pulses on display in bulk bins at a large supermarket. Resist the temptation to buy huge quantities to fill large jars with a dozen different sorts, but try small quantities of a few different beans, to use, one after another, until you find your own favourites. It is best to buy enough pulses to last you for only a couple of months, because pulses do deteriorate on long storage, although they look as though they are everlasting. Beans continue to dry out with age, and beans which are several seasons old will require much longer cooking times than beans from a recent harvest.

You may sometimes see colourful bean mixtures for sale. Although they look pretty, they are unlikely to have been selected because they have identical cooking times. If you are cooking them for soup you will not mind the fact that some of them cook more quickly than others, and turn to mush, but this will not suit you for most other bean mixtures, where it is better to cook each variety separately.

If you have not cooked dried pulses before, we suggest you start with brown lentils, cook Lentil and Tomato Sauce, (*see page 62*), then try sprouting some of them following the instructions on page 175. Next, make Hummus, (*see page 29*) using black-eyed beans, then cook kidney beans for Vegetarian Shepherd's Pie (*see page 44*).

If you become a bean enthusiast, invest in a pressure cooker! As you will see from the cooking times given on *page 175*, pressure cookers revolutionise bean cooking. With a pressure cooker you can use the valuable soya bean regularly. This cooks, without prior soaking, in 45 minutes, in a pressure cooker. It is the cheapest bean, and has the greatest food value, but is often ignored because it takes hours to cook really soft, using conventional methods.

1. PEA FLOUR:
Made by grinding peas (or beans), sometimes called channa or gram flour. We noticed no differences using flour ground from chickpeas or other dried peas. Pea flour mixed with water and flavourings makes a good batter without eggs.

2. SPLIT RED LENTILS:
Small halved lentils with their outer skin removed. Cook quickly (in about the same time as white rice) to a lighter beige-orange colour with a slightly mealy texture. Often used in soups or dahls.

3. HARICOT BEANS:
Smallish, white oval beans (referred to as Navy beans in the USA). A good all-purpose bean, used in many traditional recipes from England, France and the USA. Probably most commonly seen as the 'baked bean'.

4. GREEN SPLIT PEAS:
Skinned, halved bright green peas. Mushy when cooked, commonly used in soups and purées.

5. BLACK-EYED BEANS:
(Black-eyed peas, cow peas.) Attractive, creamy rounded beans with a distinctive black 'eye' or spot. Greatest advantage is a short cooking time without soaking. Pleasant, slightly smoky favour. Use in place of any bean if pressed for time.

6. PINTO BEANS:
Attractive beige-pink and red-brown speckled medium-sized beans. Used in much the same way as red kidney beans; pretty in salads or casseroles.

7. YELLOW SPLIT PEAS:
Halved, skinned peas. Similar in flavour and texture to green split peas.

8. ADZUKI (ADUKI) BEANS:
Small, rounded dark red beans. Often sweetened in Asian recipes. We have not found these beans to cook as quickly as is sometimes claimed.

9. WHITE LIMA BEANS:
(Butter beans in southern USA.) Large, flat white beans. Require soaking and gentle cooking to prevent breaking up. Sweet flavour, make a wonderful creamy purée.

10. RED KIDNEY BEANS:
Attractive dark red colour, raw and cooked. Cook to a nice mealy texture, good in salads, casseroles, Mexican bean recipes. Never eat these beans raw, they must be boiled rapidly for 10-15 minutes during their cooking to break down a potentially dangerous component. Available canned.

11. MUNG BEANS:
Small, roundish dark olive beans. Quick cooking without soaking but usually sprouted (most bought bean sprouts are mung beans).

12. BROWN LENTILS:
(Green lentils, continental lentils.) Whole lentils with skin. May vary in size and colour (light green to pale red-brown). Very useful as they cook quickly, retaining their shape without soaking. Good in casseroles, salads, spaghetti sauces, lasagne etc. Also good sprouted. After sprouting cook in 2-3 minutes.

13. BABY (GREEN) LIMA BEANS:
Small, pale green cousin of the white lima. Don't cook fast and tend to lose their nice green colour, but have a pleasant flavour and nice shape.

14. BLACK BEANS:
Several shapes and sizes of medium to large black beans are available (black beans, turtle beans, tiger beans, black haricots, etc.) but all seem interchangeable. Shiny and attractive when cooked, some have a smoky flavour.

15. SOYA FLOUR:
Not the same as pea flour, but made from ground soya beans. Used to boost the protein content of other mixtures, it has a distinctive, slightly bitter soya bean flavour.

16. SOYA BEANS:
Smallish, rounded whitish beans. Very high in protein but require very long cooking to soften completely, and have a distinctive 'beany' flavour that bothers some people. Their high protein content is utilised in many other soya products, e.g., soya flour, soya bean sprouts, soya milk, tofu, tempeh, etc. An enormously important crop globally, also used for edbile oil production.

17. MOONG DAHL:
Mung beans with their outer coat removed. Cook quickly without soaking; good for dahls, curries and soups.

18. MERINO BEANS:
Locally produced, these beans have an interesting piebald appearance. Have a rather coarse texture and cook fairly slowly.

19. CHICKPEAS:
(Garbanzos, Garbanzo beans.) Easily recognised by their distinctive pea shape and their protruding shoot; usually beige (but sometimes brown); cooking times seem to vary considerably. Lovely nutty flavour—traditionally used in hummus, casseroles and falafel.

SOAKING BEANS

Some types of beans and lentils may be cooked without pre-soaking (see list and table below), however, thicker-skinned beans cook faster if soaked prior to cooking.

There are two soaking methods:
1. The long soak method: Cover beans with about four times their volume of cold water and leave to stand for 8 hours or longer, in refrigerator if longer.
2. The rapid soak method: Cover beans with about four times their volume of boiling water, or bring to boil and boil for 2 minutes, then leave to stand for 1-2 hours before cooking.

COOKING BEANS

We usually pour off and discard the soaking liquid. This removes soluble impurities and some of the substances thought to cause flatulence. Replace with about the same quantity of fresh water. Bring to boil, add a tablespoon of oil to prevent excess frothing, and simmer with the lid ajar to prevent boiling over. You can flavour beans with garlic, onion, and herbs during cooking, but you must not add salt, sugar, lemon juice or tomato products until the beans are completely tender, since these toughen the beans. Beans are cooked when they are tender enough to squash with your tongue.

Important:

Beans which are undercooked will put you off recipes which are excellent if made with properly cooked beans. Nearly cooked beans are not good enough!

Approximate cooking times for the types of beans we use most frequently are given in the table. Use these as a guide only, since times vary with the age and quality of the beans. Add about ½ teaspoon of salt to 1 cup of dried beans, after cooking. Liquid drained from beans after cooking makes good stock for soups and sauces. Refrigerate up to 3-4 days.

Type of bean	soak	cook (min.)
moong dahl	no	20-30
red lentils	no	25-35
brown lentils	no	40-50
black-eyed beans	no	30-45
split peas	no	40-60
mung beans	no	40-50
lima beans	yes	45-90
pinto beans	yes	60-90
adzuki beans	yes	60-120
red kidney beans*	yes	60-90
haricot beans	yes	75-90
merino beans	yes	90-120
chickpeas	yes	90-150
soya beans	yes	120-180

*Need 15 minutes of rapid boiling during cooking. If preferred, pre-soak first six varieties and reduce cooking time.

In a hurry?

You can:
- Change bean varieties to use a quick- cooking variety which needs no soaking, e.g., black-eyed beans or brown lentils
- Use canned beans (this may also mean changing varieties)
- Soak and cook beans in bulk, in advance, then freeze them ready for use
- Use a pressure cooker
- Cook beans without soaking, remembering cooking times will be considerably longer.

The resulting recipe may differ from the original recipe, but it will usually be good, nonetheless.

Pressure-cooking beans:

Pressure cooking dramatically decreases the cooking times of dried beans. The times we recorded with a modern (German) pressure cooker were spectacular.

- *Unsoaked black-eyed beans* cooked in 15 minutes.
- *Black-eyed beans*, rapid-soaked for 1 hour, cooked in 5 minutes.
- *Unsoaked kidney beans* cooked in 35 minutes.
- *Pinto beans, merino beans* and garbanzos rapid-soaked for an hour cooked in 15 minutes to the texture of canned beans.
- *Unsoaked soya beans* cooked to very soft in 45 minutes.

It is obviously worth investing in an efficient pressure cooker if you eat beans often and want to speed up their cooking times. (A borrowed 25-year-old pressure cooker made considerable time savings, although all times were 5-10 minutes longer than those given above.)

For best results you should follow the manufacturer's instructions. If these are not available, use the following as a guide.

- Use 4 cups of water to 1 cup dried beans.
- Do not fill the cooker more than half full, since beans froth as they cook.
- Add 1 tablespoon of oil to lessen frothing.
- Let the pressure fall over 2-3 minutes.
- Cook beans without seasonings, as suggested under cooking instructions here.

Microwaving beans:
Soaked beans may be drained, generously covered with boiling water, then cooked at a low power level (30-50% power) with a lid on. Cooking times are not much shorter, and may vary, but this method may suit you, as the microwave oven turns itself off. Unsoaked beans or soaked beans cooked on high power levels can burn if they cook dry. A microwave oven is good for reheating cooked beans.

Yields and costs:
- 1 cup dried beans yields 2-3 cups drained cooked beans.
- 1 can (about 440 g) cooked beans contains about 1½ cups drained beans.
- Canned beans save a lot of time but cost 3-4 times as much as home-cooked beans.

SPROUTING BEANS

Beans and lentils will sprout and grow easily and quickly in a warm kitchen. They grow fastest in summer, protected from light.

Mung beans:
Mung beans are most usually sprouted. Put 2 Tbsp mung beans in a large coffee jar, half fill with cold tap water, and leave for 8-12 hours. Cover jar with coarse muslin or net, and hold in place with a rubber band. Pour off all the water, surround jar with a darkish paper collar to keep out some light, and keep it in a warm and visible place. Two or three times a day, pour cold water through the cloth top, then tip away all water immediately. Eat sprouted beans at any time, preferably after shoots are 2-3 cm long, and leaves are starting to grow. To stop growth, refrigerate.

Brown lentils:
Quarter fill a large coffee jar with brown lentils. Fill jar with water, leave for 24 hours, then drain and proceed as above. Shoots will be very small, compared with mung bean shoots. Lentils will be tender enough to eat raw, or will cook in 3-4 minutes, any time after 12 hours.

EATING FOR HEALTH & HAPPINESS

As well as tasting and looking good, the food you eat should be good for you.

You want to enjoy food which will make you healthy and strong, and keep you in peak condition.

You need to eat a good variety of foods, so that the nutrients that one particular food lacks are supplied by another. Including a wide variety of foods in your diet helps to make it interesting, too.

You do not need to know the composition of everything you eat, but it helps to have an idea of the foods, and the food groups from which you choose your daily meals.

If you are eating no meat, poultry or fish, you can divide your food into four groups:

- Cereals (grains, bread and pasta)
- Legumes (peas, beans and lentils), nuts, and seeds
- Fruit and vegetables
- Milk, milk products and eggs

Make sure that you eat some foods from each of these groups each day.

The foods we eat provide us with:
- Protein
- Carbohydrates
- Fat
- Fibre
- Vitamins and minerals

Protein
The proteins in our bodies are made up of amino acids. Some of these amino acids cannot be made by our bodies, so they must be supplied by the food we eat. These particular amino acids are called essential amino acids. Animal proteins contain the essential amino acids we need, so people who eat little or no animal protein need to eat combinations of different vegetable proteins to make sure they get all the essential amino acids.

If you eat meat, fish or poultry regularly, you do not need to consider these combinations of protein, or complementary proteins.

If you eat, say, an egg, a cup of milk or yoghurt, and some cheese each day, along with a variety of other foods, you need not be concerned with your protein requirements.

If you eat few or no eggs, and little or no milk or dairy foods, you should know about complementary proteins, and make sure you combine foods from any two of these five groups at one meal.

- Whole grains, e.g. wholegrain bread, brown rice, rolled oats
- Legumes, e.g. dried beans, lentils, dried peas
- Nuts and seeds, e.g almonds, walnuts, sunflower seeds, sesame seeds, peanuts
- Soybean products, e.g. soybeans, tofu, soya milk, miso, soybean flour
- Eggs and milk products, e.g. milk, yoghurt, cottage cheese

These combinations do not have to be complicated or difficult, and are often foods that seem right together, for example:

- muesli and milk or soya milk
- peanut butter sandwich
- macaroni cheese
- baked beans on toast
- toasted cheese sandwich
- pea soup and a bread roll

Carbohydrates

These include refined sugars, which are high in energy and low in fibre, and unrefined cereals, which are high in fibre and nutrients, and lower in energy. Unrefined cereals are important in a vegetarian diet.

Fat

In a vegetarian diet fat comes from oil, butter, and dairy foods. It is important to have some, but not too much. Watch that you do not use too much in cooking, dressings, etc. Be aware of the low-fat dairy products available.

Fibre

This is found in plant foods. There is usually enough in vegetarian diets.

Vitamins

If you are eating a good variety of foods from the food groups above, you should not need vitamin pills. Dietitian friends remind us that:

- Young children should not be given a diet which is too high in fibre, and should be given eggs, milk, and milk products in their diets.
- Calcium and Vitamin B 12 should be added to a vegan diet—e.g. as fortified soya milk. These nutrients are especially important for children and pregnant women.
- Women need to be especially aware that they need foods which contain iron. Egg yolk, dark green vegetables, dried fruit, cocoa, dried pulses and whole grains all contain some iron. Vitamin C helps iron to be absorbed, so this is another good reason to include fruit, fruit juice or vegetables with each meal.

CONVENIENCE FOODS

We all have times when we feel that we have worked so hard all day, and are so tired, that we simply cannot face cooking an evening meal. Apart from fasting, there are three options.

You can go out to eat. You need the energy to get there, the time to wait for the food to come, and the money to pay for it. Few of us can afford to go to our favourite restaurants too often, so, at times like this, we settle for lower priced eating places where the food is not memorable, to say the least.

You can buy takeaways. These are seldom as 'instant' as you think they are. Add up the time it takes you to get to the outlet, wait in a queue for your order to be taken, then the time it takes until you walk out the door with your meal.

Work out how much it costs you to eat out, or buy takeaways. You may find that your best value for this money is to buy some luxury food items which you can eat with little or no preparation, and which you do not buy when you do your regular shopping because you think they are too expensive.

Here are some of the foods that we buy in situations like this. Make a list of your own favourites, so you can spoil yourself, and enjoy a treat, in a park, beside a river or beach, or while you watch your favourite television programme or a video.

- A perfectly ripe avocado, a lemon to squeeze over it, and your favourite bread.
- A wedge of your favourite cheese, with bread or good crackers, and fresh fruit like cherries, or a punnet of strawberries.
- A bunch of asparagus, at the start of the asparagus season, and some soft cheese.
- A jar of really good vacuum-packed nuts, and grapes or peaches, apricots or nectarines.
- Add juice, sparkling juice, beer, or wine, and you have a luxury meal which requires almost no work, and which will probably be faster and cheaper than the first two options.

There are a number of convenience items that we have found worth buying, so that we can put together minimum- fuss meals in a short time. Again, some of these items are expensive in terms of your groceries, but are cheaper than eating food which other people have cooked.

Here are some of the semi-prepared foods we buy at times, and try to keep hidden for use when our time is more valuable than the extra money spent, or when friends arrive unexpectedly. You might like to make a cache of some of these items.

- good, ready-made spaghetti sauce
- fresh pasta (to freeze)
- at least one type of regular pasta
- Longalife vegetarian frankfurters, and other vegetarian sausages (these have a long refrigerator life)
- packs of pre-grated cheese
- green and black olives
- dill pickles
- popping corn
- uncooked tortillas (to freeze)
- good crackers
- canned beans, in brine, and in sauces
- vacuum-packed nuts
- long-life tofu
- tahini
- parmesan cheese
- canned tomato products
- canned asparagus
- frozen pita bread (which can also be used as instant pizza bases)
- dried herbs and spices (a good selection)
- Kikkoman (thick) teriyaki baste and glaze
- Kikkoman sweet and sour sauce
- canned corn
- nut butters
- olive oil
- maple syrup
- canned or bottled peppers
- capers
- hot pepper sauce
- sliced wholegrain bread (frozen)
- juices and juice concentrates
- your favourite specialty teas
- your favourite hot specialty drinks
- little pots of dairy and double cream
- sour cream and cream cheese
- hot horseradish
- Dijon mustard
- Basmati rice
- dried yeast granules (refrigerated)
- pine nuts
- lemons
- corn chips
- your favourite canned fruit
- ice-cream
- frozen stir-fried vegetables

INDEX

Adzuki beans	174
African beans	41
Alphabet soup	17
Apple and walnut cake	151
crêpes	78
crumble	156
pie	156
Artichokes	120
marinated	121
Asparagus	120
crêpes	78
egg and cheese casserole	99
roulade	99
soup	21
Aubergine casserole	79
dip	28
barbecued	124
grilled	124
Aubergines	121
Avocado dip	26
Avocados	120
Baked beans, home-style	40
Baked potatoes	52
Banana bread	148
Barbecue bread	24
Barbecued aubergine	124
corn	127
Barbecuing vegetables	123
Barley, flaked	111
pearl	111
Basic bread rolls	146
pilaf	115
Basmati rice	111
Bean and cheese casserole	45
burgers	84
cooking table	176
feast	46
salad	125
salad, cumin	125
salad, sweet-sour	124
sprouts	177
stroganoff	45
yields	176
Beans à la Grecque	124
adzuki	174
African	41

baby (green) lima	175
black	175
black chilli	41
black-eyed	176
broad	120
cooking	175
curried	45
Garbanzo	175
green	120
haricot	174
home-style, baked	40
lima	175
merino	175
Mexican	42
microwaving	177
mung	175
navy	174
pinto	174
pressure-cooking	176
red kidney	175
red with rice	46
refried	41
soaking	175
soya	175
sprouting	177
Beer, ginger	167
home-brewed	107
Beetroot	120
shredded	125
Black bean and rice soup	20
bean chilli	40
beans	174
rice	110
-eyed beans	174
Blanching	123
Blue cheese and mushroom	
packages	89
cheese ball	28
cheese dip	28
Boiled fruit loaf	150
Braised celery	127
red cabbage	125
Braising vegetables	123
Bread, barbecue	24
brown	144
brown banana	148
pita	147
pocket	147
quick bran	149

quick yeast	146
rolls, basic	47
steamed	149
Broccoli	120
Brown banana bread	148
bread	144
lentil burgers	85
lentils	174
onion soup	14
rice	111
rice and lentil loaf	114
Brussels sprouts	120
Buckwheat	111
Bulgar	110
and bean chilli con carne	49
Burgers, bean	84
brown lentil	85
mushroom	85
tofu	84
Burghul	110
Cabbage, Joanna's	126
Cabbages	120
Cake, apple and walnut	151
coffee	150
wholemeal carrot	153
zucchini chocolate	131
Camembert, crumbed	32
Cannelloni	64
Capsicum	112
Carrot and apple salad	126
and mushroom loaf	72
cake	153
soup	14
Carrots	120
Casserole, asparagus egg and	
cheese	99
bean and cheese	45
eggplant	79
potato and egg	53
Cauliflower	120
Celery	**120**
and apple salad	127
braised	127
hot mix	160
Cereals	110
Cheddar cheese fondue	101
Cheese and mushroom quiche	67
and onion soup	13
and pumpkin balls	76

180 MEALS WITHOUT MEAT

muffins	142
sauce	136
soufflé	100
spread	31
strata	100
potted	33
Cheesy potato bake	54
Chickpeas	175
Chilled tomato soup	18
Chilli bean crepes	78
con carne	49
black bean	40
Chokos	121
Chunky vegetable and tomato	
sauce on pasta	61
Coffee cake	150
Coleslaw	126
Confetti salad	130
Cooking beans	175
rice	112
Courgettes	122
Corn	121
and pea patties	41
dahl soup	22
fritters	73
meal	110
muffins	142
barbecued	122
microwave	127
Cottage cheese omelet	98
Cream of lentil soup	20
Creamy lentil and vegetable soup	15
Crêpes	**78**
apple	78
asparagus	78
chilli bean	78
mushroom	78
Oriental	78
savoury	78
spinach and cheese	79
vegetable	78
Croutons	127
Crudités	31
Crumbed camembert	32
Cucumber	121
Cumin bean salad	125
dressing	137
Curried cashew and	
carrot soup	14

kumara soup	16
rice and tomato casserole	115
Curry, lentil and vegetable	47
Dahl	48
moong	175
Deep-frying vegetables	123
Dehydrated tomatoes	171
Dip, aubergine	28
avocado	26
blue cheese	28
green bean	26
hot cream cheese	27
hummus	29
tomato and cheese	27
tomato salsa	26
Dressing, cumin	137
French	138
herb	138
sesame	137
tofu	137
tomato	138
vinaigrette	139
Easy zucchini pie	77
Egg fried rice	116
scrambled	98
Eggplant casserole	79
Eggplants	121
Eggs, Swiss	98
Eggy tofu	106
Egmont potatoes	53
Empanadas	93
Falafel	34
Fancy scones	181
Fillo pastry	80
triangles	32
Flaked barley	111
rye	111
wheat	111
Flan, leek	90
mushroom topped spinach	92
rhubarb cream	157
spinach	92
vegetable	90
Florence fennel	121
Flour tortillas	144
pea	174
soya	175
Fondue, cheese	101
French dressing	138

omelet	102
toast	101
Fresh pasta in savoury tomato	
sauce	60
tomato sauce	62
tomato soup	18
Fried rice, egg	116
Frittata, potato	56
Fritters, corn	73
Fruit mufffins	143
Gadogado salad	80
Garbanzo beans	175
Ginger beer	167
Glazed root vegetables	128
Gravy, vegetarian	136
Greek salad	131
Green bean dip	26
salad	131
sauce	137
split peas	174
Grilled polenta	116
Grilling vegetables	123
Guacamole	31
Haricot beans	174
Hearty bean pie	181
Heat-treated rice	111
Herb dressing	138
Herbed cream cheese pate	27
creamy vinaigrette	139
Home-brewed beer	166
Home-style baked beans	40
Honey bran muffins	143
Hot cereal mix	160
cream cheese dip	27
Hummus	29
Ice-cream, instant	156
Joanna's cabbage	126
Kebabs	107
vegetable	130
Kibbled rye	110
wheat	110
Kohlrabi	121
Kumara	121
patties	128
purée	128
Lasagne	64
Leek flan	90
Leeks	121
Lentil and tomato sauce	66

INDEX **181**

and vegetable curry	47	**Muffins,** cheese	142	kumara	128
loaf	114	corn	142	parsnip	128
Lentils, brown	175	fruity	143	pea flour	48
red	175	honey bran	143	**Pea** flour	174
Lettuces	121	oaty	142	flour patties	128
Lima beans	175	Mung beans	175	pods	121
Loaf, banana	148	**Mushroom** and walnut pâté	28	soup	19
boiled fruit	150	burgers	85	**Peanut** and sesame pasta sauce	67
carrot and mushroom	72	crêpes	78	sauce	80
pumpkin	148	salad	128	-sauced vegetable plate	80
red lentil	43	soup	21	Peanutty pasta salad	63
steamed high-protein	149	strudel	88	Pearl barley	111
zucchini and mushroom	73	topped spinach flan	92	**Peas**	122
Low-cal self-crusting quiche	94	**Mushrooms**	121	chickpeas	175
Macaroni cheese	62	microwaved garlic	128	green split	174
cheese, microwaved	61	Nachos	30	sugar snap	122
soup	13	Navy beans	174	yellow split	174
Maple syrup, mock	161	Nearly instant stock	12	**Peppers**	122
Marinated artichokes	124	Nuts, roast	35	stuffed	72
tofu	107	Oat bran	111	Pesto	139
tomato salad	89	**Oaty** muffins	142	Pickle, pretty	170
Marrow, stuffed	74	pancakes	161	**Pie,** apple	157
Marrows	121	**Omelet,** cottage cheese	98	easy zucchini	77
Mayonnaise	136	French	102	hearty bean	91
chilli	136	potato	102	shepherd's	44
garlic	136	Spanish	102	silver beet and cheese	89
herb	136	**Onions**	121	Pilaf, basic	115
tofu	137	sweet and sour	129	Pinto beans	174
Merino beans	175	Open sandwiches	35	Pita bread	147
Mexican beans	42	Orange milk shake	161	**Pizza** base	146
seasoning mix	42	**Oriental** crêpes	78	toppings	146
tortillas	43	tofu and noodles	66	Plain scones	145
Microwave muesli	160	Overflow bottled tomatoes	170	Pocket bread	147
Microwaved corn cobs	127	Painless pasta	60	Polenta, grilled	116
garlic mushrooms	128	Pakora vegetables	75	Popcorn	34
macaroni cheese	61	**Pancakes,** oaty	161	Popping corn	110
rice	112	potato	52	**Potato** and egg casserole	53
Microwaving beans	177	Parsnip patties	128	cakes	40
vegetables	123	Parsnips	121	frittata	56
Milk shake, orange	161	**Pasta,** painless	60	omelet	98
soya	166	and tomato bake	62	pancakes	52
Millet, flaked	110	with instant sauce	67	salads	129
Minestrone	15	to cook	60	savouries	32
Mix and match	65	zucchini and yoghurt	63	**Potatoes,** baked	130
Mock maple syrup	161	**Pastry** for pies	88	Egmont	53
Moong dahl	175	quick flaky	157	skillet	129
Muesli bars, super	162	**Pâté,** herbed cream cheese	27	spiced with peas	54
microwave	160	mushroom and walnut	28	stuffed baked	52
Swiss	160	**Patties,** corn and pea	41	Potted cheese	33

Pressure-cooking rice	112	Greek	131	Soaking beans	175
beans	175	green	131	Soufflé, cheese	100
vegetables	123	marinated tomato	132	**Soup** stock	12
Pretty pickle	170	mushroom	128	alphabet	17
Pumpkin balls	76	peanutty pasta	63	asparagus	21
loaf	148	potato	129	black bean and rice	20
soup	22	spinach	131	brown onion	14
Pumpkins	122	sweet-sour carrot	126	carrot	14
Quiche, cheese and mushroom	91	tabbouleh	131	cheese and onion	13
leek	90	Salsa, tomato	26	chilled tomato	18
low-cal self-crusting	94	Samosas	92	corn dahl	22
self-crusting	94	**Sandwiches,** open	35	cream of lentil	20
self-crusting lentil and tomato	95	toasted cheese	33	creamy lentil and vegetable	15
self-crusting mushroom	94	two-slice	36	curried cashew and carrot	14
self-crusting potato and		**Sauce,** cheese	136	curried kumara	16
vegetable	94	chunky vegetable and		fresh tomato	18
vegetable	90	tomato	61	macaroni	13
Quick bran bread	149	fresh tomato	62	minestrone	15
flaky pastry	157	green	137	mushroom	21
pizza base	146	lentil and tomato	66	pea	19
potato soup	17	peanut	80	pumpkin	22
yeast bread	146	peanut and sesame	67	quick potato	17
Raclette	55	red pepper	74	winter	16
Radishes	122	savoury tomato	60	yoghurt and cucumber	19
Rapid refried beans	41	sesame cream	34	**Soya** beans	175
Ratatouille	81	tofu and tomato	68	flour	175
Red beans and rice	46	tomato and chilli	106	milk	166
cabbage, braised	125	yoghurt	48	Spaghetti scramble	98
kidney beans	175	Sauté	123	Spanish omelet	102
lentil loaf	43	Savoury crepes	78	Special spiced rice	81
lentils	175	Scallopini	122	**Spiced** potatoes and peas	54
Refried beans	41	scones, plain or fancy	145	rice	114
Reheating rice	113	Scrambled egg	98	**Spinach**	85
Rhubarb cream flan	157	**Self-crusting** lentil and tomato		and cheese crêpes	79
Rice	111	quiche	95	and cottage cheese cannelloni	64
and tomato casserole	115	mushroom quiche	91	beet	122
spiced	114	potato and vegetable quiche	94	salad	131
to cook	112	quiches	94	triangles	32
Roasting nuts and seeds	35	Semolina	110	Spread, cheese	31
Rolled oats	111	**Sesame** cream sauce	34	Sprouting beans	177
Rolls, bread	146	dressing	137	Squash	122
Roulade, asparagus	99	sugar	161	Squiggles	37
Rye, flaked	110	Shepherd's pie, vegetarian	44	Steamed high protein loaf	149
kibbled	110	Short pastry	88	Stir-fried vegetables	132
Salad greens	121	Short-order curried beans	45	Stir-fry-steam	183
carrot and apple	126	Shredded beetroot	123	Stir-frying	183
celery and apple	127	**Silver beet**	122	**Stock**	12
confetti	130	and cheese pie	89	vegetable	12
gadogado	80	Skillet potatoes	129	Strudel, mushroom	88

INDEX **183**

Stuffed baked potatoes	52	kebabs	130	
leaves	81	stock from scratch	12	
marrow	74	Vegetables, stir-fried	132	
peppers	72	**Vegetarian** gravy	136	
zucchini	74	shepherd's pie	44	
Super muesli bars	162	Vinaigrette, herbed creamy	139	
Sushi	29	Walnut torte	158	
Sweet and sour onions	129	**Wheat** berries	110	
tofu	106	bran	110	
Sweet-sour bean salad	124	germ	110	
carrot salad	126	flaked	110	
Swiss chard	122	kibbled	110	
eggs	98	Whip, tofu-fruit	156	
muesli	160	**Wholemeal** carrot cake	152	
Tabbouleh	131	flour	110	
Takefumi rice	117	Wild rice	111	
Tempura vegetables	77	Winter soup	16	
Thick tomato savoury	170	Yams	122	
Toasted cheese sandwiches	33	Yellow split peas	174	
Tofu and tomato pasta sauce	68	**Yoghurt** and cucumber soup	19	
burgers	84	sauce	48	
mayonnaise	136	**Zucchini**	122	
sandwich spread	37	and mushroom loaf	73	
-fruit whip	156	and yoghurt pasta	63	
-shakes	162	cakes with red pepper purée	74	
eggy	106	chocolate cake	151	
marinated	107	with herb cream	132	
Oriental	66	stuffed	74	
sweet and sour	106			
tortilla stack	106			
Tomato and cheese dip	27			
dressing	138			
leather	171			
paste	171			
puree	171			
salsa	26			
sauce	60			
tofu tortilla stack	106			
Tomatoes	122			
bottled	170			
dehydrated	171			
savoury	170			
Torte walnut	150			
Tortillas	43			
flour	144			
Two-slice sandwiches	36			
Vegetable combo	75			
crepes	78			
flan	90			

"The recipes in this book have been carefully tested by the authors. The publisher and the authors have made every effort to ensure that the instructions are accurate and safe but they cannot accept liability for any resulting injury or loss or damage to property whether direct or consequential."

£ 14.99